Schubert's Song Sets

Schubert's Song Sets

Michael Hall

R Routledge
Taylor & Francis Group

LONDON AND NEW YORK

First published 2003 by Ashgate Publishing

Reissued 2018 by Routledge
2 Park Square, Milton Park, Abingdon, Oxon OX14 4RN
711 Third Avenue, New York, NY 10017, USA

Routledge is an imprint of the Taylor & Francis Group, an informa business

Typeset in Sabon by Q3 Bookwork, Loughborough.

A Library of Congress record exists under LC control number: 2001099668

ISBN 13: 978-1-138-72433-4 (hbk)
ISBN 13: 978-1-138-72432-7 (pbk)
ISBN 13: 978-1-315-19252-9 (ebk)

Contents

Part Two   The Heine set

Acknowledgements

My thanks to Elizabeth Norman McKay, Richard Morris, Nicholas Rast and the late John Reed for answering my queries so attentively and promptly, to David and Peter Lumsdaine for providing the music examples, and to my wife, Brenda, for her advice, unfailing assistance and patience. I am also most grateful to Ashgate, whose reader made valuable suggestions for improvements to my text.

List of abbreviations

Bingham — Bingham, Ruth Otto (1993), 'The song cycle in German-speaking countries, 1790–1840: approaches to a changing genre', unpublished PhD thesis, University of Cornell.

Chusid — Chusid, Martin (ed.) (2000), *A Companion to Schubert's Schwanengesang*. New Haven, CT: Yale University Press.

Companion — Gibbs, Christopher, H. (ed.) (1997), *The Cambridge Companion to Schubert*, Cambridge: Cambridge University Press.

DF-D — Fischer-Dieskau, Dietrich (1976), *Schubert: A Biographical Study of his Songs*, trans. and ed. Kenneth S. Whitton, London: Cassell.

Doc. — Deutsch, Otto Erich (1946), *Schubert: A Documentary Biography*, trans. E. Blom, London: Dent. Published in the USA (1947) as *The Schubert Reader: A life of Franz Schubert in Letters and Documents*, New York: Norton.

Frisch — Frisch, Walter (ed.) (1986), *Schubert: Critical and Analytical Studies*, Lincoln, NE: University of Nebraska Press.

Kramer — Kramer, Richard (1994), *Distant Cycles: Schubert and the Conceiving of Song*, Chicago: University of Chicago Press.

McKay — McKay, Elizabeth Norman (1996), *Franz Schubert: A Biography*, Oxford: Oxford University Press; revised paperback edition 1997.

Mems — Deutsch, Otto Erich (ed.) (1958), *Schubert: Memoirs by his Friends*, trans. R. Ley and J. Nowell, London: Black.

Prawer — Prawer, Siegbert, S. (1960), *Heine: 'Buch der Lieder'*, London: Arnold.

Schachter — Schachter, Carl (1999), *Unfoldings: Essays in Schenkerian Theory and Analysis*, ed. Joseph N. Straus, Oxford: Oxford University Press.

SSC — Reed, John (1985), *The Schubert Song Companion*, Manchester: Manchester University Press; New York: Universe Books; paperback edition 1993, London: Faber and Faber.

Steblin — Steblin, Rita (1983), *A History of Key Characteristics in the Eighteenth and Early Nineteenth Centuries*, Ann Arbor, MI: UMI Research Press.

Stein   Stein, Jack M. (1971), *Poem and Music in the German Lied from Gluck to Hugo Wolf*, Cambridge, MA: Harvard University Press.

Studies, 1982   Badura-Skoda, Eva and Branscombe, Peter (eds) (1982), *Schubert Studies: Problems of Style and Chronology*, Cambridge: Cambridge University Press.

Studies, 1998   Newbould, Brian (ed.) (1998), *Schubert Studies*, Aldershot: Ashgate.

Whitton   Whitton, Kenneth, S. (1999), *Goethe and Schubert: The Unseen Bond*, Portland, OR: Amadeus Press.

Youens   Youens, Susan (1996), *Schubert's Poets and the Making of Lieder*, Cambridge: Cambridge University Press.

Introduction

Schubert's life and work have been subject to extensive research and analysis since Otto Erich Deutsch published the first of his highly esteemed Schubert studies in 1914. Even so, our knowledge of his biography and certain aspects of his music still need to be more thoroughly examined. The purpose of this study is to draw attention to the 42 song sets Schubert compiled or specially composed for publication from 1821 until his death. It will be shown that as well as being fascinating works in their own right, they offer valuable insights into his intellectual and personal preoccupations during those seven years. Although sets containing the same number of songs share formal characteristics, the range of topics and musical features which bind them differ widely. This is why each set is examined separately in this study. It means that it can be consulted as a reference book as well as a chronological account of a neglected oeuvre.

A changing perspective

The reasons for their neglect are not difficult to find. In Schubert's lifetime, and thereafter until recently, the features binding these song sets into units have been virtually ignored and, as a consequence, they have been considered to be little more than collections arbitrarily gathered together for publication. This is true even when the binding feature is as palpably clear as that in the Op. 21 set, settings of three originally unrelated poems by Johann Mayrhofer (*Auf der Donau, Der Schiffer and Wie Ulfru fischt*), which Schubert composed at various times in 1817 and gathered together for publication in 1823. They relate to events on a river before, during and after a storm. Neither the publishers nor the critic who reviewed it in the Leipzig *Allgemeine Musikalische Zeitung* seem to have been aware of the topic. Even though only one song is concerned with fishing, the publishers advertised the set as '3 Fischerlieder von Meyerhofer [*sic*] für den Bass' (SSC, p. 436), while the critic treated the songs as being entirely independent of each other. The only interest he found in them was the unusual modulations in *Auf der Donau* (Doc. 479).

When the first complete edition of Schubert's music was published by Breitkopf und Härtel between 1884 and 1897, the 603 songs the editor had at his disposal were arranged in chronological order. The three Op. 21 songs, written within six months of each other, appeared in Volume 5. Although each was supplied with its opus number there was nothing else to suggest they constituted a set. *Auf der Donau* appears on page 92, *Der Schiffer* on page 24 and *Wie Ulfru fischt* on page 8. The sets were also broken up in the Peters Edition issued between 1885 and 1887. For commercial reasons the firm decided to arrange the 400 or so songs they selected in order of popularity, those most in demand appearing in Volume 1. This enabled them to control print runs and stock efficiently. As a result, *Der Fischer* appeared in Volume 2, *Auf der Donau* and *Wie Ulfru fischt* on pages 14 and 16 of Volume 4.

These two editions dominated the market until volumes of the *Neue Schubert Ausgabe* began appearing in 1964. In this and the 17-volume softback edition of the songs based on the new complete edition and published jointly by Bärenreiter and Henle, Walther Dürr, the editor, gave pride of place to most of the nearly 200 songs published with opus numbers assigned by Schubert. We can now study and perform the sets without having to search for them in different volumes. In the softback edition Op. 21 appears in Volume 17, the one devoted to songs for the bass voice. As in his prefaces to the other volumes in which the sets appear, Walther Dürr draws attention to what he believes to be salient features in it. However, his comments are devoted solely to Mayrhofer's poems. They are related, he says 'by a metaphor of central importance to this poet: water as a symbol of motion, of the passage of time, even of Nature. The boatman and the angler make their appearances in dialectical opposition to water; although they live from or simply entrust themselves to water, they want to subdue and dominate it'. He makes no mention of the musical and structural reasons which made Schubert decide these songs would make a coherent unit. Nevertheless comments such as these have been a stimulus to those who have wanted to probe the sets from a musical as well as a poetical point of view. Robert Winter in his article on Schubert's songs in the second edition of *The New Grove Dictionary of Music and Musicians* (2001) writes:

> The nearly 200 songs published in Schubert's lifetime are generally performed as if their groupings were of no consequence; but there is ample internal evidence that he compiled his opuses carefully. In Op. 59, a group of four songs published in 1826, Schubert opens with *Du liebst mich nicht* (D756) in A minor, followed by another heartbreaking song, *Dass sie hier gewesen* (D775), in the relative major. The third song, *Du bist die Ruh* (D776), uses a similar form of address to the first song but in a different, comforting mood, signalled by the more distant common-tone shift from the key of *Dass sie hier gewesen*, C major to E♭ major. Finally, the whimsical, bitter-sweet *Lachen und Weinen* (D777) is in A♭ major, to which the previous song's E♭ major serves as a retrospective dominant. Hence the opus skillfully groups two pairs of songs in contrasting moods but united by the general theme of love.

Winter makes no mention of the other song sets, but his comments on Op. 59 uncover the structural principles which govern several of Schubert's four-song sets. There are, however, two other facets of this particular set which help to unite it. All four poems are based on oriental models, and three contain refrains. Schubert took advantage of this by constructing the set to produce a pattern in which the position of the refrains makes the division into two contrasting yet related pairs even clearer: (1) refrain confined to the text, music through-composed, (2) refrain occurs at the end of each stanza, (3) refrain confined to the music, text through-composed and (4) refrain occurs at the beginning of each stanza.

Song sets rather than song cycles

Of the 42 sets, only nine were specially composed for publication. Most of them were either assembled from individual songs composed at various times in the past, or were a mixture of old and new. The specially composed sets all consist of settings of one particular poet, the rest vary between settings of sometimes one author but, more usually, several. As a genre they differ from *Die schöne Müllerin* and *Winterreise*, the major song cycles, in four respects. First, they are much more modest in their proportions. Ten contain only two songs, twenty, three songs, and nine, four songs. The remaining three contain five, six and seven songs respectively. Secondly, whereas it was Wilhelm Müller who decided the poetic content of the cycles, Schubert himself selected and ordered the poetic content of the sets. They represent his ideas. Thirdly, unlike the cycles, none tells a story. They are rendered coherent in other ways. Although each song represents an incident in a process, the events relate to different people rather than to one person. When they do concern only one person, as in the two sets based on lyrics in Goethe's novel *Wilhelm Meisters Lehrjahre* (Wilhelm Meister's Apprenticeship), it is virtually impossible to construe a story from them without prior knowledge of the context. Fourthly, whereas *Die schöne Müllerin* and *Winterreise* build up to a state of maximum tension, the sets begin when the tension is at its greatest. The passengers in the small boat on the Danube in Op. 21 fear for their lives when the storm threatens. In the subsequent songs the tension reduces. The storm may be at its height in the second, but the boatman defies its danger; and when the storm is over, the angler notes that throughout its course the fish appear to have been unaffected by it.

These differences are the reasons why I decided to call the 42 works 'song sets' rather than 'song cycles', the standard music dictionary term for groups of interrelated songs. The description 'song cycle' has become associated with those containing a narrative, and has been rarely employed in recent years by song composers. For example, it is not a term Britten used for *A Charm of Lullabies* or *Winter Words*, Dallapiccola for *Rencesvals* or *Quattro Liriche di Antonio Machado*, Poulenc for *Tel Jour, Telle Nuit*, or Kurtág for *The Sayings of Péter Bornemisza*. However, unlike these composers, Schubert never supplied titles for his sets; they are known only by their opus numbers.

The early nineteenth-century context

The history of interrelated song groupings in the early nineteenth century has only recently been explored. One of the most valuable accounts can be found in Ruth Otto Bingham's dissertation 'The Song Cycle in German-speaking Countries, 1790–1840: approaches to a changing genre'. Although she does not discuss Schubert's song sets other than Op. 54, the set taken from lyrics in Scott's *The Lady of the Lake*, her findings are crucial to our understanding of the context in which Schubert was working. Bingham's examples indicate that although most of his organizing principles had their source in the works of other composers, the range and depth of his sets outstrip in every way what his contemporaries produced. Bingham calls all groups of songs which cohere 'song cycles', and does not confine the term to those containing a narrative as has been done in this present study. She divides the early cycles into four categories: those based on topics, those in which the emphasis is placed on musical principles, those with an internal plot and those with an external plot.

Grouping songs on a topic was the earliest and most frequently encountered way of forging a coherent unit. Among those Bingham cites are Johann Friedrich Reichardt's cycle based on the months of the year (1796), Paul Wineberger's on flowers (1810) and Carl Maria von Weber's on the four temperaments (1816). Schubert constructed 32 sets based on topics. They range from the comic and light-hearted to all the themes Romanticism brought to the fore in German poetry: nature, wandering, longing, night, time, death, the imagination. Some are concerned with philosophical topics raised by Goethe, Mayrhofer, Schiller and the brothers August and Friedrich Schlegel in their poems. Others deal with issues of personal interest: friendship, bachelorhood, love across social barriers, the divisions within himself, facing the prospect of an early death. In all of them Schubert looks at the topic in terms of its relationship to human consciousness, the overall pattern being a progression from a state of distress to one of relative calm. But since most were drawn from his reservoir of separate songs and involve the voices of different protagonists the particular is raised to the general. As a consequence an argument can be advanced. Op. 58, for example, concerns those who mourn and seek consolation. The three poems are by Schiller, but since Schubert selected and ordered them he was responsible for the conclusion that those who mourn have to accept reality, that the departed cannot be restored to life nor do they continue to love the living. The only palliative for grief is weeping.

The precedent Bingham provides for those groups of songs which cohere 'equally or primarily on musical rather than poetic devices', and use 'techniques formerly associated with instrumental and dramatic genres' is Beethoven's *An die ferne Geliebte*, which she claims was the first of the kind (Bingham, p. 236). She believes its seamless construction, tonal plan, recapitulation of the opening and prominence given to the piano indicate a composer who thought mainly in terms of instrumental music. Schubert has been accused of thinking mainly in terms of song, but he too made use of instrumental procedures. His Op. 3 (*Schäfers Klagelied, Meeres Stille, Heidenröslein* and *Jägers Abendlied*) consists of a sonata form first movement, a reflective slow movement, a lively scherzo and, like all instrumental finales, a concluding movement based on the principle of repetition. Nevertheless the musical devices which interested him most were those associated with dramatic genres. Op. 83, for instance, has texts by Metastasio and provided the distinguished Italian bass, Luigi Lablache, with virtuoso specimens of the oratorio, opera seria and opera buffa styles. Op. 56 may not be overtly operatic, but Schubert had the words translated into Italian and composed the music in a style associated with Rossini whose operas were extremely popular in Vienna when he composed the songs in 1822–23 and again in 1826 when he published them. He was also adept at the French vaudeville style as witnessed by Op. 95, his settings of four of Johann Seidl's witty refrain songs.

According to Bingham, structures based on internal and external plots have their origins in the *Singspiel*. But whereas the narrative in internal plot cycles such as *Die schöne Müllerin* are explicit, those in external plot cycles consisting of 'musical settings excerpted from narrative works' are not. The composer relies 'on the audience's familiarity with the source for context and coherence' (Bingham, p. 86). Bingham provides examples from works by Bernard Crusell and Charlotte Veltheim, but she devotes most of her attention to Schubert's Op. 52. Scott's narrative poem, *The Lady of the Lake*, which had been translated into German in 1819, had become as popular in German-speaking countries as some of Scott's novels. Schubert selected seven lyrics from the work and published his versions in the order they appear in the narrative. This means that the last is the 'Lay of the Imprisoned Huntsman', a song for the lady of the lake's

lover, which he delivers from the turret of the castle where he is being
held captive. Since this leaves the story in suspense, the present author
contends that Schubert must have decided the best models for the set's
structure were the finales which brought the first acts of comic operas to
a close. In these, slow numbers getting progressively slower alternate
with fast numbers getting progressively faster until the fastest possible
tempo is reached and the curtain falls with the plot suspended in mid-air.
Schubert's structure may not end in the confusion that characterizes the
endings of the central finales of *The Marriage of Figaro* or *The Barber of
Seville*, but the contrast between Ellen's very slow *Ave Maria,* which
precedes Malcolm's dashing, polonaise-like 'Lay', is musically conclusive
even though it leaves the plot unfinished. Members of the audience have
to supply the story's denouement and the narrative connections between
the songs from their memories.

The two sets based on lyrics extracted from Goethe's *Wilhelm
Meister's Apprenticeship*, on the other hand, are much more in keeping
with Schubert's normal practice. Op. 12 is devoted to three of the
Harper's lyrics, Op. 62 to three of Mignon's. Although knowledge of the
context may be useful for the listener, it is not essential. The interest lies
in the characters of these mysterious people, in particular their capacity
to suffer, he from guilt, she from the necessity to keep her love for
Wilhelm secret. The capacity to suffer also lies behind two of Schubert's
other character studies. Op. 23, concerns Schubert's school friend, the
poet Johann Senn, who was cruelly punished by the school authorities for
taking part in a demonstration calling for the independence of his native
Tyrol. Later, in 1821, he was betrayed by a police spy and arrested for
being a leader of an illegal student organization. After languishing in
prison without trial for 14 months he was exiled to the Tyrol, and was
thus cut off from his friends, his career and all he valued in the Austrian
capital.

The subject of the last character study was also a poet, but Schubert
never knew Heinrich Heine and did not come across his work until
January 1828. As well as having the capacity to suffer, Heine could also
stand back from his suffering and mock it. Herein lies the poet's appeal
for Schubert for he too possessed two natures except that, in his case, the
manic depression from which he suffered produced states of mind that
were beyond his control. He could not stand back from them. As a consequence he held mockery in reserve until he reached the last song in his
Heine set. This set is as much a study of himself as it is of the poet. The
six poems come from Heine's collection *Die Heimkehr*, and Schubert
rearranged their order so that at first the set would appear to be about
the contrasting personalities of different people. Only as it unfolds does it
become clear that it is concerned with the dual nature of one person.

Finally in *Der Doppelgänger* the protagonist encounters the other side of himself. In a state of deep depression he sees his grief being aped by his mocking, manic self.

Bingham provides no precedents for these character study sets, nor for the first version of Op. 106, a group of songs based on four of the poems introduced to Schubert by Marie Pachler, his gracious hostess in Graz when he was staying there in September 1827 (*Heimliches Lieben, Das Weinen, Vor meiner Wiege* and *Eine altschottische Ballade*). He had the set published privately because he wanted it to be his personal tribute to her. Its interest lies in the fact that, although it has no topic or other device to bind it, the structure reflects Schubert's concern for balance. This is manifest in all the sets and collections he compiled. As in Op. 59 the four songs are divided into pairs, each pair containing contrasting songs. In the first pair, one lover speaks of the joy of being kissed, the other of the consolation found in tears. In the second, one son thinks of his mother lovingly, the other looks on his mother with hate. But although one pair balances the other, Schubert was even more concerned to end his sets with a song expressing in itself a sense of balance, and this *Eine altschottische Ballade* (the ballad 'Edward') fails to achieve. No man who murders his father, abandons his family and hates his mother so much can be said to be balanced. Schubert therefore replaced it with *An Silvia*, a song in praise of a woman who is 'holy, fair and wise'. Yet although this is more suitable for a tribute, the substitution does not upset the structural balance of the set, for the first and third songs contain a mixture of varied and contrasting sections, while the second and fourth are strophic.

The need for structural balance

Structural balance as an organizing principle in its own right can be witnessed in the the three substantial collections of songs Schubert gathered together in 1816: the two albums of songs he assembled to send to Goethe and the 16 songs he presented to the soprano Therese Grob as a parting gift and birthday present when their close relationship came to an end.

Only one of the two albums prepared for Goethe in April 1816 was actually sent to the poet. The first pages of this are missing, but the pagination and the way the songs are ordered suggest that the missing song is *An Schwager Kronos*, which Deutsch dates from the beginning of the year. On this assumption, the order of the 17 songs is as follows: (1) *An Schwager Kronos*, (2) *Jägers Abendlied*, (3) *Der König in Thule*, (4) *Meeres Stille*, (5) *Schäfers Klagelied*, (6) *Die Spinnerin*, (7) *Heidenröslein*,

(8) *Wonne der Wehmut*, (9) *Wandrers Nachtlied (Der du von Himmel bist)*, (10) *Erster Verlust*, (11) *Der Fischer*, (12) *An Mignon*, (13) *Geistes-Gruss*, (14) *Nähe des Geliebten*, (15) *Gretchen am Spinnrade*, (16) *Rastlose Liebe*, (17) *Erlkönig*. The songs are neither in chronological order, nor in one which would have made an immediate appeal to Goethe given his penchant for strophic settings. Schubert's purpose was clearly to create a set in which the songs are balanced by being placed in an order creating bilateral symmetry.[1] The first and the last items are both extended through-composed songs in which the narrative leads to a premature death. At the centre is *Wandrers Nachtlied* another through-composed song, but in this case, it is short and in two parts, the division functioning as the axis of the reflective symmetry. Although the symmetry refers only to the character and structure of the songs and, in the circumstances could not be exact, the ordering does indicate Schubert's efforts to attain balance. For example, *Heidenröslein*, the eighth item, is a strophic, folk-like song about a flower (that is, a girl) being 'taken' by a boy. Balancing it is *Der Fischer*, a strophic, folk-like song about a man being 'taken' by a mermaid.

The second album consists of 12 songs that are also arranged to produce a balanced structure. The first and last songs, *Sehnsucht (Was zieht mir des Herz so?)* and *Der Sänger*, each involves frequent changes of tempo and key, and alternate recitative and aria or arioso. The two central songs, *Sehnsucht (Nur wer die Sehnsucht kennt)* and *Kennst du das Land?*, relate to Mignon and are through-composed. The songs lying between the extremes and those in the centre either mirror each other or reflect each other in some other way. The light-hearted nature of *Wer kauft Liebesgötter?* and *Trost in Tränen* lying second and third, for instance, balance the two light-hearted drinking songs, *Bundeslied* and *Tischlied* lying eighth and ninth.

Schubert's organization of the Therese Grob Song Book demonstrates another kind of balance. It was undoubtedly he who organized it and not Therese as is sometimes claimed. However, Therese did insert an item which should not be in it, a setting of the same words as the fourth song, an item which has not been authenticated as being by Schubert, and is not in Schubert's hand as the others are. When this is omitted then four clearly defined groups emerge (4+4+3+5). These roughly correspond to the movements of a four-movement instrumental work. The first group has songs in moderate tempos and progresses to *Der Leidende*, which ends with the words, 'let me sink with my sorrows into

---

[1] Dürr, Walther (1978), 'Aus Schuberts erstem Publikationsplan: zwei Hefte mit Liedern von Goethe', in *Schubert Studien: Festgabe der Österreichen Akademie dem Wissenschaften zum Schubert – Jahr 1978*, Vienna, pp. 43–56.

the grave ... All hope is lost'. The second has songs in slow tempos and progresses to the graveside lament, *Am Grabe Anselmos*, which terminates with, 'See, we loved each other, and as long as I live joy will never return to my heart'. The structures and tempos of the other two groups are arranged in the ABA form of the typical scherzo and the ABACA form of the typical rondo finale (the rondo sections were specially composed for the album – all are cast in G major). In these sorrow is replaced by joy. The scherzo ends with *Lied aus der Ferne* – 'Sleep sweetly, for it is only my ghost promising you joy and peace'; the rondo with *Am ersten Maimorgen* – 'I shall rush out and shout for joy. Even the king will not stop me'.

The experimental sets

Most of Schubert's experiments in cycle and set construction took place in his early years. Of particular interest from a musical point of view are the Don Gayseros songs and the first version of the Harper's songs from *Wilhelm Meister's Apprenticeship*. Both express the essence of their texts through the way their harmony is organized. The autograph of the Don Gayseros songs is an untitled and undated draft. Deutsch thought it was an early work and postulated either 1813 or 1814. But on the evidence of the manuscript paper, Robert Winter believes it belongs to between February 1816 and June 1817.[2] The poems come from Friedrich de la Motte Fouqué's novel *Der Zauberring*. Since the story they tell is complete in itself the work should be classified as a miniature song cycle rather than a set.

The unusual feature about it is that in the course of the three songs Schubert changes key 21 times. The reason for this becomes evident as the story unfolds. It tells of the tragic love of Don Gayseros, a Moorish king, who disguises himself as a Spaniard to win the hand of Donna Clara, a devout Christian. In the first song, when he refuses to make the sign of the cross, Donna Clara becomes suspicious of his identity. When he reveals who he is in a serenade, she accuses him of being 'a false plunderer of souls' and rejects him. He then seizes her and bears her away on his horse. In the third song we learn through a narrator that her brothers have murdered him. But so great is her grief that they build a chapel for her where she can spend her life praying for the man she has never ceased to love in her heart. 'Everything in the world is in flux,' says the narrator, 'she alone is unchanging.'

---

[2]   Winter, Robert (1978), 'Schubert's undated works, a new chronology', *Musical Times*, 119, p. 500.

Schubert composed the music so that the changes of key, the fluctuations, become obvious only in the second song. Until then he goes from one key to another simply by treating a tonic as a dominant. The music starts in F major then in the next strophe goes to B♭ major then to E♭ major and so on. The second song also starts in F major, but the processes of getting from there to G major and then to A♭ major involve a more complex method of modulation. Having reached A♭, Schubert then resorts to his tactics for the first song, A♭-D♭-G♭(F♯)-B. Thereafter the process of getting from one key to another always involves the more complex method of modulation so that a state of flux becomes unmistakable. The process comes to a halt when Donna Clara's constancy is revealed. At that point the tonality becomes stabilized in E♭ major, the key prominent at the beginning of the song.

In the Harper's songs, Schubert goes to the opposite extreme. All three songs are in A minor. The Harper is obsessed by feelings of guilt, and in the course of the novel becomes deranged. Schubert clearly interprets the character as someone who lives in fear of madness and who tries to keep disruptive emotions constantly at bay. The tight rein he holds on himself is harmonically represented by the restrictions imposed on the tonality. The first song contains multiple cadences in A minor and has only one quickly controlled outburst from the Harper. In the second song he appears to have his emotions completely in check. He goes from door to door asking for food, and fails to understand why the householders should weep when they see him. Although the music never strays outside the tonic and its relative major, a tonic cadence does not occur until the end. However, in the last song, when he rails against the heavenly powers for allowing him to fall into guilt, he gives way to his emotions and reveals his impending insanity. The intensely agitated music moves to F♯ minor then to E♭ minor, the key furthest removed from A minor. To get back to the home key the music undergoes an extraordinarily wayward modulation. When A minor is eventually reached and the tremolandos cease, it sounds as if madness had only narrowly been avoided.

In order to achieve this dramatic structure Schubert had to change the order of the lyrics. Six years later, when he published the set as his Op. 12, he rewrote the song he had originally placed third and changed the order so that it came second. The sense of impending derangement was removed, and the cadence bringing the vocal line to a close resolves in the major. His last song is *An die Türen will ich schleichen* and in this new context it sounds as if the Harper has found a measure of inner peace, and has become more balanced as he goes from door to door begging for food.

Schubert was probably also experimenting when he produced an undated fair copy of four songs which he signed and entitled 'Four

German songs for solo voice with pianoforte accompaniment'. On the evidence of the paper, Robert Winter believes the manuscript dates from October 1819.[3] This is probably when Schubert composed his second version of Goethe's *An den Mond*, the third song in the group. The date of the second song, Goethe's *Hoffnung*, is uncertain. It may have been written much earlier. The other two definitely were. The first, Klopstock's *Dem Unendlichen*, dates from September 1815 and the last, Mayrhofer's *Abendlied der Fürstin*, from November 1816.

John Reed suggested that, as Schubert wrote fair copies and signed the manuscript, he intended to send the songs to a publisher (SSC, p. 89). But in October 1819 the only song that had appeared in print was his setting of Mayrhofer's *Erlafsee*, which came out in February 1818 as a supplement to the annual *Mahlerisches Taschenbuch* (Pictorial Pocketbook). That a publisher would be interested in four relatively unknown songs when *Erlkönig* had been turned down suggests that Schubert was placing them in meaningful sets in anticipation of when his songs would be published.

The structure is based on the sequence of images in the first song. These images are taken up one by one in the subsequent songs, but in the last song there is a sudden, unexpected change of mood. *Dem Unendlichen* makes a splendid beginning. It starts with a dramatic recitative contrasting the joy the soul feels when it thinks of the 'Infinite One' with the sorrow it experiences when it turns in on itself. In the following aria we hear that the swaying trees, murmuring streams and 'resounding suns' direct their praise towards God. To end the poem Klopstock calls on worlds to 'thunder forth, trumpet choirs to ring out in praise'. *Hoffnung* takes up the image of the trees, *An den Mond*, the murmuring streams. Both poems focus on the solace to be found in nature. But although the beech trees stand silent and the stream murmurs softly in the evening glow at the beginning of *Abendlied der Fürstin*, in this poem the thunder that Klopstock associated with praise in the first song shatters the peace. 'Every pleasure turns to grief and pain', Mayrhofer concludes. 'Where are you, sacred evening glow? Where are you gentle Hesperus?'

Although Schubert was to use this organizing principle on several occasions in his published sets, it never resulted in such a pessimistic volte-face again. Op. 3, the first of them, has poems taken from the album sent to Goethe in 1816. It too lacks a topic. As in the 'Four German songs' the poetic continuity comes from following up images in the first poem. But here the sequence progresses from sorrow to a situation where peace prevails.

---

[3] Winter, 'Schubert's undated works', p. 500.

Taking heed of the market

The decision to send the first album of Goethe songs to the poet in April 1816 had been made by Josef von Spaun and other friends. No publisher had expressed interest in Schubert so they decided to bring out his songs and instrumental works themselves. It was an ambitious plan, and they knew that it would not succeed unless it had the endorsement and support of someone as eminent as Goethe. The album was sent on 17 April 1816 along with a letter from von Spaun outlining the 19-year-old's remarkable talent for composition and listing the kinds of publications the friends had in mind. Their intention, he said, was to start with eight volumes of songs. Although more than 70 collections of songs had been published in Vienna in the first 15 years of the century,[4] in all probability their models were the volumes of Zumsteeg and Reichardt songs Breit-kopf und Härtel had brought out between 1800 and 1811. Spaun wrote as if the contents had already been planned. 'The first two (of which the first is enclosed as a specimen) contain poems by Your Excellency', he said, 'the third contains poems by Schiller, the fourth and fifth by Klop-stock, the sixth by Matthison, Hölty, Salis, etc., and the seventh and eighth contain songs from Ossian, these last excelling all the others' (Doc. 81).

Spaun had chosen the poets with care because they were those Goethe was known to admire. But it was clearly a mistake to suggest that Ossian's verse had inspired Schubert to write songs superior to the ones inspired by Goethe himself. It is not known whether Goethe looked at the songs or read the letter, but he failed to reply and the album was returned without comment (Whitton, pp. 138–42). The project was therefore dropped. Yet even if Goethe had taken an interest in it and agreed to give his support, Spaun and the friends would have had to dig deep into their pockets for it is doubtful whether the project would have been viable commercially. The ballads and songs of Zumsteeg and Reichardt were widely known and admired throughout the German-speaking world, but Schubert's had only been heard by his friends. It was foolhardy to believe they could be issued in volumes of 17 or more.

Fortunately the next person who tried to get Schubert published, Leopold von Sonnleithner, was more businesslike. The volumes he arranged to have printed contained no more than five songs, and before he embarked on the venture he ascertained there was a market for them. His father had put him in charge of the regular concerts held fortnightly in his home during the winter months to an audience consisting usually

---

[4] West, Ewan (1994), 'Schuberts Lieder im Kontext: Einige Bemerkungen zur Lied komposition in Wien nach 1820', *Brille*, 12, pp. 5–19.

of about 120 invited guests. On 1 December 1820, *Erlkönig* was included in the programme. It was the first of Schubert's songs to be performed in public, and was a huge success. 'Suddenly', Sonnleithner reported, 'Schubert's name was talked of in all the musical circles, and people were asking why his songs were not published'. During the following three months *Der Wanderer* (D489), *Gretchen am Spinnrade* and *Der Jüngling auf dem Hügel* were also performed to great acclaim. Yet when Sonnleithner attempted to get *Erlkönig* published it was turned down on the grounds that the composer was unknown and the piano accompaniment too difficult. He and three friends therefore paid the firm of Cappi and Diabelli to engrave and print the song, and to act as their agents. It was issued on 2 April 1821 as Schubert's Op. 1.

At the next concert nearly 100 copies were sold. The proceeds enabled the friends to cover the expense of having *Gretchen am Spinnrade* published as Schubert's Op. 2, and during the following 18 months they were responsible for bringing out ten more 'books', each with its own opus number. Apart from Op. 11, a set of part songs for male voice quartet, all were for solo voice. The number of songs in each book varied between two and five. Sonnleithner clearly wanted to keep them roughly the same size as Op. 1 and Op. 2 for which he charged 2 florins and 1 florin 30 kreuzer respectively, the price difference being related to the amount of engraving involved. This meant that Op. 3 containing four songs, Op. 4 containing three and Op. 5 five could all be bought for 1 florin 30. Song books of this size had become fairly standard in Vienna at the time, and were to remain so throughout Schubert's life. The 20 songs of *Die schöne Müllerin* came out in five books, and the seven of *The Lady of the Lake* in two. The one exception occurred in January 1828 when the 12 songs making up the first part of *Winterreise* came out in a single volume, but by that time Schubert had become well known as a song writer.

Cappi and Diabelli printed 600 copies of *Erlkönig*, 500 copies of *Gretchen am Spinnrade*, 400 copies of the Goethe set Op. 3, and 300 copies of each of the other sets. The enterprise proved so successful that the overall profits enabled the friends to pay Schubert's debts and to give him what Sonnleithner called 'a considerable sum in cash'. The success was in part due to the business acumen of Sonnleithner and his friends. It was doubtless they who insisted that Schubert should dedicate at least the first few works to people of influence, should begin each set with something that had proved to be, or was likely to be, particularly attractive, and should draw on his reservoir of Goethe settings as much as possible. The first five 'works', for example, contain 12 of the 17 songs Spaun sent to Goethe in 1816. In addition Op. 12 contains the three Harper's songs, Op. 14 two songs from the *West-östlicher Divan*.

Op. 14 was the last work published under this arrangement. The success of the venture meant that publishers were prepared to publish Schubert themselves. In November 1822 Cappi and Diabelli bought five manuscripts from him, the Wanderer Fantasy, two sets of male-voice quartets, a collection of Waltzes, Ländler and Ecossaises, and another set of Goethe songs later published in 1825 as Op. 19. But at the end of 1822 Schubert had contracted syphilis, and presumably needed money to pay doctor's bills. He therefore sold to Cappi and Diabelli for a relatively modest lump sum the plates and all his rights in respect to Opp. 1–7. This meant he would no longer receive any commission on such valuable assets as *Erlkönig* and *Gretchen am Spinnrade*. A few weeks later when he needed more money, he tried to sell them the rights for the remaining works Sonnleithner and his friends had subsidized, but he quibbled at the amount the publishers offered him, and as a consequence wrote them on 10 April 1823 a rather tetchy letter accusing them of being dishonest in their dealings with him and informing them that he had entered into a fixed agreement with another publishing house (Doc. 356). This was the firm of Sauer & Leidesdorf, and the agreement was that they would publish five books per year for two years and pay him a sum of 200 florins for each of them. In the second year, the five books were those *Die schöne Müllerin* had been divided into. Thereafter Schubert made use of several publishers, but always on an ad hoc basis. However, as Sonnleithner observed in his memoir of the composer, Schubert lacked all sense of money matters 'so that, when he was short of cash, the publishers bought his works for a trifling sum and gained a hundredfold thereby' (Mems, p. 109).

Music for the home rather than the concert hall

Perhaps it was on account of his indifference to money matters that Schubert made no effort to promote his sets. Although Michael Vogl and Baron Schönstein performed his songs to his accompaniment at private gatherings, and sometimes in public, to the best of our knowledge none of the sets was included in their programmes. On one occasion in 1825 Vogl and Schubert performed the five solo songs in *The Lady of the Lake* set at a private concert in Gmunden. The omission of the two part-songs meant that they had to be given in an order different from the one in the published version. Schubert was always in awe of Vogl, and doubtless had to give way to the famous singer's taste for the theatrical. To make an 'entrance' to capture the audience's sympathy Vogl began with Ellen's *Ave Maria*; and to make an 'exit' to promote applause he ended with the rousing song Norman sings as he marches off to war.

Schubert had the ideal opportunity to present a set to the public when he organized a private concert of his music in Vienna on 26 March 1828. The songs in the programme were interspersed between instrumental items. After a performance of the first movement of the G major String Quartet, D887, Vogl sang a group of four songs, but they were not one of the four-song sets, and only two of them, *Der Kreuzzug* and *Die Sterne*, were new. Once again Vogl's theatricality won the day, for *Der Kreuzzug*, the first in the group, is also devotional, and the last, the highly dramatic *Fragment aus dem Aeschylus*, another song he could perform in a manner that would bring the house down.

With the exception of Op. 83, the set written for Luigi Lablache, Schubert seems to have designed his sets for domestic rather than public performance. Publishers accepted his music for publication only if they thought it would appeal to, and be bought by, amateur musicians. This was probably one of the reasons why he ended most of his sets in an intimate manner. Several were written specially for friends or for those who were the dedicatees of the sets. But the care he lavished on all his sets suggests that, as well as compiling them to satisfy his innate desire for coherence, he also felt impelled to uphold the principles he and his friends had believed in during their formative years when they embarked on a programme of self-education.

The principles of the Bildung circle

Living during the period when the Classical Viennese style of Haydn, Mozart and Beethoven was gradually giving way to Romanticism, Schubert had a foot in both camps, and nowhere is this more in evidence than in the song sets. The individual songs may be Romantic, but the way the sets are structured reflects the spirit of Classicism.

In his essay 'The Romantic Lied: Romantic Form and Romantic Consciousness' (Frisch, pp. 200–34), Lawrence Kramer begins with the statement: 'In Schubert's hands the German Lied became the first fully developed genre of Romanticism in music.' He believes Schubert's development of it rested on 'two imperatives'. The first was to break away from the dramatic opposition of tonic and dominant by loosening 'the grip of the dominant and its dominants', and replacing it with a dramatic movement which Charles Rosen calls 'simple and indivisible'. The second was 'to align music with the widespread effort of literary and philosophical Romanticism to represent subjectivity in action':

> This expressly means that the purpose of the Romantic song is not simply to enhance the emotional force of the text, nor even, as writers

on the Lied traditionally claim, to evoke the meaning of the text, whether directly or ironically. The purpose is to represent the activity of a unique subject, conscious, self-conscious, and unconscious, whose experience takes shape as a series of conflicts and reconciliations between inner and outer reality.

Kramer's view has to be set against the deep opposition to Romanticism of Schubert and his youthful friends when they were educating themselves for life. Among the members of this circle of friends which McKay calls the Bildung circle (McKay, pp. 45–7) were Anton and Josef von Spaun, Mayrhofer, Josef Kenner, Anton Ottenwald and Franz von Schober. In 1817 and 1818 they gathered their ideas together in two year-books published under the title *Beyträge zur Bildung für Jünglinge* (Contributions towards the Education of Young Men). The programme they proposed involved carefully directed activity, reading, writing (and, in Schubert's case, composing), study of great men and ideas of the past, and the belief that the 'good' combined reason and feeling, that head and heart should always be in balance. According to David Gramit they considered themselves Classicists, and looked on Romanticists as being 'cut off from reality and given over to a non-productive dream world.'[5] 'Mayrhofer', says Gramit,

> contrasted the 'distortions and blunders of the German school' of artists to the 'canon of the beautiful and truthful, in a word, the classical,' which had been lost since the fall of Rome; Anton von Spaun criticized the 'completely incoherent, chaotic longing of the heart' characteristic of modern poetry; and Anton Ottenwald castigated critics who 'most often lead a petty, perhaps perverted life, let history count for nothing, know of nothing but the dreary night of absolute everything-and-nothing doctrine, over which the will-o'-the wisps and spooks of Romanticism hover'. (Companion, p. 62)

Their ideas stemmed in the main from Goethe's *Wilhelm Meister's Apprenticeship*, written in the wake of the Romantic excesses of *Sturm und Drang*, the German literary movement prominent during the 1770s. It represents in fictional form the transition from *Sturm und Drang* to the classical canons of order and balance which Goethe, along with Schiller, wanted to follow thereafter. The novel concerns Wilhelm's education for life by life itself. In the first half he searches for it in the theatre and through people who have completely given themselves over to their feelings. Mignon and the Harper are introduced to represent extreme cases of the subjectivity which absorbed *Sturm und Drang*. About halfway through the novel Wilhelm realizes that their subjectivity, their 'romantic beauty' becomes sterile when taken to such an extreme. 'The decisive

---

[5] Gramit, David (1987), 'The intellectual and aesthetic tenets of Franz Schubert's circle', unpublished PhD thesis, Duke University, p. 68.

turning-point in the education of Wilhelm Meister', said Georg Lukács, 'consists precisely in his abandonment of a merely internal, merely subjective attitude toward reality, and in his working toward an under-standing of objective reality and active participation in reality just as it is.'[6]

In the second half of the novel the figures who embody what he now seeks, Lothario and Natalie, represent those who have achieved harmony and balance within themselves, and can consequently live in harmony with the world, and as a result can lead active, useful lives.

The position taken by Goethe and the Bildung circle represents a narrow view of Romanticism. They failed to see that, as Virgil Nemoianu makes clear,[7] the essence of High Romanticism was the desire for an expansion of consciousness so that it can embrace the universal, an ideal they too wanted to achieve in their different ways. Schubert gives evidence of it through the extraordinary range of consciousness his songs and song sets cover. In fact Schubert and Franz von Schober never rejected Romanticism as wholeheartedly as the older members of the Bildung circle. Later when his circle of friends lost some of its older members and new ones were added, strong links were established with the group of overtly Romantic writers and thinkers who were living in Vienna, notably Friedrich von Schlegel.

One of the most important tenets of these writers and thinkers was the value they placed on the imagination. To illustrate this H.G. Schenk draws on Schubert's diary entry for 29 March 1824 as being representa-tive of a view held by most Romantic writers, visual artists and composers of Schubert's generation: 'Oh imagination, supreme jewel of mankind, inexhaustible source from which artists and scholars drink! Although recognized by only a few, abide with us, preserve us from that so-called Enlightenment, that ugly skeleton without flesh and blood!'[8]

Later, in 1826 and 1827, Schubert assembled four sets in which he modified his effusion. Op. 60 suggests that the imagination is at its most valuable in old age; Op. 88 that its main purpose is to reach out to what lies beyond us; Op. 57 that imagination and reality should be kept in balance; Op. 58 that in certain circumstance the imagination must give way to reason. In other words, contrary to what he wrote in his diary, the principles of the Enlightenment should not be rejected out of hand.

Nowhere is this belief more in evidence than in his composite

---

[6]   Lukács, Georg (1968), *Goethe and his Age*, trans. R. Anchor, London: Merlin Press, p. 59.

[7]   Nemoianu, Virgil (1984), *The Taming of Romanticism: European Literature and the Age of Biedermeier*, Cambridge, MA: Harvard University Press, p. 7.

[8]   Schenk, H.G. (1979), *The Mind of the European Romantics*, Oxford: Oxford Univer-sity Press, p. 5.

instrumental works. With the exception of the Unfinished Symphony, which eventually and perhaps unintentionally came to be seen as the essence of Romanticism, all his symphonies, sonatas and chamber works are tightly contained within the classical structures established by Haydn and his contemporaries during the heyday of the Enlightenment. Schubert may have begun some of his instrumental works with broad, song-like material, he may have modified the proportions within movements, but he nevertheless preserved to the letter the relationship between them. He hardly ever deviated from the pattern in which a diverse, dramatic first movement is balanced by a predominantly homogeneous finale, and a reflective slow movement is balanced by a mainly extrovert scherzo. A vivid example of the way he applied the relationship between first and last movements in his song sets can be witnessed in Op. 24, a two-song set consisting of settings of Schiller's *Gruppe aus dem Tartarus* and Mayrhofer's *Schlaflied*. The group in Tartartus, the deepest part of Hades, are the souls of the dead condemned to spend eternity yearning to be released from their suffering. They are the furthest removed from Nature as it is possible to be. The boy snuggling down to sleep in *Schlaflied*, on the other hand, rests on the bosom of Nature, and has been healed of his suffering. Unlike the condemned, he is in harmony with himself and the world. The first song is through-composed, declamatory, restless and highly dramatic; the second a gentle lullaby in strophic form, the simplest of all homogeneous structures. But unlike the finale of a typical symphony, sonata or string quartet, the tempo is relatively slow, the dynamic soft and the end unemphatic. These features characterize most of Schubert's terminating songs. They not only indicate that the sets were intended for intimate circumstances, they also confirm that after one of the most tortured of his songs he was compelled to end with an affirmation of classical poise.

Even those songs which fail to end in this manner, nevertheless give the impression that this condition is about to be attained. Op. 4 is a three-song set assembled from settings of Schmidt's *Der Wanderer*, Werner's *Morgenlied*, and Goethe's *Wandrers Nachtlied* (*Der du von dem Himmel bist*). In three-song sets, the second song functions as a transition between the distressed mood of the first and the more relaxed third. As often as not it supplies the conditions on which the transformation can take place. Schmidt's Wanderer is convinced he will always be a stranger, will never be released from his suffering. Werner's birds, on the other hand, accept their lot, even those who are old and sit huddled in their nests are at peace with themselves. They supply the condition which enables Goethe's Wanderer to overcome his striving and to call on 'sweet peace' to enter his heart. In this instance, the last song is through-composed, but when 'sweet peace' is called for, the Wanderer's words are

repeated and the music becomes repetitive and simple. In addition, the
tempo accelerates so that the final strains sound not unlike the chorus of
rejoicing the birds had been singing.

The musical co-ordination in the sets

When selecting the songs for his sets, Schubert took care to make sure the
music was as coherent as the poetry. Inevitably contrast is needed, but so
too is good continuity, some feature to suggest the songs are linked.
Usually the most effective way is with something simple and unobtrusive,
a common pitch, interval or rhythmic figure. Ideally it should suggest
development is taking place. The piano part at the end of *Der Wanderer*,
for instance, has a group of four quavers which fall then rise to make a
dipping shape. It also singles out the E, C$\sharp$ and A in the last three bars by
accenting the E, swelling to the C$\sharp$, and making the final A an appoggiatura.

The opening of the next song, *Morgenlied*, contains a variant of the
dipping shape. Emphasis is also given to the fall from E to A, except that
here C$\sharp$ is replaced by C.

The link between the end of *Morgenlied* and the beginning of *Wandrers
Nachtlied* is less obvious. It relies on a three-note figure found in most, if
not all, of Schubert's songs, a segment of an arpeggio combined with a
segment of a scale. If the figure is sufficiently well defined to retain its
identity when varied it becomes a motif. At the end of *Morgenlied* the

unit of a rising third followed by a falling second is present in every bar other than the last (see previous page, bar 85ff).

During the first three bars of *Wandrers Nachtlied* a simple variant of the figure is present in the notes Gb-(Ab)-Bb-Ab and then Ab-(Bb)-Cb-Bb. But since they cut across the phrasing, the listener may only be conscious of the connection subliminally. In bars 3 and 4, however, the figure becomes recognizable even though the rising third has become a fourth: Bb-Eb-D then Gb-C-Bb.[9]

In his penetrating essay 'Motive and text in four Schubert songs', Carl Schachter discusses how Schubert uses motifs to reflect the central images in the poems he sets (Schachter, pp. 209–20). Three of his examples are taken from songs included in these sets. In all of them the motifs are simple, frequently encountered figures. *Dass sie hier gewesen* (Op. 59, No. 2) uses a descending four-note scale. Initially it is split into two units (F-E / D-C#), both units being harmonized by the same diminished seventh chord. They first appear in a high register on the piano. Eleven bars later another version is introduced. Here the scale is transposed, the notes joined up (C-B-A-G), and given to the voice. By harmonizing it with chords on the dominant and tonic of C major, the tonality is clarified. Schachter compares this development of the motif with the images the words evoke. He focuses on the first two lines of the poem: 'The east wind blows gently, scenting the air; and so it tells me that you have been here.' He believes the first scale represents the scent, the second the person. The first is 'a melodic idea barely perceptible as such, floating in an improbably high register within a context of the utmost ambiguity'. The person, the 'you', on the other hand, is represented by 'the same melodic idea but now with distinct outlines, a definite rhythmic shape, the greatest possible clarity of tonal direction. Certainly many

---

[9]   Schubert followed the usual practice of confining most of the performance markings to the piano part. However, when only vocal lines are given as examples in this study, markings in the piano part such as dynamics, hair-pins and accents are supplied on the assumption that singers would inevitably refer to them.

compositional elements contribute to this astonishing example of text setting', he continues: 'rhythm, texture, register, and tonal organization, as well as motivic design. But only the motivic aspect conveys the *connection* between perfume and person, conveys the notion that, in a sense, the two – sign and signified – are one'.

In *Nacht und Träume* (Op. 43, No. 2) the motif consists of three notes of a rising chromatic scale, F#-Fx-G# followed by the same three notes in reverse order, G#-G-F#. The difference between Fx and G, Schachter points out, is crucial to the way Schubert expresses the subject of the poem, the ephemeral nature of dreams. At first both Fx and G are passing notes, but in the second part of the song G becomes the root of a solid major triad. Later, when the poem speaks of dawn awakening, it changes into Fx which still has its status as a passing note. It reappears in the piano's postlude after the words 'Kehre wieder' (come back), but on this occasion it no longer has the stability it had eight bars earlier for now it is a minor sixth requiring resolution.

Schachter refers to the motif A-Bb-G-A in *Der Tod und das Mädchen* (Op. 7, No. 3) as a 'double-neighbour figure'. In D minor, the song's key, Bb is the minor sixth and A the dominant. 'Its most prominent tones, A-Bb-A,' he says, 'form a musical idiom that has had an age-old association with ideas of death, grief, and lamentation.'[10] These particular notes are used only when the girl speaks. When Death speaks the G comes back, and when the key moves into D major for his words 'sollst sanft in meinen Armen schlafen' (you shall sleep softly in my arms) Bb becomes B. 'At the Maiden's death,' says Schachter, 'the double neighbour figure appears in its original rhythmic shape for the first time since the introduction. It decorates a major chord, and both neighbour notes lie a whole step from the main note. In this final statement there is no half-step, no strongly goal-orientated progression; the music, like the Maiden, is at peace.'

Given the attention Schubert devoted to the development of a motif within an individual song, it would have been inconsistent of him not to have given cognizance to the development of a motif within a set, even in those sets compiled from songs written independently of each other. It may indeed have been one of his prime concerns when selecting what items should be included. As Schachter makes clear, a motif can be made from the simplest, most unobtrusive gesture. Schubert's death motif, for example, is merely a slowly descending chromatic scale usually in the

---

[10] Schubert made extensive use of the minor sixth degree of the scale; it can be counted among the hallmarks of his style. Essentially it belongs to the minor mode, but he frequently employs it in major keys to provide a darker hue to the harmonic colour, as in the closing bars of *Nacht und Träume*.

bass. He employs it on a number of occasions in his songs, but nowhere as effectively as across the two songs in his Op. 22 set: *Der Zwerg* and *Wehmut*. The topic is the transience of existence, and three notes of the scale (F♯-F-E) are introduced in the bass near the beginning of the first song when the words speak of the dim light of the mountains fading away. Later, when the queen dies, five other slowly descending notes appear in the bass: D-C♯-C-B-B♭. Near the beginning of *Wehmut* the descending scale appears unobtrusively in a middle voice: A-G♯-G-F♯-F-E. But it is not until the end of this second song that the motif comes fully into its own. Here the words are 'All shall vanish and perish'. In the bass comes an extension of the scale introduced in *Der Zwerg*, G-F♯-F-E; overlapping it in the pianist's right hand, but now prominent, there is an extension of the scale heard near the beginning of *Wehmut*, A-G♯-G-F♯-F-E♭-C♯-D, the missing E appearing almost immediately afterwards. Taken together over the course of the two songs, the scales cover all the chromatic notes contained within an octave. In other words the motif, like the transience of existence, is all-embracing.

In all probability the songs in Op. 22 were composed as a unit, but not those in Op. 108. And yet, as in the earlier set, the principal motif is present in all three songs. *Über Wildemann* dates from 1826, *Todesmusik* from 1822, *Die Erscheinung* from 1815. The motif is simply a rise from the tonic to the mediant through the supertonic and back again. In every instance it is the mediant, the highest note, which receives emphasis. But the mediant varies according to whether the mode is major or minor. In the first restless and deeply troubled song the minor mode prevails. Here the first three notes of the motif receive most attention. The major mode is only touched on when the protagonist thinks fleetingly of happier things. The second song is preoccupied with the hope that happiness will be attained. After the announcement of the whole motif in the major mode, Schubert focuses this time on its last three notes. He returns to the first three notes in the closing bars, and from there the music can slip almost imperceptibly into the last song, a song in which the reiteration of the major form of the motif confirms that happiness has been achieved.

On two occasions Schubert also employs the double neighbour-note figure as a motif covering the whole set. In both instances the neighbour notes are the semitones above and below the dominant so that in the key of D minor, for example, the figure would be A-B♭-A-G♯-A, a figure expressing a fairly high degree of tension because both the B♭ and the G♯ are strongly goal orientated. As in *Der Tod und das Mädchen* the main emphasis is given to the minor sixth, the second note, which functions as an appoggiatura resolving on to the dominant. Although traditionally this expresses anguish or grief, in Op. 19, as in *Der Tod und das Mädchen*, such negative feelings are ultimately transcended, at least in two of the songs. Only Mignon in the second song fails to escape the dark shadows represented by the double neighbour-note figures lying deep in the accompaniment. The set concerns young people who face an early death. The first song changes the minor sixth into a major sixth when the protagonist, having lived his short life up to the hilt, peremptorily knocks at death's door intoxicated. The third song is about Ganymede being taken up to Olympus in a state of ecstasy to embrace his father Zeus. At the climax of his song the second note no longer receives the greatest emphasis. The key is F major and the motif pivots around D, the sixth degree of the scale: (D)-Eb-D-C#-D. Although Schubert accents the Eb, he nevertheless gives greater emphasis to the C# by making it an appoggiatura that aspires upwards for resolution.

The double neighbour-note figure also features in Op. 21, the set about storms on a river. Here the development depends on the degree of dissonance the appoggiatura on the minor sixth receives. When the passengers in the boat on the Danube realize that the storm might plunge them to their deaths, the dissonance is high. When the boatman defies the storm and the minor sixth is used to express his courage in facing what could be his death, the note is accented, but its harmonization is less dissonant. Finally, when the fisherman looks at the fish swimming in the river after the storm, the accent is removed and the mild dissonance conveys merely his disappointment at not being able to catch any that day.

Motifs are not the only way in which Schubert co-ordinates a set. Several of his two-song sets are unified by both songs being underpinned by a rhythmic ostinato. Examples of these are the sets devoted to Goethe, Scott and Schulze, Opp. 14, 85 and 93. In some cases the ostinato represents the repetition of an action such as rowing or the trotting of a horse, in others it serves to reveal an almost obsessive preoccupation with an idea. In all three sets the second ostinato relaxes the tension created in the first. Both the songs in the Matthäus von Collin set Op. 22 make extensive use of measured tremolos indicating insubstantiality, as do those in Op. 43 which also includes a von Collin setting. Opp. 36 and 37 contain songs based on operatic set-pieces. Op. 36 concerns people who go to their deaths singing, and in typical operatic fashion Schubert has them singing full-blown arias as they do so. The other set casts the stories of young men who are unable to fulfil their ambitions and are forced to accept reality in the form of multi-sectional dramatic scenes.

Stylistic features in three-song sets usually involve a progression from one state to another. Op. 65, for example, varies the placing of the voice within the texture to impart a progression from darkness to light across the set. Op. 13 expresses a sense of increasing intimacy by making the contrasts within the songs less extreme as the work unfolds. But perhaps the most interesting examples of progressions leading to fulfilment occur in four-song sets. Throughout Op. 8, for instance, quavers are grouped in threes. The topic is the desire for the ultimate attainment of an ideal, and the fairly easygoing quavers eventually become associated with the river of time. The first three songs place the groups of quavers in duple or quadruple metres; the last, however, contains them in triple metre and in a faster tempo than hitherto. By increasing the sense of flow, the song creates the impression that the river is at last reaching its destiny and the ideal might be fulfilled. However, nowhere is the sense of fulfilment or enrichment more striking than in Op. 88 where the topic concerns the evocation of worlds lying beyond reality through the medium of sound. The first three songs are devoted to what can be gleaned through distant or ghostly sounds; the last to what can be encountered through music. In terms of style the first three songs are limited in their range of expression. The poems necessitate that either their rhythms or their melodies should be restricted, held on a tight rein. But this throws into relief the rhythmic subtlety, the sweeping melody that characterizes the ultimate song, *An die Musik*.

Schubert often composed or compiled sets based on similar ideas one after the other. Opp. 80 and 81, for example, both make use of different types of genre. The first progresses from a simple folk song with a guitar-like accompaniment to an elaborate art song with an impromptu-like piano part which would make a perfectly satisfactory piece by itself. Op. 81 reverses this procedure. From an extremely refined art song, it moves through a strophic song with a lute-like accompaniment to a tavern song in which the piano is there simply to provide the basic harmony without any elaboration.

The keys of the three songs in Op. 81 are A major, D major and A major again. Having the second movement in the sub-dominant of the work's main key is a standard practice in classical instrumental music. The Piano Sonata in A major, D664, for example, has the same scheme. But such coherent schemes are rare in the song sets. They usually occur in those works Schubert composed specially for publication. Those he compiled from individual songs follow the practice observed in eighteenth-century and early nineteenth-century operas, where keys were usually selected because they were suitable for the mood of the individual items rather than for the structure of the work as a whole. Schubert's choice depended on his own predilections as well as the stock of key associations that had been accumulating ever since the tonal system came into existence. In opera, modulating from the key of one number to that of the next was undertaken in the recitatives. The lack of these in the song sets meant that Schubert had to take extra care in selecting songs to ensure that the continuity from one to the other was either smooth or dramatically pertinent.

Another example of a specially composed set with an overall tonal plan is Op. 62 containing three of Mignon's songs. Here the keys are A minor, E minor and B major, a sequence of ascending fifths. The choice was almost certainly determined by the fact that in the third song Mignon, dressed as an angel for a children's party, is on the point of death. She imagines that she has already risen above human existence, and B major was the key Schubert invariably used for transcendence of the spirit. The ascending fifths suggest that the whole of Mignon's short life was fated to lead up to this moment. Schubert also set the first song, *Nur wer die Sehnsucht kennt*, as a duet for Mignon and the Harper. In this instance the words relate to Wilhelm Meister as well as to them. They mirror the dark thoughts that go through Wilhelm's mind as he lies in a reverie: 'Only he who knows longing knows what I suffer.' Schubert must therefore have considered it more appropriate that the song should be in B minor, the key which Beethoven in a sketch for the Cello Sonata, Op. 102, No. 2, called 'black'.

Moving through a section of the cycle of fifths had long been a standard practice in tonal music, but with equal-tempered tuning at his disposal Schubert could also make use of cycles of major thirds. *Der zürnenden Diana* (Op. 36, No. 1) is an example of how he employs a cycle of descending major thirds in the context of an individual song. The four sections are in, respectively, A♭ major, E major, C major then A♭ major again. In Op. 92, the last of his Goethe sets, he extended this procedure by having a cycle of major thirds span the whole work. As always his purpose was to find a musical device that fitted the words, and to do it he had to transpose all the songs to keys which are different from their original ones. The topic is restlessness of spirit. During the course of the first two songs (*Der Musensohn* and *Auf dem See*) and the opening section of the third (*Geistes-Gruss*) it would appear that the restlessness will never cease. But halfway through *Geistes-Gruss* a change occurs. The Ghost of the Hero high up on his cliff tells the passing boat of mankind that although he was restless when young, in his later life he found tranquillity. At that stage the music becomes dignified and calm. Schubert's tonal plan underpins this volte-face. *Der Musensohn* alternates between G major and B major, but ends in G major. Since *Auf dem See* is in E♭ major, listeners may well be in doubt about whether the major thirds are descending or ascending. If descending, then the sequence will be B-G-E♭-B; if ascending G-B-E♭-G. Because it was more usual to modulate to keys a major third lower rather than a major third higher, listeners may expect that the most likely sequence will be the first. But in fact Schubert chose the second, for *Geistes-Gruss* ends in G.

In three sets Schubert co-ordinated the songs by referring to a specific note throughout the work. In one song it might be a dominant, in another a leading note or indeed any degree of the major or minor scale. This procedure had the advantage of enabling him to change the note's function in the context of the set, and by implication its meaning in relation to the text. He made limited use of the idea in *Die schöne Müllerin* and *Winterreise*, but the technique proved more suitable for short rather than long structures so in these Schubert had to use a variety of co-ordinating methods. Op. 6 and Op. 58 have only three songs, the Heine set six. Although the importance of A♭ in the first two songs of Op. 6, *Memnon* and *Antigone und Oedip*, may have been fortuitous, Schubert must have chosen to end the set with *Am Grabe Anselmos* rather than one of his other graveside songs because it too makes significant use of that note. At first A♭ becomes associated with the desire for death. It is established by being reiterated in the rhythm associated the first movement of the Unfinished Symphony, another of Schubert's death motifs. But Memnon is doomed never to die so that A♭ is still present at the end of the song. Oedipus, on the other hand, does find release from life. His C major duet with Antigone reaches its climax in another emphatic reiteration of A♭, but this is the key's minor sixth rather than its dominant as it had been in the first song. When Oedipus dies it resolves. But its resolution down to G is immediately 'corrected' at the beginning of the last song. Here the key is E♭ minor, and the music begins with an A♭ immediately followed by a G♭, this key's 'depressed' minor third. Attention has switched from someone who seeks death to someone who mourns. Schubert casts the song's central section in A♭ minor which has G as its leading note. This means that when G♭ comes back in the final section its depressed character is enhanced. For the mourner death is not a release from suffering, it is the cause of it.

Op. 58 is also about those who mourn, and it too focuses on A♭. Andromache's query as to whether Hector will continue to love her after his death begins in F minor. When he asserts that he assuredly will, her depressed minor third becomes the root of an A♭ major aria for his affirmation. But during the following song his certainty is undermined not only by the poet but also by Schubert's destabilization of A♭ major when it appears. On its reappearance in the last song it is undermined still further. As the minor sixth in the key of C minor, A♭ becomes the note associated with lamentation. All the bereaved girl can do is weep for her dead lover.

The Heine set, which Schubert composed a few months before his death represents the most elaborate use of what can be termed a 'structural pivot'. The keys of the six songs are respectively, G minor, B♭ minor, A♭ major, C minor, C major and B minor. The note which co-ordinates them is F♯ or its enharmonic equivalent G♭. In either one or the other of its 'spellings' it functions as the essential note in the gesture encapsulating the essence of each song. When spelled as F♯ in G minor, C minor and C major it resolves up to G, when spelled as G♭ in B♭ minor and A♭ major it resolves down to F. The only key in which it is stable and need not resolve is B minor, the key of the last song, *Der Doppelgänger*. This may be one of the most harrowing songs Schubert composed but, since F♯ functions as an inner pedal virtually throughout the song and ultimately becomes part of the B major tonality bringing the song to an end, it resolves the tensions it has been associated with hitherto and attains the stability to close the set in a spirit of relative calm.

The Heine set is undoubtedly Schubert's masterpiece in the genre, and since the early 1950s, when Dietrich Fischer-Dieskau began performing it as a unit separate from the other songs in *Schwanengesang* where it is included, it has received, unlike the other sets, a great deal of critical attention and as much controversy as the Unfinished Symphony. Elizabeth Norman McKay is not alone in believing that the songs show Schubert to be 'at the summit of his powers as a composer of songs' (McKay, p. 313). Jack M. Stein, on the other hand, is also not alone in maintaining that Schubert failed to grasp Heine's irony or subtlety, and that none of the songs 'is in any way a real synthesis of poetry and music' (Stein, p. 81). But the most damaging criticism comes from those Schubert scholars who believe that Schubert's ordering of the songs is haphazard and that, as such, they 'can make no claim to the autonomy of a self contained work' (Kramer, p. 125).

To contest these negative criticisms the second part of this study is devoted to a detailed assessment of the Heine set. These criticisms would never have arisen had the detractors been aware of the set's precedents among the 41 other song sets Schubert devised.

PART ONE

Sets with opus numbers assigned by Schubert

Opus 3

Four songs to poems by Johann Wolfgang von Goethe. Published on commission by Cappi and Diabelli, 29 May 1821. Dedicated 'with high regard' to Ignaz, Edler von Mosel.

1. *Schäfers Klagelied* (Shepherd's Lament), D121 (version b, 30 November 1814)[1]
2. *Meeres Stille* (Calm Sea), D216 (21 June 1815)
3. *Heidenröslein* (Wild Rose), D257 (19 August 1815)
4. *Jägers Abendlied* (Huntsman's Evening Song), D368 (?early 1816)

Although the decision to launch the publication of Schubert's songs by drawing on the volume Spaun sent to Goethe in 1816 may have been made for commercial reasons by Leopold von Sonnleithner and the friends who clubbed together to finance the venture, the selection and arrangement of those songs into sets was unquestionably the responsibility of the composer. They bear his stamp and no one else could have compiled them.

Most of Schubert's sets progress from a state of stress to one of tranquillity. Those containing four songs are divided into pairs, each pair consisting of contrasting songs. In this set the storm the distressed shepherd is sheltering from contrasts with the eerie calm of the sea; the destructive liveliness of the boy plucking the rose contrasts with the tranquillity of the huntsman. But since the calmness of the sea produces anxiety, the first pair completes the progression only in terms of the external circumstances. As in other four-song sets, the progression takes place in two phases, the state of inner calm being reserved for the final song.

Op. 3 is unusual in that it lacks a clear topic, but images in the first song – travelling over the sea, aimlessly picking flowers, going grimly through the countryside – are followed up in the other songs.

Texts

1. *Da droben auf jenem Berge.* Six quatrains.

---

[1] The dates of the songs are those given in the Second Edition of *The New Grove Dictionary of Music and Musicians*, eds S. Sadie and J. Tyrrell, London: Macmillan, 2001.

(1) I have stood a thousand times on yonder hill, leaning on my staff and looking down into the valley.

(2) I have followed the grazing flock watched over by my dog, and have come down here without knowing how.

(3) The whole meadow is full of lovely flowers. I pick them without knowing to whom I shall give them.

(4) I shelter under the tree from rain, storm and tempest. The gate over there stays closed, but alas it is all a dream.

(5) It looks as if a rainbow were standing over that house. But she has moved away to distant regions.

(6) To distant regions and beyond, perhaps even over the sea. Move on, you sheep, move on. Your shepherd is so wretched.

2. *Tiefe Stille herrscht im Wasser.* Two quatrains.

(1) A deep calm reigns over the waters, the sea is motionless, and the sailor looks anxiously at the glassy surface all around him.

(2) No breeze from any quarter! A fearful, deathly stillness! No wave stirs in the vast expanse.

3. *Sah ein Knab ein Röslein stehn.* Three seven-line stanzas each ending with the refrain: 'Wild rose, wild rose, wild rose red, Wild rose in the heather.'

(1) A boy saw a wild rose growing in the heather, as young and lovely as the morning. He ran swiftly to see it more closely, and what he saw gave him joy.

(2) Said the boy, 'I shall pluck you, wild rose in the heather'. Said the rose, 'I shall prick you so that you will always remember me. I will not suffer'.

(3) The rough boy plucked the rose, and the rose pricked the boy. But her cries were of no avail. She had to suffer.

4. *Im Felde schleich ich still und wild.* Three quatrains.

(1) As I stalk through the fields, grim and silent, gun at the ready, your sweet image hovers brightly before me.

(2) Perhaps you too are wandering gentle and silent through the field and lovely valley. Does my fleeting image appear to you at all?

(3) When I think of you it is as if I were gazing at the moon. A peaceful, inexplicable tranquillity descends on me.

Music

Musical factors were also important in the choice of these songs for this set. Schubert would have seen that he could make from them a structure resembling the composite instrumental design of a symphony, string quartet or sonata: dramatic movement in sonata form, slow movement, scherzo and finale. The only difference from this pattern is that to be suitable for the home the finale had to reflect the calm, intimate atmosphere of the circumstances.

Of particular significance is the way one song enhances the character of the next. This means that, apart from the first, the songs are more vivid in the context of the set than they are when performed individually. The first song, a quasi-sonata form movement in C minor, contrasts with the second, a through-composed slow movement in C major, not only in its form, tempo and key, but because of the insistence on the note E♭ throughout its course, it throws in relief the following song's equally insistent use of E natural.

1. *Schäfers Klagelied*

C minor. Moderate 6/8 ($\flat$ = 120).

The music for the six stanzas is arranged in the pattern A^1-B^1-C-D-B^2-A^2, A being the equivalent of a first subject in the tonic, B a second subject starting in the relative major (E♭), and C and D a dramatic development moving from A♭ major to A♭ minor (via D♭ major/minor), then, for the climax of the song, when the shepherd alludes to the rain, storm and tempest, to C♭ major. The recapitulation is unorthodox in that the second subject comes before the first, and it is not transposed to the tonic. But this reversal is essential for the drama Schubert imposes on the text. Throughout the exposition and development he gives the impression that everything is in a state of change. For instance, the two phrases used for the first two lines of stanza 1 (Cm) come back in varied form for the first two lines of stanza 2 (E♭) and then with even greater variety for the first two lines of stanza four (C♭). But the prospect that change may continue to take place is dashed in the recapitulation. By reversing the first and second subjects Schubert returns the music to its starting point. In effect the music mirrors the shepherd's dashed hopes when he sees that the door of his sweetheart's house remains locked, and all he can do is to tell his sheep to move on.

E♭ is present in the tonic chords of all the principal keys touched on. *Schäfers Klagelied* was not originally intended to precede *Meeres Stille*, but, as the only significant difference between its last chord and the next song's first is the shift from E♭ to E, the connection is remarkably smooth.

2. *Meeres Stille*

C major. Very slow, anxiously 2/2 ($\bullet$ = 72).

As Lawrence Kramer points out in his analysis of the song (Frisch, p. 210), Goethe's poem seems to have two narrative styles. In the first stanza the voice seems to be that of an impersonal narrator, in the second an anxious sailor. Schubert ignores the stanzaic division and writes a through-composed song reflecting Goethe's observation of the scene from different perspectives by dividing it into four four-bar phrases, each being rhythmically a variant of the durational pattern of the first. He therefore personalizes the text, makes it seem the voice of someone who also experiences extreme anxiety. That this is fear of death becomes clear when for the words, 'No breeze from any quarter! A terrible, deathly stillness!', Schubert introduces his death motif, a descending chromatic scale in the bass.

As Kramer notes:

> *Meeres Stille* is music that barely moves. Schubert's tone painting of Goethe's calm sea involves immobility in every expressive dimension. Both the vocal line and the accompaniment are depressed in register; the highest note in the song is c. There is no change in dynamic level and, in the accompaniment, no change in rhythm; the voice suspends itself over dull arpeggios, one to a measure, in steady *pianissimo*. Even the words fail to move in the usual sense; the singer's long notes make taffy of the text at the tempo indicated. Only the harmony is not static, but while the arpeggios vary in tonal function their sonority is monotonous, an almost unbroken succession of close-position chords and octave basses. (Frisch, p. 210)

Yet although the song is through-composed and only the harmony gives the impression of movement, the opposing pole of attraction to the key's tonic is not the dominant but the median, E minor or E major. In other words, Schubert avoids a strong harmonic dialectic. Halfway through the song he cadences ephemerally on the sub-dominant. The episode quoted above which follows it indicates that it is actually part of a progression towards the dominant of the mediant. Since a progression to a key a third away is considered weak in tonal music, E minor, E major and A minor, the other keys he veers towards, offer no real challenge to the authority of the tonic. Ultimately the listener comes to realize that the harmony also floats in stillness. As in the first song, the sense that change is taking place is unfulfilled. Consequently it is perhaps appropriate that the last words of the poem, 'reget keine Welle sich' (not a wave stirs) should be intoned on one note.

The other pair of songs, the structure's scherzo and finale, are both in repetitive, non-developing strophic form so that musically they too are fundamentally changeless.

3. Heidenröslein

G major. Lieblich (lovingly, charmingly) 2/4 ($\downdownarrows$ = 69).

The key is C major's dominant which had been scarcely touched on in the previous song. Although Goethe is primarily concerned with the distress and plight of the rose, Schubert reflects the light-hearted mood of the boy. As in *Meeres Stille*, he personalizes the text, making it seem like the voice of the boy flirting with the rose (hence the instruction 'lovingly'). The first bar of the song sounds as if the boy were cheekily picking up the quasi-liturgical chant at the end of *Meeres Stille*. Later, in the refrain, the slowing down of the tempo during his rising scale suggests he is teasing the rose before 'deflowering' it.

Rös-lein, Rös-lein, Rös-lein— rot,   Rös-lein auf der Hei - den.

The last four notes of that scale when the boy is most loving will throw new light on a recurring figure in the accompaniment of the last song.

4. Jägers Abendlied

Db major. Very slow, gently 2/4 ($\eighthnote$ = 63).

Goethe's poem actually consists of four stanzas. Schubert's simple strophic setting omits the third stanza because in it the huntsman suspects that his sweetheart will think him ill-humoured and peevish for leaving her, and this would disturb the sense of inner peace the composer wanted to establish. John Reed (SSC, p. 287) reminds us that the sliding sixths in the accompaniment have usually been thought to represent the huntsman 'slinking' through the fields, but in the context of the set, having just heard the boy sing the words 'Röslein rot' to a rising four-note scale, these rising four-note sixths will strongly suggest that, behind his opening words, the huntsman has his sweetheart in mind.

Opus 4

Published on commission by Cappi and Diabelli, 29 May 1821 (the same day as Op. 3). Dedicated 'with respect' to Johann Ladislaus von Pyrker, Patriarch of Venice.

1. *Der Wanderer* (The Wanderer) Georg Philipp Schmidt, D489 (version c, *c.* 1816)
2. *Morgenlied* (Morning Song) Zacharias Werner, D685 (1820)
3. *Wandrers Nachtlied I* (Wanderer's Night Song) Johann Wolfgang von Goethe, D224 (5 July 1815)

Der Wanderer was second only to *Erlkönig* in popularity during Schubert's lifetime. This alone would have been reason enough for the composer to give it prominence in a set he wanted to be a commercial as well as an artistic success. He also needed something to justify ending the set with *Wanderers Nachtlied I*, one of the songs sent by Spaun to Goethe in 1816.

The figure of the Wanderer has had a long history in European literature, and has meant different things to different writers. Schmidt came from Lübeck in what is now Schleswig-Holstein, and it was there in 1542 that the Bishop of Schleswig claimed to have met the Wandering Jew, the man who, according to legend, had been condemned to wander endlessly through the world, lonely and homeless, for urging Christ to walk faster to Calvary. Doubtless this would have influenced Schmidt's version of the figure, but he may also have had in mind those who wandered through the countryside feeling alienated and homeless as a result of being displaced by the effects of the population explosion during the second half of the eighteenth century, especially in rural areas.

Goethe's Wanderer is much closer to the spirit of Romanticism. He represents the man who cuts himself off from the hurly-burly of city life and travels through the countryside in order to find fulfilment and peace of mind in nature. Schubert's setting of the poem is frequently accused of being at odds with Goethe's words, for it makes it appear that the Wanderer has already found the peace of mind he claims to be seeking (DF-D, pp. 43–4 and SSC, p. 429). But this is precisely why it makes a fitting conclusion to the set. It represents a transformation of Schmidt's distress. As in most of Schubert's three-song sets, the second song provides the reason for the transformation. Werner's birds, instead of striving for something beyond their grasp like Schmidt's Wanderer, find contentment in simply being who they are and where they are.

Texts

1. *Ich komme vom Gebirge her.* Five quatrains.

   (1) I have come from the mountains. The valley steams, the ocean roars. I wander on silent and joyless, and my sighs forever ask: Where?

   (2) Here the sun seems so cold, the flower has faded, life is old, and what men say has an empty ring. I am a stranger everywhere.

   (3) Where are you my beloved land, sought after, dreamed of, yet never known? The land so green with hope, the land where my roses bloom,

   (4) where my friends roam together, where my dead friends rise again; the land that speaks my own tongue. O land, where are you ... ?

   (5) I wander on silent and joyless, and my sighs forever ask: Where? In a ghostly whisper comes the answer: 'There, where you are not, there is happiness.'

2. *Eh' die Sonne früh aufersteht.* Four stanzas of varying length.

   (1) Before the sun rises in the morning, when the red flags of dawn flutter over the misty sea and march ahead with gleaming spears, little birds flit to and fro singing merrily here and there a song of jubilation.

   (2) 'What makes you all so happy, little birds, in the warm sunshine?' 'We are happy because we live and we are, and because we are the companions of the air. In time-honoured tradition we flutter merrily through the bushes caressed by the sweet morning breeze; and the sun, too, rejoices.'

   (3) 'And why do you little birds sit so dumb and hunched up in your mossy nests under the roof.' 'We sit here because the sun is not looking at us; night has already dipped it in the waves. The moon alone, that sweet light, that sweet reflection of the sun, never forsakes us in the dark so that we remain happy and tranquil.'

   (4) 'Youth, cool time of morning when with hearts wide open and senses waking we took pleasures in the freshness of life, you have fled, alas. We old ones sit huddled in our nests; but the sweet reflection of youth, when we rejoiced in the dawn, never forsakes us even in old age, the calm, pensive time of happiness.'

3. *Der du von dem Himmel bist.* A single eight-line stanza.

You who are of heaven, who cure all grief and suffering, and fill him who is doubly wretched with double rapture, O, I am weary of strife! What use is all this pain and joy? Sweet peace, come, O come into my breast.

Music

This is the set in which Schubert establishes the principle of progressing towards a state where the tension expressed in the first song is resolved by the conditions described in the second. Everything is therefore moving to the passage where Goethe's Wanderer calls out for peace to enter his heart.

1. *Der Wanderer*

E major. Very slow 2/2 ($\sqcup$ = 63).

Schubert's song is a scena in five episodes roughly corresponding to the poem's five stanzas. The first is tonally ambiguous, for E major is not reached until bar 16. The first key to be established is F♯ minor. The song's 'tune', the melody in C♯ minor, which Schubert was later to use in the Wanderer Fantasy, appears in the second episode. After this, when the Wanderer thinks of the land he dreams of, the key returns to E major and the tempo becomes increasingly more animated. The first tempo comes back in the final episode, when an overwhelming feeling of alienation overcomes him; he hears the ghostly voice telling him that happiness lies where he is not. To ensure that the voice has a ghostly timbre, Schubert takes the music down to a register normally too low for a tenor or high baritone.

2. *Morgenlied*

A minor – major. Fairly slow 2/2 ($\sqcup$ = 63).

The metronome mark is the same as the opening and closing sections of *Der Wanderer*, but because the metre is two rather than four in the bar, the tempo appears to be brisker. Schubert casts the song in modified strophic form, each of the three verses moving from minor to major for a chorus of rejoicing. This varies in length, but is always childlike – simple, diatonic and repetitive.

3. *Wandrers Nachtlied I*

Gb major. Slow, with expression 4/4 ($\sJ$ = 50).

Although Schubert writes the song in Gb, the listener, having just heard a
song ending in A major, will undoubtedly interpret it as being in F♯
major, a major chord on A major's submediant, a tonal relationship
indirect but close. In the broader context of the set, F♯ major relates
directly to the first key in *Der Wanderer*, F♯ minor. The song is through-
composed. Schubert repeats the poem's last line, and for the closing
phrases removes all the chromaticisms, increases the tempo and takes the
voice to a higher register than hitherto. Though it could hardly be called
childlike, it is nevertheless as simple, diatonic and repetitive as the birds'
chorus of rejoicing in the previous song.

Opus 5

Five songs to poems by Johann Wolfgang Goethe. Published on commission by Cappi and Diabelli, 9 July 1821. Dedicated to Antonio Salieri.

1. *Rastlose Liebe* (Restless Love), D138 (version a, 19 May 1815)
2. *Nähe des Geliebten* (Nearness of the Beloved), D162 (version b, 27 February 1815)
3. *Der Fischer* (The Fisherman), D225 (version b, 5 July 1815)
4. *Erster Verlust* (First Loss), D226 (5 July 1815)
5. *Der König in Thule* (The King of Thule), D367 (early 1816)

Having just published seven of the songs contained in the volume sent to Goethe in 1816, Schubert had a severely limited number to choose from for this set. All are comparatively modest in length, which meant that five were needed to match what had become the standardized size of the booklets in which his songs were being published. His choice was determined by the nature of *Rastlose Liebe*, a song about the restless, all-consuming nature of first love. Being entirely devoid of tranquillity, it is the one best suited to come first. As Schubert's only five-song set, the structure is unique. Overall it progresses from first love to a song about the undying love of an old man on the point of death. The internal division is organized to produce the pattern $A^1A^2B^1$-A^3B^2, the three songs designated A being personal and musically highly expressive, the two B songs narratives in the folk idiom and more objective in style. Both tell of a man who dies believing he will soon be united with the woman he loves, and both involve the sea.

Texts

1. *Dem Schnee, dem Regen.* Four stanzas of respectively six, four, four and six lines.

   (1) Against snow, rain and wind, through the steaming mists of ravines – on and on, without rest or peace.
   (2) I would rather battle my way through sorrow than suffer so much joy.
   (3) This affection of one heart for another, oh how strangely it creates pain.
   (4) How shall I escape? Further into the forest? It is all in vain. Love, you are the crown of life, happiness without peace.

2. *Ich denke dein, wenn mir der Sonne Schimmer.* Four quatrains.

   (1) I think of you when sunlight glints from the sea. I think of you
        when the moon's glimmer is reflected in streams.
   (2) I see you when dust rises on distant roads, when the traveller
        trembles on the narrow bridge at dead of night.
   (3) I hear you when the waves surge up with a dull roar. I often go to
        the silent grove to listen when all is quiet.
   (4) I am with you however far away you may be. You are close to
        me. The sun sets, soon the stars will shine forth for me. O, that
        you were here!

3. *Das Wasser rauscht', das Wasser schwoll.* Four eight-line stanzas.

   (1) The water murmured and swelled; a cold-hearted fisherman sat
        by the bank calmly watching his rod. And as he sat and listened
        the waves surged up and parted. From the turbulent depths a
        water nymph arose.
   (2) She sang and spoke to him: 'Why do you lure my kind with
        human guile and skill to the fatal heat? If you only knew how
        happy the little fish are down in the depths, you would descend
        just as you are, and at last be made whole.
   (3) Do not the dear sun and moon bathe themselves in the ocean?
        Are they not twice as beautiful reflected in the waves? Does not
        your own face draw you down here into the dewy depth of eter-
        nity?'
   (4) The water murmured and swelled moistening his naked foot. His
        heart was full of longing, for it was as if his beloved had called to
        him. She sang and spoke to him, and then it was all over. Half
        dragged, half willing, he sank down and was never seen again.

4. *Ach, wer bringt die schönen Tage.* A single nine-line stanza.

   Ah, who will bring back those beautiful days, those days of first love?
   Ah, who will bring back but one hour of that sweet time? Alone, I nurture
   my wound and forever renew my lament mourning my lost happiness.
   Ah, who will bring back those beautiful days, that sweet time?

5. *Es war ein König in Thule.* Six quatrains. (This is the ballad Gretchen
   sings to herself while undressing to go to bed and reflecting on her
   meeting with Faust. The story comes from Norse legend, and
   presumably she is singing it to convince herself that lovers can be
   faithful.)

(1) There was once a king of Thule, faithful to the grave, who was given by his dying mistress a golden goblet.

(2) Nothing was more precious to him; he drained it at every feast, and every time he drank from it his eyes filled with tears.

(3) And when he came to die, he counted all the towns in his realm and gave everything he had to his heirs except this goblet.

(4) In his castle by the sea, he sat at a royal banquet in his lofty ancestral hall surrounded by his knights.

(5) The old tippler stood up, drank life's last glowing draught, and hurled the sacred goblet into the waves below.

(6) He watched it fall and fill, and sink deep into the sea. His eyelids closed, and never more was he to drink a drop.

Music

Schubert will have been aware of the listener's desire to find connections between songs contained in the same context, and this is why he always appears to have chosen items which make the task relatively easy. Usually the most effective connections are the frequently used building blocks of music. In the opening bars of the first song in this set, the four-note scalic units in the pianist's left hand will bind together the first three songs, while the upper notes in the pianist's right hand, a rising minor third followed by a falling second, will be significant in the last two songs.

1. *Rastlose Liebe*

E major. Quick, with passion 2/4 ($\s3 = 152$).

The song is through-composed. For the more reflective third stanza, Schubert modulates to G major and replaces the accompanying semiquavers with triplet quavers. He is therefore able to mirror the sentiment of the text without losing too much impetus. Shortly before moving into G major, for the words 'so much joy', he converts the four-note diatonic scale heard in the bass at the beginning of the song into a four-note chromatic scale in the same register. Then for 'This affection of one heart for another' another chromatic scale appears, this one containing six notes.

When the music returns to E major a variant of the original diatonic version of the four-note scale is rhythmically amended to suit the words, 'Liebe, bist du'. This is the first time the all-important word 'Liebe', the subject of the song, has occurred, so its appearance, and the music associated with it, is bound to be noted by the listener.

A few bars later Schubert repeats the line, and extends the scale chromatically to take the song to its climax.

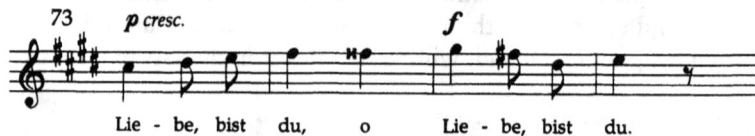

2. *Nähe des Geliebten*

Gb major. Slow, solemnly with grace 12/8 (♩. = 50).

This is more meaningful in the context of this set than by itself. The essence of the poem is the certainty of the poet's love for the distant beloved, and Goethe contrasts his feelings for her by using images that are uncertain, never still: 'sunlight glinting on the sea', 'the moon's glimmer reflected in streams', 'dust rising on distant roads', 'the traveller trembling on the narrow bridge'. Schubert makes a similar contrast, for the stability of the song after the singer enters is markedly different to the ambiguity of the piano's introduction. It begins as though it might be in Eb minor, but in the second bar the possibility that the key is Fb major arises. Since we have just heard a song in E major, Fb major's enharmonic equivalent, we may be tempted to believe that Fb major will be confirmed. Even so the last chord in the second bar could be interpreted aurally as being a German augmented sixth in E♭ minor rather than a dominant seventh in F♭ major. Nevertheless, whatever key the chord implies, the top G♭ has to resolve; it has to either move up or move down. In fact it does neither for Schubert renders its instability stable; 'I think of you' is the beginning of a passage that is emphatically in G♭ major.

Melodically the first two bars feature rising chromatic scales. With *Rastlose Liebe* still in our minds we may associate the six-note scale in the middle voice with 'This affection of one heart for another' in the previous song, and the scalic rise to a G♭ with the scalic rise to an F♯ when the singer sang 'This, Love, is you'. Later in *Nähe des Geliebte* diatonic four-note scales predominate. Each strophe ends with the scale at its most stable (D♭-E♭-F-G♭), its stability intensified by being balanced by its inversion (G♭-F-E♭-D♭). The scale is also uppermost in the horn call in bars five and six (G♭-A♭-B♭-C♭). After the singer's high, strong call in bars two and three, the horn call appears to be coming from the distance. In the eighteenth and early nineteenth centuries, horn calls were associated either with the arrival and departure of the post-chaise, or with hunting, the presence of man in nature. The images that evoke the horn call in the first three stanzas of Goethe's poem are the glittering sea, the rising dust, the surging waves. But in the last stanza it immediately follows 'Du bist mir nah' (you are near me). This is the essence of the poem. The beloved is near because the lover is aware of her presence through what he sees in nature.

3. *Der Fischer*

B♭ major. Moderate 2/4 (♩ = 60).

A strophic song in folk idiom. Like the following two songs and many other early Schubert songs, it lacks a piano introduction. However, the singer will have no difficulty in finding the opening notes (F and B♭) because both are present in the last bar of the previous song. So too, in the third bar, is the four-note horn call, here sounding less evocative, more matter of fact. Its reference is to the call of the water nymph, and then to the fisherman's belief that he is being summoned into the water by his distant sweetheart.

4. *Erster Verlust*

F minor. Very slow, sadly 4/4 (♩ = 54).

The form is ternary (ABA). The first section modulates from F minor to its relative major, Ab, the second from Ab back to the home key for the words 'Mourn my lost happiness'. Schachter considers that F minor represents the unhappy present, and the relative major, the memory of a happier past (Schachter, p. 24). When the first section returns it is shortened by cutting out its central four bars and restating only its opening and closing phrases. This means that, as before, the music modulates from its home key to its relative major. To bring it to a close in F minor, Schubert simply transposes the cadence into Ab major down a third. The result is an ending full of poignant regret.

The first three bars of this passage are a repetition of those which opened the song. In the context of the set they refer to the melodic line in the pianist's right hand in the first four bars of *Rastlose Liebe*, except that here the rising minor third, C-Eb, then another rising minor third followed by a falling second, Bb-(C)-Db-C, are used to express the loss of first love rather than the restlessness associated with it.

5. Der König in Thule

D minor. Rather slow 2/4 ($\downarrow$ = 66).

Schubert's setting groups the six stanzas in pairs to create three strophes. Thule was the name given by the ancient Greeks to an island considered to be the extreme northern limit of the world. To capture the ancient spirit, Schubert casts the melody in the Dorian mode, and has it accompanied by simple chords in root position. As in *Erster Verlust*, the song opens with a rising minor third and in its third bar stresses the same note (C♯ being enharmonically the equivalent of Db). However, in this instance the note is not harmonized as an expressive appoggiatura but as the third of a simple triad (see over).

Etwas langsam

Es war ein Kö - nig in Thü - le,   gar— treu bis an— das Grab

pp   simile

Opus 6

Published on commission by Cappi and Diabelli, 23 August 1821. Dedicated to Johann Michael Vogl 'out of high regard'.

1. *Memnon* (Memnon) Johann Mayrhofer, D541 (March 1817)
2. *Antigone und Oedip* (Antigone and Oedipus) Johann Mayrhofer, D542 (March 1817)
3. *Am Grabe Anselmos* (At Anselmo's Grave) Matthias Claudius, D504 (version a, 4 November 1816)

Michael Vogl (1768–1840) was the leading baritone at the Vienna Hoftheatre when Schubert met him in March 1817. He had sung the role of Pizarro at the first performance of Beethoven's *Fidelio*, and Schubert, who had no one but himself to sing his songs at musical gatherings, had for some time wanted to interest him in his music and, if possible, work with him. Eventually a meeting was held at the house of Franz von Schober. Among those present was Josef von Spaun, who later wrote about it.

> Vogl, full of dignity, arrived at Schober's house on the agreed hour, and when the small insignificant figure of Schubert made rather a clumsy bow and, in his embarrassment, stammered a few disconnected phrases about the honour of meeting Vogl, the singer wrinkled his nose rather disdainfully and the meeting seemed to portend disaster. At last Vogl said, 'Now, then, what have you got there? Accompany me'. Then taking up the first manuscript, Mayrhofer's *Augenlied*, a pretty, very singable, but rather insignificant song, he hummed rather than sang it and said non-committally, 'Not bad!' When after that he was accompanied in *Memnon*, *Ganymed* and other songs, all of which he sang only *mezzo-voce*, he became noticeably friendlier, although he left without promising to return. (DF-D, pp. 94–5)

In fact Vogl had been deeply impressed, and was soon to become one of Schubert's most ardent champions. The composer's choice of *Memnon* to be the first song in this set dedicated to him was his tribute to the moment when the singer first warmed to him. *Antigone und Oedip* was composed immediately after it and was probably one of the other songs Spaun alluded to. Together with *Am Grabe Anselmos* they make a set that challenged Vogl's dramatic and vocal skills to the full. In the first draft of *Antigone und Oedip*, Antigone's line was written in the treble clef and Oedipus's in the bass clef, suggesting that Schubert may have intended the song to be a duet. In the published version, however, only a single singer is intended, for both lines are in the treble clef. Schubert writes the music for Antigone in a relatively high tessitura, and that for Oedipus in a relatively low one. But a copy of the song annotated 'Altered by J. M. Vogl' in the Witteczek-Spaun collection indicates that Vogl also differentiated the two voices by means of the embellishments he added. Matthias Claudius does not indicate whether the poetic voice in *Am Grabe Anselmos* is that of a man or a woman, but since the vocal range of Schubert's song is more or less the same as the vocal range he selected for Antigone, we can assume that the mourner is a woman.

The set is the first of eight involving poems by Schubert's friend Johann Mayrhofer (1787–1836), who exercised a great influence on the composer's intellectual development between autumn 1816 and late 1820, when, for some unexplained reason, they became estranged. Mayrhofer was a tortured person beset by self-hatred and consequently deeply melancholic. His only consolations were nature, poetry and the belief that after death we will gain access to 'ein milder Land', a gentle land of pure spirit. Schubert, being subject to bouts of deep melancholia himself, was broadly sympathetic to his ideas. He set 47 of Mayrhofer's poems, more than those of any other poet except Goethe. The eight sets contain 16 of them. This one reflects Mayrhofer's interest in classical mythology. *Memnon* was the hero who perished during the Trojan war and whose spirit was incarcerated in a statue. Mayrhofer saw him as being tortured like himself, a spirit who gives voice to his suffering in song, and who craves to be released from his earthly existence and attain a condition of pure love. By following it with *Antigone und Oedip,* Schubert shows another tortured man longing to be released from his suffering. He, however, achieves his desire, for at the end of the poem death summons him. When he is dead he will be mourned by Antigone. Schiller does not give us her lament, but it may have been expressed in the same language as that of the mourner in *Am Grabe Anselmos.*

Texts

1. *Den Tag hindurch nur einmal mag ich sprechen.* Four quatrains.

(Memnon, Prince of the Ethiopians, was slain by Achilles during the Trojan war. His mother, Aurora, the goddess of the dawn, begged Zeus to resuscitate him, but Zeus would only allow the rays of the early morning sun to give the statue of Memnon on the west bank of the Nile a few minutes of life each morning. Some Greeks believed that the strange sound which came from the Colossus of Memnon every morning was the voice of Memnon, others that it was like a lyre string breaking.)

(1) I am doomed to eternal silence and grief, only once during the day can I speak, and that is when Aurora's lovely crimson rays break through the night-begotten walls of mists.

(2) To the ears of men this is music, and because I proclaim my grief in song and transfigure its harshness in the fire of poetry, they imagine joy flowers within me.

(3) Yet within me, I am clutched by the arms of death, snakes writhe in the depths of my heart. I am nourished by the anguish of my thoughts, and almost maddened with restless desire.

(4) Oh to be united with you, goddess of the dawn, and, far from this vain bustle, to shine down as a pale silent star from spheres of noble liberty and pure love.

2. *Ihr hohen Himmlischen erhöret.* Seven quatrains.

Antigone:

(1) You gods on high, hear a daughter's heartfelt plea. Let the cool breath of comfort waft into my father's great soul.

(2) Take this young life to assuage your wrath; let your avenging blow destroy this deeply distressed sufferer.

(3) Humbly I clasp my hands. The sky is calm and clear; only mild breezes rustle through the ancient grove.

(4) Why does my pallid father sigh and moan? I sense that some dreadful vision disturbs his light sleep. He starts up from the grass and speaks.

Oedipus:

(5) I dream a troubled dream. Did not this right hand wield the sceptre? But mighty forces brought the majesty of this old man to dust.

(6) In happy days, amid the songs of heroes and the blare of horns in my ancestral halls, did I drink, O Helios, your golden light

(7) which now I can never see again? From every side I hear destruction call: 'Prepare yourself for death, your earthly task is done.'

3. *Dass ich dich verloren habe.* A single stanza of eight lines.

That I have lost you, that you are no more, ah, that my Anselmo lies here in this grave, that is my sorrow. See, we two loved each other, and as long as I live joy will never return to my heart.

Music

This is the first set which Schubert co-ordinated through his references to a specific pitch. He may have taken advantage of the coincidence that in *Memnon* he refers to A♭ frequently during the course of the song, that he dwells on it at the climax of *Antigone und Oedip*, and that taken together they make it musically clear that Memnon failed to find release in death and that Oedipus did. His choice of *Am Grabe Anselmos* as a song of mourning may have been determined by the significance it too places on A♭.

1. *Memnon*

D♭ major. Very slow, passionately 2/2 (♩ = 50).

Schubert made no attempt to find a musical image to represent the strange sound which came from the Colossus of Memnon each morning. The piano introduction has a melodic line lying within an A♭ octave pedal reiterated to sound like the type of muted military call associated with the summons to a funeral. This is verified when the singer enters with music characteristic of a funeral march.[2]

Den Tag hin-durch nur ein-mal mag ich spre-chen, ge-wohnt zu schwei-gen im-mer und zu trau-ern

The song is through-composed, divides into two parts, and within these each stanza has its own characteristic music. The first part culminates in a lyrical episode in F major, when Memnon speaks of the harshness of his grief being transfigured by the fire of poetry. The second, which becomes faster in tempo, leads to a broad, passionate melody in D♭ major when Memnon dreams of being a star.

In the last stanza, the rhythm of the military call, which has been intermittently present throughout the song, is evened out to become a consistent pattern of triplet quavers. To round off the song, the piano's introduction comes back transformed. It no longer has the military call; the melody, articulated in triplets, lies in the upper register, and the A♭ pedal is confined to the middle register. The implication is that memories of military life have no place in the mind of someone who imagines he has already joined his mother in spheres of 'noble liberty' and 'pure love'.

---

[2]   Mahler, who was au fait with Austrian military calls, opens the first movement of his Fifth Symphony, which he entitles 'Death March: Like a Funeral Procession', with a fanfare beginning with the same triple rhythm.

2. *Antigone und Oedip*

C major. Slow 4/4 (♩ = 54) – recitative (slightly faster) – moderate 4/4 (♩ = 104).

A dramatic scene consisting of two arias divided by a recitative for Antigone when she hears her father groan and sees him wake up. Her aria lies between the E above middle C and the F♯ a ninth higher, and consists of long phrases accompanied in the main by undulating arpeggio figures. Oedipus's lies between the G below middle C and the C♯ an eleventh higher, and has an accompaniment based on horn-like figures. When he wakes and remembers he was once a king, the piano plays a type of fanfare associated with trumpets. Although flamboyant rather than muted and sombre, this fanfare may put the listener in mind of the military call in *Memnon*. But a closer relationship between the two songs occurs when Oedipus hears the voice of death at the end of the song.

The passage is in two parts. For the words, 'Prepare yourself for death', the pedal on A♭ and the chords on the piano in bars 76 and 77, even though in the minor, take us back to Memnon's preoccupation with death at the opening of the previous song. But when A♭ becomes G♯ and the music returns to C major via A minor for the words, 'Your earthly task is done', the switch implies that Oedipus has found the release Memnon is denied. Schubert reinforces this in the piano's postlude by bringing back A♭ as the root of an accented augmented sixth chord resolving on to G, C major's dominant.

3. *Am Grabe Anselmos*

Eb minor. Slow 3/4 (♩ = 50).

After a song in C major, Eb minor sounds particularly sombre. The song begins in what appears to be the middle of a phrase. The first thing that might strike the listener is that Ab resolves on to a note a semitone lower than it did at the end of the previous song, on to Gb, the key's depressed minor third.

The leaning notes and the irregular pattern of accents create the impression of emotional disturbance. In the context of the set, the melodic line in the second and third bars (Gb-F-F-Eb) relates to the moment when the voice enters in *Memnon* and we are given a passing reference to a funeral march (Ab-G-G-F). More directly, the whole of this piano introduction could be considered a continuation of the passage in *Antigone und Oedip* when we hear the ominous words, 'Prepare yourself for death'. All that needs to be done is to transpose bar 76 and the first chord in bar 77 in the previous song up an octave and adjust the tempo and metre. Even those listeners who fail to identify the connections may, nevertheless, be intuitively aware that *Am Grabe Anselmos* has its genesis in the previous songs.

Schubert repeats the first five lines at the end to make an ABA structure, the central section modulating to Ab minor for the words 'joy will never return to my heart'. This means that once again Ab becomes prominent in the set. He also gives emphasis to the sub-dominant in other graveside songs, notably *Bei dem Grabe meines Vaters* (D496) and *Ihr Grab* (D736). In minor keys the sub-dominant triad contains the minor sixth, the note traditionally associated with lamentation, in this case Cb. The melody as in all Schubert's graveside songs is characterized by his use of the notes of the tonic arpeggio. The 'open' sonority this produces helps to provide Claudius's lament with great dignity.

Opus 7

Published on commission by Cappi and Diabelli, 27 November 1821.
Dedicated 'out of high regard' to Ludwig Count von Széchényi.

1. *Die abgeblühte Linde* (The Faded Linden Tree) Ludwig Count von
   Széchényi, D514 (?1817)
2. *Der Flug der Zeit* (The Flight of Time) Ludwig Count von Széchényi,
   D515 (?1817)
3. *Der Tod und das Mädchen* (Death and the Maiden) Matthias Claudius, D531 (February 1817)

As high steward to the Archduchess Sophie and a prominent member of
the Philharmonic Society, Count Széchényi was a person Schubert would
want to please. His poems were not published until after these songs were
composed, so Schubert must have had access to Széchényi's manuscripts.
From a commercial point of view the attraction of the set was the inclusion of *Der Tod und das Mädchen*, a song which had made a deep
impression on Schubert's friends when he first sang it to them in 1817.
Although the second edition of *The New Grove Dictionary of Music and
Musicians* suggests that the Széchényi poems may also date from 1817,
John Reed believed that this seems improbable, if only because Schubert
can hardly have been in touch with the author before 1820. 'The more
likely hypothesis', he suggested, 'is that the songs were written in 1821
with the publication (and the dedication) in mind' (SSC, p. 148).
Széchényi's poems may have been selected to go with *Der Tod und das
Mädchen* because they concern the passing of time, and therefore make a
suitable introduction to the set.

Matthias Claudius was probably at his best in his nature poems and in
those poems which hover between a love of life and a desire to welcome
'Friend Hain', his name for death. *Der Tod und das Mädchen* was the
most famous of these. It was first published in 1775 and remained
popular for over 50 years not only for its simplicity, but because it helped
to dispel the long-held medieval symbol of death as a grotesque skeleton
who came to punish. Its irony in the context of the set is that, whereas
Die abgeblühte Linde and *Der Flug der Zeit* lead us to expect that the
final song will concern the death of someone old, it actually concerns the
death of someone whose hair has not turned white, who has had only
limited experience of the flight of time.

Texts

1. *Wirst du halten, was du schwurst.* Four quatrains.

   (1) Will you still abide by what you pledged to me when time has made my hair white? Since you have gone over the mountains our meetings are rare.
   (2) Time is the child of change, and when we part this threatens us. What the future offers us is a paler glow of light.
   (3) The linden tree is still flowering as you take your leave today. You will find it here when you return, except that then the west wind may have stripped it of its blossom.
   (4) It will stand alone, people will pass it by indifferently, hardly noticing it. Only the gardener will remain faithful, since he loves the tree for itself.

2. *Es floh die Zeit im Wirbelfluge.* Three quatrains.

   (1) Time flew by like a whirlwind carrying away with it all life's plans. It was stormy on the journey, often difficult and unpleasant.
   (2) It passed through each age, the childhood years, the happiness of youth; through valleys where joy lies, now remembered with longing.
   (3) Until, with gentler flight, it reached the shining uplands of friendship, and there at last it folded its wings in sweet repose.

3. *Vorüber, ach vorüber.* Two quatrains.

   The Maiden:
   Pass by, ah, pass by! Away, savage skeleton. I am still young. Go away, dear fellow. Do not touch me.
   Death:
   Give me your hand. I am your friend and not to be feared. You shall sleep softly in my arms.

Music

Mayrhofer, in his obituary for Schubert, considered how he treated each poet differently.

> If the wealth of melody he invented justly astonishes, the amazement is further heightened by the clear-sightedness, the certainty and the

felicity with which he penetrated into the life of the words and, I should say, into the personality of each poet. How differently and yet how characteristically does he deal with Goethe, Schiller, Müller, Rückert, Schlegel, Scott, Schulze and others! (Doc, p. 863)

Although this statement has to be modified in the case of those poets whose work embraces a wide range of literary styles and topics, such as Goethe and Schiller, it does hold true for lesser poets. *Die abgeblühte Linde* and *Der Flug der Zeit* are Schubert's only Széchényi settings. Both are operatic in style, binary in form, have a principal subject based on the notes of the tonic chord and make significant use of the chord of the German augmented sixth. These features are not unusual in themselves, but together they provide the songs with a characteristic identity.

However, in this instance, the identity may not have been originated by something in Széchényi's literary style, it may have come from the salient features of *Der Tod und das Mädchen*. As Christoph Wolff says in his analysis of the song, 'the technical vocabulary of the music is taken from opera'. The first stanza 'follows in its design the traditional pattern of an *accompagnato* recitative', while the voice of Death in the second employs 'the oracle *topos* of eighteenth-century *opera seria*' (Studies, 1982, p. 156). Moreover, like *Die abgeblühte Linde* and *Der Flug der Zeit*, the song ends by offering assurance and consolation.

1. *Die abgeblühte Linde*

The first stanza is cast as an *accompagnato* recitative in A minor, moderato 4/4 ($\quarternote$ = 92), the following three as a binary aria in C major, moderato 2/2, the lines about the gardener remaining faithful being repeated to form a coda in a somewhat faster tempo. These lines are the clue to the song, for in style and structure its music emphasizes solidity and security, a feature encapsulated in the aria's opening bars.

Between the recitative and the coda there are three diatonic statements, and in each their solidity is enhanced by being preceded by an unstable passage in the minor. For the third statement Schubert moves through F minor, G minor and A minor to A major (the key of the next song). In the coda the return to C major is approached through a German augmented sixth which has E♭ among its notes. The purpose of this being to make the E on which the word 'Gärtner' is articulated as bright as possible.

2. Der Flug der Zeit

A major. Rather fast 6/8 (♩. = 112).

When the tonic returned after the development section in the previous song, the tempo became faster. Here it becomes slower. The rhythm is that of a barcarolle so that when Schubert reaches the words 'and there at last it folded its wings in sweet repose' the music sounds as if the gondolier were reaching his destination. As in the previous song he highlights the crucial word, in this case 'süsser', by approaching it through a German sixth.

3. Der Tod und das Mädchen

D minor – major. Moderate 2/2 (♩ = 54).

This tempo applies to the opening funeral march and the music for Death. The girl's recitative has to be slightly faster. Christoph Wolff suggests that Schubert's model for the song was the oracle scene in the first act of Gluck's Alceste:

The solemn, quasi-psalmodic pitch-repetition, the trombone-like low register accompaniment – so uncharacteristic of pianoforte writing – the strictly regulated rhythmical declamation and the cadential formulae; the preparation of the oracle by an *accompagnato* recitative: all those very characteristic elements of the Schubert song find their logical explanation in the connection with the scene in *Alceste*. (Studies, 1982, pp. 156–7)

Absent from Gluck's scene is the funeral march which frames the song. Initially it is cast in the minor, but when Death has completed his declamation it comes back in the major so that it sounds as if the girl has found consolation.

As Schachter points out, the double neighbour-note figure the piano plays at the opening of the song (A-B♭-G-A) binds it together, for as well as being transposed into the major when the girl peacefully expires in death's arms, its most characterisic feature A-B♭-A, a move from the dominant to the minor sixth and back, is used when she expresses her anxiety before being pacified by death (Schachter, pp. 213–15). The minor sixth is the root of the German augmented sixth chords in the first two songs. It cannot have been a coincidence that these chords are also used to lead into the most important word in them.

Opus 8

Published on commission by Cappi and Diabelli, 9 May 1822. Dedicated 'out of deep respect' to Johann Karl Esterházy von Galántha.

1. *Der Jüngling auf dem Hügel* (The Youth on the Hill) Heinrich Hüttenbrenner, D702 (November 1820)
2. *Sehnsucht* (Longing) Johann Mayrhofer, D516 (?1816)
3. *Erlafsee* (Lake Erlaf) Johann Mayrhofer, D586 (September 1817)
4. *Am Strome* (By the River) Johann Mayrhofer, D539 (March 1817)

In this, the second set involving poems by Mayrhofer, Schubert focuses on the importance of nature for the poet. Nature was where he could glimpse the *milder Land* he yearned for, the gentle land of pure spirit he would discover after death. But on the grounds that he had not yet reached his Platonic ideal, he found sadness as well as happiness in nature. To paraphrase the opening of *Erlafsee*, 'wohl' was interwoven with 'weh'. As in many of the sets, especially the reflective ones, Schubert begins with a song in which the issues are expressed in simple, graphic terms. Following his normal practice, he groups the four songs into related pairs. The first is descriptive, the second inward looking. Thus *Der Jüngling auf dem Hügel* contrasts with *Sehnsucht*, *Erlafsee* with *Am Strome*.

In the anthology of Mayrhofer's poems published in 1824, *Erlafsee* has six stanzas containing 36 lines. The song Schubert composed in 1817 consists of two stanzas containing 14 lines. Susan Youens in her analysis of the song (Youens, pp. 198–202) offers two speculative reasons for this: 'Schubert either found nothing *brauchbares für Musik* (usable for music) in the other four stanzas ... or else Mayrhofer might have interleaved additional stanzas to an originally much shorter poem before the publication of his anthology in 1824' (Youens, p. 198). This set suggests, however, that when Schubert compiled it early in 1822 he was acquainted with these four stanzas, for the last two have a direct bearing on why he chose to bring it to an end with *Am Strome*. Susan Youens translates these stanzas as follows:

(5) The lake's border is a ribbon woven of light green: it is the river that must drive the saw-mill further down.
(6) Unwillingly it writhes along the narrow path, distant from its beautiful mother, and flees to far-away lands. Love will you too, with gentle hands, entwine the singer's grave, rocky land with blossom-red?

These lines are obscure; the images need to be pondered over. Consequently, had Schubert seen the stanzas in 1817, he would have considered them unsuitable for music. *Am Strome*, however, offers a simple, eminently settable version of their contents.

Texts

1. *Ein Jüngling auf dem Hügel.* Nine quatrains.

   (1) A youth sat on a hill with his sorrow, his eyes becoming dim and moist with tears.
   (2) He watched lambs gambolling happily on the green hillside, and brooks rippling merrily through the bright valley.
   (3) Butterflies sipped at the red mouth of the flowers; clouds scudded about like morning dreams.
   (4) Everything was so cheerful, bathed in happiness; only his heart was untouched by the light of joy.
   (5) Just then the muffled death-knell sounded in the village, and in the distance there echoed a mournful song.
   (6) He saw the lights shining and the black cortège. He began to weep bitterly for they were bearing away his Rosie.
   (7) Now they lowered the coffin. The gravedigger came to return to the earth that which God had once made from it.
   (8) Then the youth ceased lamenting and looked upwards in prayer, foreseeing happier days when they would meet again in bliss.
   (9) And as the stars came out and the moon sailed heavenwards, he read in those stars a message of hope.

2. *Der Lerche wolkennahe Lieder.* Two eight-line stanzas.

   (1) Winter flees and the songs of the cloud-soaring lark ring out; the earth wraps itself in velvet and fruit forms from the blossom. Only you, storm-tossed soul, only you do not flower; turned in on yourself you are consumed by longing even in the golden radiance of spring.
   (2) What you desire will never sprout from this earth, alien to ideals, for the earth defiantly opposes its raw strength to your fairest dreams. You wear yourself out wrestling with its harshness, consumed by the burning desire to journey to a kinder land as an aspiring companion to the cranes.

3. *Mir ist so wohl, so weh'.* Two stanzas, one with eight lines, the other with six.

(1) I am so happy, so melancholy by the calm waters of Lake Erlaf. A sacred silence amid the pine branches; motionless the dark depths. Only the shadows of clouds float across its glassy surface.

(2) Cool breezes gently ruffle the water, the sun's golden corona grows paler. (Schubert then repeats the first two lines of the poem: I am so happy, so melancholy by the calm waters of Lake Erlaf.)

4. *Ist mir's doch, als sei mein Leben*. Three quatrains.

(1) My life, it seems, is linked to the lovely river; for have I not known joy and sorrow on its banks?

(2) Yes, you are like my soul, sometimes green and tranquil, and at other times, when the wind blows, foaming, agitated, furrowed.

(3) Unable to find a home here, you flow to the distant sea. I yearn for a kinder land, for I too can find no happiness on earth.

Music

The musical structure clarifies Schubert's division of the set into two related pairs. The first two songs involve thoughts and feelings which change. Both structures have four sections each in a different key and containing different material. Both songs end in G major, and both go into C major for the sections dealing with nature in springtime. The third and fourth songs, on the other hand, begin and end in the same mood, and are therefore ternary in structure, their contrasting central sections being in a faster tempo than the ones that enclose it.

The songs are united by their use of quavers grouped in threes. In the first three songs this grouping occurs within either duple or quadruple metres, simple or compound; in the last in triple metre. This means that crotchets as well as quavers are grouped in threes. As a result *Am Strome* sounds more flowing and relaxed than the previous songs. Because it represents the river of time flowing to the destiny Mayrhofer and Hütten-brenner's young men yearn for, its course runs more smoothly. The song also makes a clearer distinction between 'wohl' and 'weh' than hitherto. The first two songs both begin and end with 'wohl' foremost, and move into and out of 'weh' by means of a transition. The opening line of *Erlafsee*, on the other hand, demands that 'wohl' and 'weh' should be closely interwoven so that a mere chromatic inflection is enough to convey the frequent moves from one into the other. This throws the clean separation of them in *Am Strome* into sharp relief. It creates the impression that although storms may happen on rivers and in the life of the poet, they are mere incidents. Ultimately the sought-for destination will be reached.

1. *Der Jüngling auf dem Hügel*

The song's four sections are: (1) E minor. Not too slow 6/8[3] (the young man's sorrow), (2) C major. Moderate 4/4 (his sight of the lambs, brooks and butterflies), (3) G minor. Slow 4/4 (the funeral of his sweetheart), G major. Somewhat faster 6/8 (his conviction that they will eventually be united in joy).

2. *Sehnsucht*

The tempo is a slow 12/8 throughout.

The four sections are: (1) C major (the beauty of the spring landscape), (2) a rapid modulation from A♭ major to the dominant of B minor via G♯ major (the poet's storm-tossed soul and sense of longing), (3) B minor (the earth as being alien to ideals), (4) G major (the longing to be a companion to the cranes).

Although *Der Jüngling auf dem Hügel* and *Sehnsucht* have several features in common, they differ in that one uses the third person and the other the first person singular, making the setting of Hüttenbrenner's poem considerably less introspective and less vivid than that of Mayrhofer's. In the first song, for example, when the young man catches sight of the funeral and is at his most distressed, Schubert illustrates the scene by interrupting the syncopations representing the young man's distress to insert a two-bar, quasi-liturgical gesture in the rhythm of a funeral march (bars 59 and 60). But at a corresponding place in *Sehnsucht* his musical images have to appear to come from inside the poet/singer. For the lines *Nur du, o sturmbewegte Seele, /nur du bist blütenloss, in dich gekehrt ...* (Only you, storm-tossed soul, only you do not flower, turned in on yourself ...) he also interrupts one progression to insert, in bars 14 and 15, another. But these strongly emphatic two bars for *Nur du, o sturmbewegte Seele* speak directly of Mayrhofer's anguish. And, as Susan Youens points out, by prolonging the '*du*' Schubert is able to call attention to what she calls 'the sufferer's self-obsession' (Youens, p. 197) (see over).

---

[3] For this and all the following sets Schubert did not supply metronome markings. An account of Schubert's metronome markings can be found in Clive Brown's essay, 'Schubert's tempo conventions', in Studies, 1998, pp. 1–15.

Both *Der Jüngling auf dem Hügel* and *Sehnsucht* end with the piano playing a line which runs in rhythmical unison and parallel with the vocal line to represent, on the one hand, the young man's hopes of being united with his Rosie and, on the other, Mayrhofer's hopes of becoming a companion to the cranes. In the closing bars of *Sehnsucht*, however, Schubert introduces the flattened sixth of the key to suggest *weh* in the presence of *wohl*. This inflection and the contour of the last three notes in the line (F♯-A-G) will be taken up in *Erlafsee*.

3. *Erlafsee*

F major. Rather slow – faster – tempo 1 6/8.

Schubert makes the two stanzas into a ternary structure by repeating the words and the music of the first two lines at the end. This repeat offers a good illustration of how the song develops the ending of *Sehnsucht*. The minor sixth in *Sehnsucht* is E♭, here it is D♭, but the first chromaticism in *Erlafsee* is E♭, and it is this note which provides the first link with the previous song. The contour made by F♯-A-G in close position comes back as B♭-(C)-D♭-C when the opening phrase is inflected to convey 'weh'. D♭ is also prominent in the penultimate bar.

4. *Am Strome*

B major. Moderato 3/4.

The design is ternary, the central section marked fast 4/4. F major and B major are at opposite ends of the tonal spectrum, but since the opening of *Am Strome* simply raises the F-B♭ in the melodic line at the end of *Erlafsee* up a semitone to F♯-B the succession feels natural (see over).

Like many composers in the eighteenth and early nineteenth centuries, Schubert frequently associated F major with the pastoral. He uses B major when the words speak of spiritual transcendence, of rising above one's normal frame of mind. In this instance its use suggests that in *Am Strome* Mayrhofer had considered his entry into the gentle land to be imminent. However, key alone cannot convey this, and this may be why Schubert cast the central section in a different tempo and metre. It creates the impression that Mayrhofer's thoughts about being lashed by storms have interrupted his peaceful meditation The vehemence of his outburst relates the song to the insert in *Sehnsucht* outlined above. But in this song the way the piano takes up and transforms the singer's concluding notes in preparation for the return of the opening section suggests that the poet has put his troubled feelings behind him.

Opus 12

The Songs of the Harper from Goethe's *Wilhelm Meister's Apprenticeship*. Published on commission by Cappi and Diabelli, 13 December 1822. Dedicated 'out of respect' to Johann Nepomuk von Dankesreither, Bishop of St Pölten.

1. *Wer sich der Einsamkeit ergibt* (He who gives himself up to solitude), D478 (version b, 1822)
2. *Wer nie sein Brot mit Tränen ass* (He who has never eaten his bread without tears), D480, No. 3 (version c, 1822)
3. *An die Türen will ich schleichen* (I shall steal from door to door), D479 (version b, 1822)

Wilhelm Meister's Apprenticeship was published in 1795–96 and deals with a young man's apprenticeship for life. Goethe held that, although we are free to fashion our development in the way we want, our aim should be to achieve harmony within ourselves and be of use to others. Wilhelm sets out on his voyage of discovery by joining a theatre troupe, and the characters he encounters on his journey have in their various ways either achieved what Goethe regarded as the human ideal, or failed to do so. Those who have achieved the ideal are the aristocratic figures of Lothario and Natalie, who appear in the second half of the novel: those who have not, and are consequently at odds with themselves, are the homeless, romantic and pathetic figures of Mignon and the Harper.

Wilhelm first encounters the Harper when the mysterious man is performing at a dinner party. Later, when Wilhelm feels restless and wants 'to allay the evil spirit that torments him' he visits him in his attic. As he climbs the stairs to the man's bleak lodging he hears him singing the song *Wer nie sein Brot mit Tränen ass* (number 2). On entering his room he asks him to sing again. This time the song is *Wer sich der Einsamkeit ergibt* (number 1). This establishes a bond of sympathy between the two men, for Wilhelm, believing that his mistress has betrayed and deserted him, feels that the sentiment relates to himself. As a consequence he asks the Harper to join his entourage. But as time goes on the Harper behaves more and more strangely until eventually he becomes unhinged and commits arson. It is after this that he sings *An die Türen will ich schleichen* (number 3). According to Wilhelm, this 'had for its subject the consolation of a wretched being, conscious that he was about to fall into insanity'. We are not told why the Harper's guilt should have led to this condition until the end of the novel, when it is revealed that he has had an incestuous relationship with his sister and that Mignon is his daughter. Meanwhile Wilhelm arranges for him to be cared for by a sympathetic doctor and clergyman. Eventually, when he becomes well enough to teach, the old man finds that he too can be of use to others, and he ends his days in a state of relative tranquillity.

Texts

1. *Wer sich der Einsamkeit ergibt.* Two eight-line stanzas.

   (1) The man who takes to solitude, ah, he is soon alone; each man lives, each man loves, and leaves him to his agony. Yes, leave me to my suffering for once I am truly alone I shall not be lonely.

   (2) Just as a lover steals up softly to discover whether his beloved is alone, so my miseries steal up on me to torment me day and night. They will leave me alone only when I lie in the grave.

2. *Wer nie sein Brot mit Tränen ass.* Two quatrains.

   (1) He who has never eaten his bread without tears, who has never spent anxious nights weeping on his bed, knows you not, heavenly powers.

   (2) You bring us into life, let us fall into guilt and then abandon us in our agony, for all guilt is avenged on earth.

3. *An die Türen will ich schleichen.* A single eight-line stanza.

   I shall go from door to door, and when a kind hand offers me food I shall go on my way. Men will think themselves happy when they see me standing before them. They will shed a tear, yet I shall not know why they weep.

Music

Schubert set *Wer sich der Einsamkeit ergibt* (number 2) twice and *Wer nie sein Brot mit Tränen ass* (number 1) three times. The first version of *Wer sich der Einsamkeit ergibt* dates from 13 November 1815 and is a simple song in A minor marked *Klagend* (plaintive). It brings out what Goethe called the 'sad, heartfelt' quality of the Harper's singing. The following September Schubert composed his first version of *Wer nie sein Brot mit Tränen ass*, also a simple song in A minor marked *Klagend*. He must then have seen the possibilities of creating a dramatic set from all three poems. To do so he changed Goethe's order and wrote new versions of the songs he had already composed. Goethe's second song came first, his third second and his first last. The reasons he chose to do this are discussed in the introductory section of this study.

When he came to publish the set in 1822, Schubert rewrote *Wer nie sein Brot mit Tränen ass* again and placed it second. This third version is less highly charged than the second one, and serves as an ideal transition between the intense first song and the even-tempered third. In its new position *An die Türen will ich schleichen* gives the impression that the Harper has gone beyond feeling separated from himself and the world, and become as naive as a child. In this respect the song looks forward to the final song in *Winterreise*.

1. *Wer sich der Einsamkeit ergibt*

A minor. Very slow 2/2.

Through-composed. Harmonically the most striking feature of the song is the way it constantly returns to A minor. When the first version of the set was discussed in the introductory section, it was suggested that Schubert chose to cast all the songs in this key, not only because he associated it with pathos, alienation and derangement, but because it could serve as a frame to indicate the Harper's attempts to hold his potential madness in check. In the first somewhat hesitant section of this song, where the Harper seems to be gathering his thoughts after every phrase, there are no fewer than four paragraphs cadencing in A minor. Later, when the Harper becomes more sure of himself and the accompaniment more harp-like, the paragraphs are longer. The only time he gives way to the intensity of his emotions is when he sings *sotto voce* 'Ah when I lie lonely in the grave' against Schubert's chromatically descending death motif in the bass, and then raises his voice to *fortissimo* for 'then they will leave me alone'. But he quickly controls himself, for when he repeats the words he returns to singing softly.

2. *Wer nie sein Brot mit Tränen ass*

A minor. Slow 2/2.

Schubert goes through each stanza twice, the second occasion being musically a highly modified version of the first. Once again he exaggerates the dynamics at the climax of the song. When he comes a second time to 'for all guilt is avenged on earth', he makes a huge crescendo on a single note from *pianissimo* to *fortissimo* in a bar and a half. The song ends in A major. After being in the minor mode for so long it should sound bright and stable. But Schubert weakens it by introducing a B♭ into his elaboration of the final chord, so that it sounds as if it could be the dominant of D minor. It is difficult to think of a more imaginative way to suggest the Harper's agony and instability of mind at one and the same time.

3. *An die Türen will ich schleichen*

A minor. In a moderate walking tempo 2/2.

Schubert divides the eight lines into two strophes, the first with the pattern A-B-C-D, the second with the pattern E-B-C-D. This is the simplest of the three songs. Apart from an occasional accent, the dynamics rarely rise above *pianissimo*. The texture is consistently legato, and instead of having a harp-like accompaniment, a 'walking' bass line takes the song to its A minor destination. The clue to the Harper's naïveté comes from the vocal line's tessitura, for it is confined to the upper register of a tenor's or high baritone's voice. Furthermore, there is no display of emotion in the song. Its simplicity suggests that either the Harper has total control over his emotions or else he has transcended them.

Opus 13

Published on commission by Cappi and Diabelli, 13 December 1822.
Dedicated to Josef von Spaun 'out of friendship'.

1. *Der Schäfer und der Reiter* (The Shepherd and the Horseman)
   Friedrich de la Motte Fouqué, D517 (version b, 1822)
2. *Lob der Tränen* (In Praise of Tears) August Wilhelm von Schlegel,
   D711 (version b, 1822)
3. *Der Alpenjäger* (The Alpine Huntsman) Johann Mayrhofer, D524
   (version c, January 1817)

Cappi and Diabelli brought out this set on the same day as the Harper's
Songs Op. 12 and the two songs from Goethe's *West-östlicher Divan* Op.
14. As with several of his other sets, Schubert selected songs he knew
would appeal to the dedicatee. In this instance, however, he consulted
Spaun beforehand. This must have been before September 1821 because
in that month Spaun left Vienna to take up a government post in Linz for
five years. On 7 December 1822 Schubert sent copies of the Opp. 12 and
13 sets to Spaun and in an accompanying letter wrote: 'I hope to give you
some pleasure by the dedication of these songs ... you will like their
choice, for I selected those which you indicated yourself' (Doc. 328). He
then went on to say that Op. 14 was still with the engraver, and that he
had composed a Fantasy for pianoforte (the Wanderer Fantasy) which
was also to appear in print.
   Why Spaun selected these particular songs is strange, for they are not
mentioned in the long obituary notice he wrote for Schubert, where he
singled out those songs he considered to be outstanding (Doc. 865–79).
The explanation may lie in the autograph of *Lob der Tränen* on which
Schubert scribbled in pencil 'Spaun! Don't forget Gahy and the Rondo.'
The reference is to the Rondo in D major, D608 for piano four-hands,
which he composed in 1818 and played with his favourite duo partner,
Josef von Gahy. John Reed believed the note refers to a forthcoming
performance of it (SSC, p. 324). Alternatively, it could refer to the music
itself. If it does, then Schubert must have been alluding to his revised
version of the Rondo, which Diabelli published in 1835. The manuscript
for this has not survived, but it may have contained the subtitle Diabelli
included in his publication: *Notre amitié est invariable* (Our friendship is
constant). Scholars consider this revised version and the subtitle may
have been the result of Diabelli's characteristic tinkering, but the piano's
refrain in *Lob der Tränen* suggests otherwise. In the revised version, the

Rondo ends with the *primo* playing the rondo theme's first phrase in canon with the *secondo* two bars later. The *secondo* plays it in a register lying between a fifth and a thirteenth above middle C, the *primo* an octave higher. To play its phrase, *secondo*'s right arm has to cross over *primo*'s left arm, which has an accompanying figuration to execute in the middle register. This crossing of hands has always been taken to be a symbol of friendship. It could be likened to two people linking arms.

Although this gesture cannot be replicated in *Lob der Tränen*, the pianist can nevertheless allude to it. For most of the time the simple piano part is confined to the bass register. This throws its extremely high refrain into relief. In this the first phrase lies in the same register as the phrase given to *secondo* in the Rondo and, as in the Rondo, it is then repeated two bars later an octave higher.

'Don't forget Gahy and the Rondo' may have been a reference to Gahy's surprise and delight at Schubert's gesture of friendship when they performed the revised version of the Rondo for the first time. Had this taken place in Spaun's presence, he would have understood the allusion when he received the autographed copy of the song. Furthermore there are other gestures of friendship in the song. Dietrich Fischer-Dieskau believes Schubert's music clothes Schlegel's reflective poem 'in a veil of melodic intimacy' (DF-D, p. 67). It may also be noted that throughout the song the voice's dotted rhythm contrasts with the piano's triplets. The two work in harmony with each other yet keep their separate identities.

Schlegel's poem maintains that the pleasures we obtain through our senses do not satisfy the heart. We cannot discover the ocean of love until pleasures are united with tears. The idea of being different yet united is therefore the essence of the poem. To make this the centrepiece of a progressive structure, Schubert opens the set with a song in which the shepherd and horseman have nothing to unite them, and concludes with one in which a sense of unity is experienced even though the partner is absent.

Texts

1. *Ein Schäfer sass im Grünen.* Seven quatrains.

   (1) A shepherd sat in the greenery, his sweetheart in his arms; through the tops of the beech-trees shone the sun's warm rays.
   (2) Joyfully, blithely, they talked sweet nothings. Then past the happy pair rode an armed horseman.
   (3) 'Dismount and find some shade', called the shepherd to him. 'Soon the sultry midday heat will bid you rest quietly.'
   (4) 'Here bush and flower still smile in the radiance of the morning, and my sweetheart will pick the loveliest of flowers to make you a garland.'
   (5) Then the gloomy horseman spoke: 'Woods and meadows can never delay me. My fate drives me onwards, and, ah, my solemn vow.'
   (6) 'I gave up my young life for vile money. I can never aspire to happiness, only at best to fame and gold.'
   (7) 'So trot on briskly, my steed, past where the flowers bloom. Perhaps some day a peaceful grave will reward my toil and strife.'

2. *Laue Lüfte.* Four 12-line stanzas.

   (1) Gentle breezes, fragrant flowers, all the pleasures of spring and youth; sipping kisses from fresh lips, nestling against a soft breast; stealing nectar from grapes, dancing, games and banter – but do the pleasures of the senses ever satisfy the heart?
   (2) When eyes glisten with the gentle dew of sadness, the fields of heaven become reflected in them. Swiftly, refreshingly, every fierce passion is quelled. Just as flowers are revived by rain so weary spirits revive.
   (3) Prometheus created man out of earth not with sweet water, but with his tears. We are at home with longing and pain. To earth-bound senses these springs are bitter, yet when they arise they take us beyond our limits to the ocean of love.

(4) Eternal longing flowed in tears and encircled the lifeless world, which now holds this symbol of mercy in its watery embrace for ever. If man is to rid himself of earth's dust he must be united with the holy source of love through tears.

3. *Auf hohen Bergesrücken*. Three stanzas of respectively five, seven and six lines.

(1) High on the mountain ridge where everything is greener and fresher, it is the huntsman's delight to look down through the drifting mists to the landscape below.

(2) As the paths wind their way up more steeply and dangerously, the more exultantly beats his heart. He thinks more tenderly of his beloved still at home.

(3) And when he reaches his goal a sweet image fills his mind in the stillness. The golden sunbeams weave a portrait of his chosen one down in the valley.

Music

Just as *Lob der Tränen* contrasts the dotted rhythm of the singer with the triplets of the pianist, so too do the other songs contrast two types of musical procedure. Indeed, the set progresses from a situation where the two types are kept strictly separate from each other (*Der Schäfer und der Reiter*) to one in which they are closely integrated (*Der Alpenjäger*).

1. Der Schäfer und der Reiter

Schubert characterizes the shepherd's music with a figure representing birdsong, and the horseman's with the rhythm of his galloping steed. The song is a scena cast in four sections: (1) E major. In a moderate tempo, brightly 4/4 (the description of the shepherd and his sweetheart), (2) E minor modulating to G major. Swiftly 6/8 (the arrival of the horseman and the shepherd's salute), (3) G major. Tempo 1 (the shepherd's promise of a garland of flowers), (4) E minor. Tempo 2 (the horseman's reply).

2. Lob der Tränen

D major. Rather slow 3/4.

Schubert casts the song in strophic form, and this, combined with the fairly insistent dotted rhythm running through the vocal line, makes Schlegel's philosophical musing sound somewhat detached. There is no musical difference between the 'pleasures of the senses' and being 'at home with longing and pain'. The only attempt Schubert makes to find a musical image to reflect the words occurs in the refrain quoted above. Here the switch from the key's minor subdominant (G minor) to its dominant and tonic could be said to mirror the lines: 'Just as flowers are revived by rain so too are weary spirits revived.' In the context of the set this note of detachment provides a foil for the emotional involvement of the Alpine huntsman.

3. *Der Alpenjäger*

F major. Lively, but not too fast 6/8.

Mayrhofer's poem consists of three stanzas, but Schubert divides the poem's 18 lines into two nine-line stanzas. The first ends with 'the more exultantly beats his heart', and deals with the huntsman's ascent up the mountain; the second, more reflective one, takes place at the top of the mountain and deals with the way the sunbeams seem to be painting a portrait of his beloved. One is characterized by hunting horns, the other by the sound of an Alpine horn echoing across the mountains. Although these are different in type, there is a close identity between them. This is because most of their phrases involve a strongly accented amphibrach. These are the lively hunting horns:

And this is the Alpine horn:

The song contains features linking it to the previous songs. Like *Lob der Tränen* it has phrases in the accompaniment echoed an octave higher. More significantly perhaps *Der Schäfer und der Reiter* prefigures its ending. Schubert turns *Der Alpenjäger* into an ABA structure by repeating the whole of the first section, which means that the song ends with the huntsman's exultation. As it turns out, its last two bars are very similar to the last two bars of *Der Schäfer und der Reiter* except that the tempo is slightly slower and the key is F major rather than E minor.

Opus 14

Published on commission by Cappi and Diabelli, 13 December 1822. Dedicated to Franz von Schober.

1. *Suleika I* (Suleika's first song) Marianne von Willemer, D720 (version b, *c.* 1821)
2. *Geheimes* (The Secret) Johann Wolfgang von Goethe, D719 (March 1821)

Both poems come from Goethe's *West-östlicher Divan*, a collection inspired by the lyrics of the fourteenth-century Persian poet, Hafiz (1326–90), which had been translated into German prose and published in 1812–13. Hafiz's principal work is the *Divan*, a collection of 200 short poems in alphabetical order on conventional subjects such as wine, flowers, love and nightingales. Most of them are sensuous, even erotic, and this led to the belief that they were mystical allegories, a 'breeze' being that which brings sweet odours or messages from God, an 'amorous glance' the act of devotion when the eye glances upward to God, the True Beloved. Modern scholars, however, are inclined to take them literally, as did Goethe. His *Divan* mainly concerns his relationship with the actress Marianne von Willemer in 1814–15; indeed several of the poems in the section called *Buch Suleika* were written by her. Goethe altered them slightly, not always to the benefit of the poem, and included them in his collection without acknowledgement of her.

Schubert set four poems from the *West-östlicher Divan*. The two by Marianne von Willemer, *Suleika I* and *Suleika II*, relate directly to her affair with Goethe, *Suleika I* being sketched when she was travelling eastwards to meet him. On the other hand, the two by Goethe, *Geheimes* and *Versunken*, are what he believed a sensuous Persian lover prone to eroticism might fantasize about. In *Geheimes* he focuses on her glances, in *Versunken* on her hair. The two songs in this set represent opposite sides of the same coin. In both the lovers are looking forward to their next meeting. The two poems reflect in their own way the formal strictness of the ghazal, the poetic structure Hafiz brought to perfection. All the lines contain eight syllables divided into four trochees, all stanzas, apart from Goethe's second, have a strict rhyming scheme, and most of them can be divided into couplets.

Texts

1. *Was bedeutet die Bewegung?* Six quatrains.

    (1) What is the meaning of this stirring? Does the east wind bring me good news? The refreshing touch of its wings cools the deep wound in my heart.

    (2) It plays caressingly with the dust, throwing it up in light clouds; it drives away the happy swarm of insects to the safety of the vine-leaves.

    (3) It gently tempers the burning heat of the sun, and cools my hot cheeks. In passing it kisses the vines decking the fields and hills.

    (4) And its soft whisperings brings me a thousand greetings from my beloved; before these hills grow dark I shall be greeted by a thousand kisses.

    (5) Now you may pass on to serve the happy and the sad; there, where the high walls glow, I shall soon find my dearest beloved.

    (6) Ah, the true meaning of the heart, the breath of love and the renewal of life, can come to me to me only from his lips, from his breath.

2. *Über meines Liebchens Äugeln.* Three quatrains.

    (1) Everyone wonders at my darling's meaningful glances, but I, knowing the secret, understand full well what they mean.

    (2) They are saying that he is the one I love, not this one or that one. So, good people, cease your wondering and your longing!

    (3) Indeed, she does cast mighty powerful glances about her, but she wants only to give him a foretaste of the next sweet meeting.

Music

Rhythmic ostinatos underpin both songs. *Suleika I* has two, the second being a development of the first. This in turn is developed into the one that dominates *Geheimes*. The main problem in setting verse in which every line has four trochees is avoiding metric monotony. Schubert achieves it by varying the length of his phrases and harmonizing the ostinatos so that the harmonic stress falls in different places.

1. *Suleika I*

Brahms called this 'the loveliest song that has ever been written'. It is cast in two parts, the first (rather lively 3/4) sets the first five stanzas in the form ABACD and alternates between B minor and B major; the second part (somewhat slower) dealing with the last stanza, functions as an extended coda and is unambiguously in B major. By alternating between the minor and major modes of the key, Schubert reflects, on the one hand, Suleika's words about the deep wound in her heart, and, on the other, her hope for renewed life. Similarly, the rhythmical ostinato under-pinning the first part contains two elements: a *moto perpetuo* in the pianist's right hand and a more ominous figure in the pianist's left hand. This is dropped when the words speak of the wind bringing her a thou-sand kisses from her beloved. It comes back when she looks at the high walls where she will meet him. The relationship to the ostinato in the second part (beginning at bar 109) subsequently becomes clear.

This new ostinato preserves the mood of expectancy, but is calmer and more overtly sensuous. The F♯ in the pianist's left hand is held as a pedal through to the end of the song. During the last few bars the A-C♯/B-D♯ figure in the piano is altered to C♯-E/B-D♯, and it is this which relates to the opening and closing of *Geheimes*.

2. Geheimes

Ab major. Rather swiftly, sweetly 2/4.

Enharmonically Ab is G♯, B major's submediant, so that the keys are more closely related than they would seem to be on paper. Indeed the relationship is made overt in the song's central section which contrasts with the outer sections by moving to different harmonic areas, the sequence being Eb major – Eb minor – Cb major (that is, B major) – Ab minor – Ab major.

The rhythmic ostinato is an exaggerated form of the trochee metre running through the poem. But it could also be said to reflect the sly, darting glances the woman is directing at the man. Perhaps this is why Schubert asks the pianist to play it with rubato (see over).

Apart from cadences the trochaic pattern runs right through *Geheimes*. Schubert casts the song in ternary form, the central section and a passage near the end being in A♭ minor, in which C is lowered to C♭, so that the return to C, when the key reverts to the major, reinforces the tonal brightness and by implication the lover's anticipation of the next sweet hour.

Opus 19

Three songs to poems by Johann Wolfgang von Goethe. Published by Diabelli and Co. (formerly Cappi and Diabelli), 6 June 1825. Dedicated to the poet 'in veneration'.

1. *An Schwager Kronos* (To Coachman Time), D369 (1816)
2. *An Mignon* (To Mignon), D161 (version b, 1815)
3. *Ganymed* (Ganymede), D544 (March 1817)

Schubert attached great importance to this set. It was one of five manuscripts he sold to Diabelli some time during November 1822, the others being the Wanderer Fantasy Op. 15, two sets of male-voice quartets Opp. 16 and 17, and the Waltzes, Ländler and Ecossaises Op. 18. Diabelli published Opp. 15 and 18 in February 1823 and Opp. 16 and 17 the following October. He probably delayed publishing Op. 19 because Schubert had gone behind his back and had negotiated a contract with Sauer & Leidesdorf to produce five song sets a year for two years for a fixed fee,[4] and because he knew that when the contract expired he had an extremely valuable asset with which he could restore relations with the composer. These had broken down in April 1823, when Schubert accused him of dishonesty. The delay proved beneficial. Soon after the publication of Op. 19, Schubert sold Diabelli a number of scores, including the Mass in C major (D452). He also asked him to print two special copies of this set on satinated paper with a gold border. These he had dispatched to Goethe, and in an accompanying letter he wrote: 'If I should succeed in giving evidence of my unbounded veneration of Your Excellency by the dedication of these compositions of your poems, and possibly in getting some recognition of my insignificant self, I should regard the favourable fulfilment of this wish as the fairest event of my career' (Doc. 557). Goethe received the consignment on 16 June but, as happened in 1816, he failed even to acknowledge receipt of it. On the same day he also received from Mendelssohn copies of the 16-year-old composer's three Piano Quartets Opp. 1–3, one of which was also dedicated to the poet. Shortly afterwards Goethe sent Mendelssohn, whom he addressed as Felix, a long letter of thanks.

If *An Schwager Kronos* was the missing first song in the volume sent to Goethe in 1816, then Schubert must have considered it appropriate

---

4   The five sets published in 1824 were the five sections of *Die schöne Müllerin*: songs 1–4 (the arrival at the mill), 5–9 (the awakening of the miller's love), 10–12 (the return of his love), 13–17 (the appearance of the huntsman) and 18–20 (the miller's death in the brook).

that his second attempt to win the poet's approval should begin with the same item. Goethe wrote the poem in a post-chaise. *Schwager* means brother-in-law and is a colloquial term for postilion. Goethe intended the poem to indicate that he would 'rather go to hell quickly while young and drunk, than become a gray beard in a slow trot' (Whitton, p. 209). *An Mignon* is also about someone who wants to die young. Mignon is the young dancer in Goethe's novel *Wilhelm Meister's Apprenticeship*. This poem, however, was written after its publication. The title suggests that Mignon addresses the poem to herself in order to distance herself from her suffering. In contrast, the last song in the set concerns a young person who is actually experiencing his death as a mortal. Ganymede was the handsome Phrygian youth who was loved by Zeus and transported to Olympus by an eagle to become cup-bearer to the gods.

Elizabeth Norman McKay (McKay, p. 164) believes the onset of syphilis, the disease which led to Schubert's death six years later, was probably late November 1822. If this is correct and if he compiled the set just before he sold it to Diabelli, then he may have been facing the possibility of an early death himself when he selected the items.

Texts

1. *Spute dich, Kronos!* Seven rhymeless stanzas of unequal length.

(1) Make haste, Chronos, on at a rattling trot! The road runs downhill; your dawdling makes me giddy. Be brisk. Over the sticks and stones, never mind the bumps – headlong into life.

(2) Now once more toiling uphill out of breath – up then, no slacking, onwards, striving and hoping.

(3) High, wide and glorious is the view of life around us. The eternal spirit soars from peak to peak, full of intimations of eternal life.

(4) A shadowy doorway beckons you to linger and cross the threshold of a girl's house, her eyes promising refreshment. Refresh yourself! For me too, girl, that foaming draught, that fresh, healthy glance.

(5) And now down, down faster! Look, the sun is sinking! Before it sets, before the marsh-mist envelops me in my old age, toothless jaws gnashing, limbs tottering,

(6) snatch me, drunk with the sun's last ray, a sea of fire boiling up before my eyes, blind and reeling through the dark gate of hell.

(7) Blow your horn, coachman, rattle on noisily at a trot. Let Orcus know we are coming, so that mine host will be at the door to welcome us.

2. *Über Tal und Fluss getragen* Five sixains. Every fourth line ends in *Schmerzen* (sorrows), and every fifth line rhymes with this – *Tief im Herzen* – *Still im Herzen* – *Fest im Herzen* – *Herz im Herzen* – *Meinem Herzen.*

(1) Over the valley and stream the sun's pure chariot passes on its way. Ah, in its course it stirs your sorrows and mine deep in our hearts, new again each day.

(2) The night no longer comforts me, for then my dreams come in mournful guise. Silently in my heart I feel the secret power of these sorrows grow.

(3) For many a long year I have watched the ships below each sailing to its appointed place. But the abiding sorrows that cling to my heart are not borne away by the waters.

(4) I must come in fine clothes; they are taken from the closet, for today is a holiday. No one guesses that in my heart of hearts I am cruelly wracked by pain.

(5) Always I must weep in secret, and yet outwardly I can seem so cheerful, even ruddy with the glow of health. But if these sorrows could be fatal to my heart I would be long since dead.

3. *Wie im Morgenglanze.* Five stanzas of respectively eight, two, nine, two and ten lines.

(1) When you shed your light on me in the radiance of the morning, Spring, my beloved, the sacred sense of your eternal warmth, infinite beauty, fills my heart with a thousand thoughts of love.

(2) O that I might clasp you in my arms.

(3) I lie languishing on your breast, and your flowers, your grass, press close to my heart. O lovely breeze of morning you slake the burning thirst within me. The sweet song of the nightingale is borne upon it from the misty valley.

(4) I come, I come! But whither, whither?

(5) Upwards, strive upwards! The clouds drift down yielding to yearning love. I come, I come up to your arms, embracing and embraced, all-loving Father.

Music

Although composed at different times, it is difficult to believe, that these songs were not designed to be a unified set from the beginning. The feature of particular interest is the double neighbour-note figure oscillating around the dominant which is introduced at the opening of the first song and reappears in varied forms at decisive moments in all the songs. It represents another example of the way something very simple and frequently encountered can be so effective in helping to unify a set.

1. *An Schwager Kronos*

D minor – major. Not too fast 6/8.

This song involves constant development, the basic material appearing in the piano's introduction. The double neighbour-note is labelled x.

Once D minor is established as the home key, the music plunges into a series of modulations, the most characteristic being to keys lying a major third lower enharmonically altered, E♭ major to B major, F minor to C♯ major, for example. D minor comes back for stanza 5, when the sun sinks and the traveller urges the postilion to keep up the pace. It turns into D major for the final section when the coachman is told to blow his horn and knock on hell's door. Here Schubert breaks the *perpetuum mobile* of quavers representing the 'rattling trot' of the horses and brings back motif x transposed to the major (B-A-G♯-A), the knocking on the door being represented by *sforzandos*.

2. *An Mignon*

G minor. Rather fast 6/8.

A strophic song opening with rising figures in the piano's introduction (B♭-C-D and F♯-G-A) which listeners will recognize as being legato variants of figures prominent in the introduction to the previous song. The tempo is slower than in the first song, but the metre is the same and Schubert also has a regular and even rhythmic figure running through it (semiquavers on the piano). This may represent the untroubled course of the sun mentioned in the first line of the poem. Mignon, on the other hand, feels her life has been far from untroubled, and whenever the varied

refrain occurs in the fifth line after the word *Schmerzen* (sorrows)
Schubert turns to A♭, the key's flattened supertonic, to colour the
harmony. He resolves it by making use of motif x transposed to A♭-G-F♯-
G in the accompaniment.

3. Ganymed[5]

Ganymed is in progressive tonality: A♭ major for the first stanza, then a
modulation through C♭ major to E major when the song of the nightingale is heard in the third stanza, and a fairly rapid modulation to F major
for the last stanza, when Ganymede ascends to Olympus. The tempo
throughout is rather slow 4/4. The song opens with phrases with a strong
resemblance to this one in *An Mignon*:

In *Ganymed* that becomes:

Thereafter most of the material in the song stems from those first three
bars for the singer, particularly the expressive prepared appoggiatura in
bar 11. The song's climax is reached after two sets of rising chromatic
scales are used to represent Ganymede's ascent upwards. The first results
in the return of motif x in the pianist's left hand act as an anacrusis to an
equally expressive unprepared appoggiatura (see next page, bar 79ff).

The second rising chromatic scale takes the music to a phrase where
Ganymede introduces the climactic words 'alliebender Vater' ('all-loving
Father'). The piano plays a transformed version of motif x. It now
revolves around F major's major sixth, greater emphasis being given to
the third note (C♯) rather than the first (E♭), an emphasis heightened by

---

[5] A detailed analysis of *Ganymed* by Lawrence Kramer can be found in Frisch, pp. 224–
34.

C♯ being an upward resolving appoggiatura. However, the minor sixth still lingers on in the closing bars. Yet as the piano takes the music ever higher it loses its usual mournfulness. Furthermore, although it could have been a member of the chord in the penultimate bar containing the appoggiatura from the beginning of the song, it is not. Ganymede has transcended sorrow.

Opus 20

Published by Sauer & Leidesdorf, 10 April 1823. Dedicated to Frau Justine von Bruchmann.

1. *Sei mir gegrüsst* (I greet you) Friedrich Rückert, D741 (between end of 1821 and autumn 1822)
2. *Frühlingsglaube* (Faith in Spring) Ludwig Uhland, D686 (version c, November 1822)
3. *Hänflings Liebeswerbung* (The Linnet's Wooing) Friedrich Kind, D552 (version b, c. 1817)

Schubert must have compiled this set in November 1822 before Op. 19. As soon as he had put the songs together, he asked his friend Josef Hüttenbrenner to deliver them to his new publishers for engraving, but on the 31 November he requested him to return them to him: 'As I have to make very important alterations in the songs handed to you, do not give them to Herr Leidesdorf yet, but bring them out to me. Should they have been already sent, they must be fetched back immediately' (Doc. 322). On making the alterations he returned the songs to Sauer & Leidesdorf and assigned the opus number for the set after selling to Diabelli the four manuscripts he had listed as Opp. 15–19.

Normally Schubert would check the songs he had selected for a set, make amendments if necessary and write out fair copies for the engraver before sending them to the publishers. For some reason he failed to do so on this occasion. He must then have remembered that among other things *Sei mir gegrüsst* and *Frühlingsglaube* were in the same key and needed to be more clearly differentiated. He therefore transposed *Frühlingsglaube* from B♭ to A♭ major (which actually made the song easier for a soprano or tenor), and added ornaments to the vocal line to give it a more distinctive identity. He also changed the tempo indication from *Mässig* to *Etwas langsam*, and that of *Hänflings Liebeswerbung* from *Lieblich* to *Etwas geschwind*. In addition he defined some of the dynamic shadings more precisely.

All three poems refer to spring and contain refrains, a device used to create certainty as to what is being expressed. In the first song the lover calls to his beloved and sends her his kisses across time and space to express his continued love for her. In the second song the person addresses himself. He tells his tormented heart that now spring is coming 'all will change'. Finally with the arrival of spring the Linnet can boldly woo the 'loveliest of sisters' in the certainty she will respond.

Texts

1. *O du Entriss'ne mir und meinem Kusse.* Five quatrains.

   (1) You who were torn from me and my kisses, I greet you, I kiss you. Although out of reach apart from my message of love, I greet you, I kiss you.
   (2) You who were given to this heart by the hand of love, you who were taken from my breast. With this flood of tears I greet you, I kiss you.
   (3) In spite of the distance that has imposed itself like an enemy between us, and in defiance of the envious power of fate, I greet you, I kiss you.
   (4) As in love's fairest springtime you once came to me with greetings and kisses, so with all the fervour of my soul I greet you, I kiss you.
   (5) One breath of love, and time and space dissolve: I am with you, you are by me; I hold you closely in my arms, I greet you, I kiss you.

2. *Die linden Lüfte sind erwacht.* Two sixains.

   (1) The gentle breezes are awakened, they rustle and stir day and night, and are creative. O fresh fragrances, new sounds! Now, poor heart, never fear, now everything, everything must change.
   (2) The world grows lovelier each day. We do not know what is yet to come, the flowering knows no end. Now, poor heart, forget your torments, now everything, everything must change.

3. *Ahidi! ich liebe.* Four sixains.

   (1) Tra-la-la, I'm in love. The sun smiles gently, the west wind blows mildly, the stream murmurs softly, the flowers scent the air. I'm in love, tra-la-la!
   (2) Tra-la-la, I'm in love. I love you my tender one with your soft silken feathers and your shining little eyes. Loveliest of sisters, I'm in love, tra-la-la.
   (3) Tra-la-la, I'm in love. See how the flowers lovingly greet one another, lovingly nod to each other. O love me in return! I'm in love, tra-la-la.
   (4) Tra-la-la, I'm in love. See how the ivy embraces the oak tree with loving arms. O love me in return. I'm in love, tra-la-la.

Music

All three songs are in major keys, and to bring out the positive nature of their refrains Schubert 'darkens' the tonalities immediately before they appear. In each case he does so by giving stress to the key's minor third: Db in Bb major, Cb in Ab major and C in A major.

1. *Sei mir gegrüsst*

Bb major. Slowly 3/4.

Schubert's accompaniment, in which the pianist's hands lightly alternate in a dance-like fashion, is muted throughout. The publishers brought out a version for the guitar, and in his memoirs of the composer the singer Ludwig Cramolini recalled that when he sang it with harp accompaniment he was coached by Schubert (Mems, p. 262). John Reed called it 'an idealised serenade', and noted that the physical passion of the verses hardly sounds in it (SSC, p. 383). Strong emotions do surface immediately before the refrain in stanzas 2–5, yet they are quickly suppressed. What takes precedence is the tenderness of the greeting and the kiss.

This refrain remains the same for each verse, but the music preceding it varies, the purpose being to gradually intensify the passionate outbursts. For the words 'I hold you closely in my arms' in the last verse, Schubert modulates to Cb major and insistantly reiterates Gb, the key's fifth. This means that when Gb is enharmonically transformed into F♯, the significance of this note in the refrain is intensified.

sei mir ge - grüsst,   sei   mir   ge - küsst,

2. *Frühlingsglaube*

Ab major. Rather slow 2/4.

Here Schubert has in effect two refrains, the first for the piano placed at the beginning of the song, between the two strophes and at the end of the song, the second for the voice at the end of each strophe. The character of the piano's refrain stems from the sonority of its texture, rich in prepared appoggiaturas. They lie on degrees of the scale which according to Deryck Cooke express 'pleasurable longing'.[6]

Ziemlich langsam

The vocal refrain, on the other hand, although ornamented is devoid of appoggiaturas. It expresses the confidence that everything will change, its confidence being enhanced two bars before it begins by the Cb for 'Nun armes Herze' (now poor heart).

nun muss sich al-les, al - -les wen-den,   nun muss sich al-les, al-les wen - den.

---

[6]   Cooke, D. (1959), *The Language of Music*, Oxford: Oxford University Press, p. 90.

3. *Hänflings Liebeswerbung*

A major. Rather fast 6/8.

The simplest and most repetitive of all the songs in the set. John Reed considered it to be 'as fresh and innocent as a daisy' (SSC, p. 256). Schubert later adapted it for the third of his Three Deutsche for Piano (D972), a Deutsche being a dance for couples in a fast triple meter. As in the previous songs the refrain is enhanced by being approached from the key's flat side, in this case Bb major.

Opus 21

Three songs to poems by Johann Mayrhofer for bass and piano. Published by Sauer & Leidesdorf, 19 June 1823. Dedicated 'to the author of the poems by his friend Franz Schubert'.

1. *Auf der Donau* (On the Danube), D553 (April 1817)
2. *Der Schiffer* (The Boatman), D536 (version b, ?1817)
3. *Wie Ulfru fischt* (Ulfru fishing), D525 (January 1817)

This publication was advertised as '3 Fischerlieder von Meyerhofer [*sic*] für den Bass' (SSC, p. 436), but only the last song is about fishing. As a set the songs make a dramatic sequence covering the beginning, climax and aftermath of a storm on a river. Susan Youens, in her analysis of *Auf der Donau* (Youens, p. 188), says:

> The tableau of the river, the ancient castles, and the pine forests – the stuff of travel posters – here inspires an Angst-ridden meditation on Time. Mayrhofer resorts to a commonplace metaphor in which a small boat gliding on the water is emblematic of individual human life on the river of Time, a metaphor tinted in blackest nihilism.

However, the prospect of doom in the poem's last line is not followed through in the other songs. Indeed it could also be argued that they represent Schubert's personal alternatives to Mayrhofer's black state of mind. In the winter of 1822–23, when he compiled the set, he too must have been in a state of deep melancholy following the appearance of syphilis. The boatman, however, faces the possibility of his imminent doom with defiance and courage; the angler looks on the fish who have evaded his rod and line with a degree of humour.

Texts

1. *Auf der Wellen Spiegel schwimmt der Kahn.* Three eight-line stanzas in alternating trochaic trimeters and dimeters to produce what Susan Youens calls 'poetic units surrounded by emptiness'.

    (1) The boat glides on the mirror of the waves; ancient castles soar heavenwards. Pine forests stir like ghosts – and within our breasts our hearts grow faint.

    (2) For all men's creations perish. Where now are the towers, the gates, the ramparts? Where now are the strong ones who stormed out in their armour to battle or to hunt?

(3) Mournful brushwood grows rampant, the power of the myths of the brave fades. And in our little boat we grow afraid, for the waves, like time itself, threaten doom.

2. *Im Winde, im Sturme befahr' ich den Fluss.* Four quatrains.

(1) In wind and storm I row on the river, my clothes soaked by the pouring rain. I lash the waves with powerful strokes, hoping for a fine day.

(2) The waves pursue the creaking boat, ahead lie the whirlpool and the reef, rocks tumble down from the cliff top, fir trees sigh like moaning ghosts.

(3) So must it be; I willed it so. I would detest a life that goes on comfortably. And even if the waves engulf the groaning boat, I should cherish the way I chose.

(4) So let the waves roar in impotent rage; a fountain of bliss wells up in my heart, renewing my courage. What heavenly joy to brave the storm like a man.

3. *Die Angel zuckt, die Rute bebt.* Three eight-line stanzas.

(1) The rod trembles, the line quivers, but it comes up easily. You capricious water-sprites provide no supper for the fisherman. His clever tricks are of no use to him. The fish dart away mockingly. He stands spellbound on the bank; he cannot enter the water for the land holds him fast.

(2) The smooth surface is ruffled, stirred by the scaly folk that swim blithely in the safe waters. The trout dart to and fro, but the fisherman's hook remains empty. They can feel what freedom is; the fisherman's age-old skill is fruitless.

(3) The earth is surpassingly beautiful, but it is not a safe place. Storms blow from the icy mountain peaks; at one stroke hail and frost destroy the golden corn and the lovely roses. But the little fish under their soft smooth roof are pursued by no storm from the land.

Music

In the introduction it was also pointed out that all three songs make expressive use of the minor sixth degree of the scale, and that when this functions as an appoggiatura resolving on to the fifth degree, the dominant, it usually expresses anxiety or grief. Here anxiety predominates, but in the course of the three songs it successively diminishes.

1. *Auf der Donau*

Eb major – F# minor. Slowly 2/4.

Schubert casts the three stanzas in ABA form. Normally this is a stable structure, but here he undermines its stability to mirror the growing tension in the boat and the feeling of imminent destruction. He does it by modulating from Eb major to F# minor at the end of the first and during the central sections so that when the first part returns, what was once in the major is now in a minor key traditionally considered 'gloomy' in character (Steblin, p. 272). In addition, the piano accompaniment becomes increasingly more chromatic and agitated, and at the end of the song Schubert adds a coda in which the voice repeats the word *Untergang* (destruction) against a figure on the piano which he almost invariably uses to indicate the presence or threat of death – a slowly descending chromatic scale in the bass.

In Eb major the minor sixth is Cb. After alluding to it throughout the first part of the song Schubert eventually cadences in Cb major, when the words speak of the passengers' hearts growing faint. In F# minor the minor sixth is D, and in the middle section, when the dominant of F# minor is reached and the poet asks where the brave men who stormed out the fight or hunt now are, he has a series of low, ominous trills on the note.

2. *Der Schiffer*

Eb major. Fast and impassioned 2/4.

The constant semiquaver movement in the accompaniment throughout the song drives the music forward as relentlessly as the waves drive the boat towards the whirlpool and reef. It is a strophic song, but the repetitions of the basic tune are never the same so that it lacks the predictability normally associated with this structure. The only phrase that returns unchanged is the one setting the third lines in stanzas 1–3, and the fourth in stanza 4. It is here that Schubert brings to the fore the flattened sixth which was such a feature of the first song, except that now it expresses the boatman's determination and courage in the face of death.

und   schlän - gen die   Wel - len den   äch - zen - den   Kahn,

3. *Wie Ulfru fischt*

D minor. In a moderate tempo 2/2.

A strophic song in which the music is repeated exactly. The constant quaver movement suggests that the river is in a docile mood. Schubert's very first gesture is to focus on the key's flattened sixth, Bb. As in the previous song it is presented as part of a pattern of notes oscillating around the dominant, Bb-A-G#-A. But here no great significance is attached to it. Ulfru is spellbound; his emotions are not highly charged. It will be noticed that when the pattern first appears neither the Bb nor the G# is accented; the accents fall on the stable notes on the weak beats of the bar. What matters in this instance is the twitching of Ulfru's line.

Opus 22

Two songs to poems by Matthäus von Collin. Published by Sauer & Leidesdorf, 27 May 1823. Dedicated to Matthäus von Collin.

1. *Der Zwerg* (The Dwarf), D771 (?1822 or 1823)
2. *Wehmut* (Melancholy), D772 (?1822 or 1823)

Sauer & Leidesdorf destroyed most of Schubert's manuscripts of the songs they published soon after the engraver had finished with them, so these are difficult to date precisely. Deutsch's numbering indicates that he believed they were written one after the other. If so they were probably intended to be a set. The painter Franz Stohl said that *Der Zwerg* was sung at a reception given by Karl Pinterics towards the end of 1822 (Mems, p. 374). On the grounds that this song has strong resemblances to the opening of the Unfinished Symphony, John Reed believed the two songs may date from November 1822 (SSC, p. 143). It was then that Schubert's symptoms of syphilis became manifest.

The topic is the transience of existence, the examples being the fleetingness of beautiful things. Originally Matthäus von Collin called the first song *Treubruch* (Perfidy) and the second *Naturgefühl* (Feeling for Nature). Schubert changed these titles presumably because he did not want to give the impression that the songs were about anything else but transience. In fact his full title for the second was *Wehmut – Alles Vergeht* (Melancholy – Everything Perishes).

Texts

1. *Im trüben Licht verschwinden schon die Berge*. Nine stanzas, the first eight being tercets, the ninth a quatrain.

   (1) In the dim light the mountains are fading away; the ship drifts on the sea's smooth swell with the queen and her dwarf on board.
   (2) She gazes up at the high arching vault, at the far blue distance, interwoven with light, crossed by the pale band of the Milky Way.
   (3) 'Stars, you have never yet lied to me', she cries. 'Soon I shall perish. You tell me so; yet in truth I shall die gladly'.
   (4) Then the dwarf comes close to the queen, begins to tie the red silk cord about her neck, and weeps as if he would go blind with grief.

(5) He speaks: 'You yourself are to blame for this wrong because you have forsaken me for the king. Now only your death can kindle any joy in me.

(6) 'Though I shall always hate myself for bringing about your death by my own hand, yet now you must grow pale for an early grave.'

(7) She lays her hand on her heart so full of youthful life, and heavy tears flow from her eyes, which she raises to heaven in prayer.

(8) 'May you reap no sorrow from my death', she says. Then the dwarf kisses her pale cheeks, and forthwith her senses fail.

(9) The dwarf gazes at the lady in the grip of death. He lowers her with his own hands into the sea. His heart burns with longing for her. He will never set foot on any shore again.

2. *Wenn ich durch Wald und Fluren geh'*. A single 11-line stanza.

When I walk through the woods and fields I feel so happy and yet so sad in my uneasy heart – so happy, so sad when I behold the meadows in all the fullness of their beauty, all the joy of spring. For all that blows and echoes in the wind, all that towers up to heaven, and man himself, so fondly linked with the beauty he beholds, all shall perish and disappear.

Music

The relationship between these songs is strong. In the first place, their keys (A minor, D minor) are closely related. Furthermore, both songs begin and end with an interval of a fifth in their vocal lines; both make use of measured tremolo and Schubert's death motif (a slowly descending chromatic scale), and both are formal structures containing material in a constant state of development.

1. Der Zwerg

A minor. Not too fast 4/4.

This is cast in binary form, the first part covering the first six stanzas, the second the last three. The tension and sense of fate are conveyed by a measured tremolo which continues throughout the song, and an ominous rhythmic figure which closely resembles the one in the first movement of the Unfinished Symphony. The descending semitones in the bass prefigure the death motif which will come in full later in the song as well as at the end of *Wehmut.* Here they are harmonized in a manner which anticipates Wagner when he wanted to convey his characteristic mixture of latent eroticism and impending tragedy.

The music becomes particularly ominous when the dwarf ties the cord about the queen's neck. The key is the 'black' key of B minor; the voice, doubled by the piano, takes over the rhythmic figure associated with the Unfinished Symphony and develops it.

Minor keys prevail. The only time Schubert touches on a major key is

2. *Wehmut*

D minor. Slow 2/2.

This song is cast in ternary form, but as mentioned earlier its material is constantly developing, the last section being far from a replica of the first. It alludes to it only in its texture and the harmony of its first two bars. Schubert reserves the measured tremolo for the song's central section devoted to the beauty of all that blows and echoes in the wind. The relationship to *Der Zwerg* is immediately apparent in the rising fifth, by the discords in the second and fourth bars, and a descending chromatic scale present but unobtrusive in a middle voice.

The change from major to minor for the phrase 'so wohl und weh' ('so happy and sad') in bar 6 is echoed on a number of occasions in the song. In the last section it occurs twice. For the words 'Entschwindet und vergeht' ('vanish and perish') Schubert brings back his death motif first in the pianist's left hand and then in the right. The notes F♯-F-E refer to the opening of *Der Zwerg*; those in the piano's upper voice to the opening of this song. Against the second appearance of the motif the voice repeats the last two words of the text as if they too were vanishing and perishing (see over).

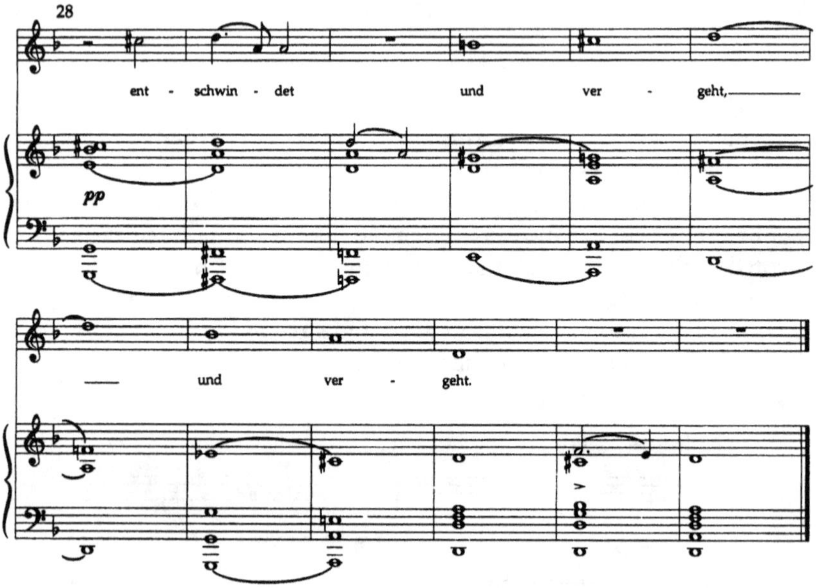
28
ent - schwin - det und ver - geht,
pp
und ver - geht.

Opus 23

Published by Sauer & Leidesdorf, 4 August 1823.

1. *Die Liebe hat gelogen* (Love has Lied) August von Platen-Hallermünde, D751 (by 17 April 1822)
2. *Selige Welt* (Blessed World) Johann Chrysostomus Senn, D743 (Autumn 1822)
3. *Schwanengesang* (Swan Song) Johann Chrysostomus Senn, D744 (Autumn 1822)
4. *Schatzgräbers Begehr* (The Treasure-Hunter's Request) Franz von Schober, D761 (November 1822)

The set revolves around two poems by Schubert's friend, the Tyrolean poet Johann Senn. Although Senn was five years older than Schubert, the two had been friendly when they were schoolboys at the Stadtkonvikt. Senn lost his scholarship to it for defending a fellow Tyrolean, who had been cruelly punished by the school authorities for taking part in a demonstration calling for Tyrolean independence. Josef Kenner, a fellow pupil, called Senn 'a splendid, warm-hearted young man of restrained power, a stubborn philosopher, candid with his friends, reserved with others, frank, passionate, a hater of imposed constraint' (Mems, p. 88). After leaving the Konvikt, Senn rapidly made a name for himself as a lyric poet of importance; indeed, according to Deutsch, his poem 'The Red Eagle of the Tyrol' celebrating the fervour of Tyrolean resistance to Napoleon brought him considerable fame (Doc. 162f).

By 1820 he had become a leading figure in the Freshmen Students' Association which met to discuss liberal and nationalist ideas. Such associations were banned by the infamous Karlsbad Decrees of 1819, and the authorities had been keeping the Association under surveillance ever since the decrees came into force. At a social gathering to say farewell to one of Senn's friends, a police informer was recognized and ejected for being an uninvited guest. Shortly afterwards, in March 1820, the police came to search Senn's rooms and, according to the police report, his behaviour towards them was both 'stubborn and insulting' (Doc. 162). Senn was arrested along with Schubert, Franz von Bruchmann and Josef von Steinsberg, who were present in his rooms at the time. Schubert got away with a reprimand and a black eye, but Senn was imprisoned for 14 months without trial. He was then exiled to the Tyrol, his career ruined. He continued to be held in great affection by his Viennese friends who thought of him as being a hero and martyr.

In September 1822 Bruchmann visited him in Innsbruck, where he was working in a cadet school. A letter from Bruchmann to Franz von Schober dated 8 September mentions that Senn had 'plans to release himself from Austrian claws', and that 'the expected change in his situation in a few months time will afford us an opportunity to act' (DF-D, p. 157). The meaning of this has never been explained, but whatever it was nothing came of it. Senn never escaped Austrian claws; he remained in exile all his life.

On his return to Vienna Bruchmann brought with him these two poems. In all probability Schubert set them to music immediately, scoring *Selige Welt* for bass and *Schwanengesang* for tenor. Although he clearly thought of them as being separate songs, both are in Ab major and continually vacillate between major and minor. The decision to place them in a set, score them for one voice and have them published may have been made some time in November 1822. Along with Platen's *Die Liebe hat gelogen*, which Bruchmann had given Schubert earlier that year, and Schober's *Schatzgräbers Begehr*, which bears evidence of being specially written for the occasion, he was able to represent the complex, contradictory nature of his friend's personality without falling foul of the censor.

As a set of four, the songs are arranged into two related pairs of opposites. The first pair contrasts the sense of being betrayed with the need to have faith in whatever life offers. We can only assume this relates to Senn's arrest and subsequent imprisonment and exile. The second pair contrasts the experience of being in two minds with that of being totally single-minded. The evidence that Schober wrote *Schatzgräbers Begehr* specially for the set is purely circumstantial. No date has ever been assigned to the poem, but John Reed speaks of 'the curiously personal and informal tone of verses two and four' (SSC, p. 372). The reference to an ancient law is also strange. Richard Capell thought it might refer to some unattainable Schillerian ideal.[7] Reed suggested love or fame. It could even refer to an actual law concerning Tyrolean independence which Senn hoped to bring to light. The most likely explanation, however, is that Schober employed it as a fiction to bring out those features of Senn's personality his friends held in affection and drank to on every festive occasion, features which Schubert wanted to focus on at the end of the set, notably Senn's integrity and indomitability.

---

[7] Capell, R. (1928), *Schubert's Songs*, London: Benn; 3rd edition revised by M. Cooper (1973), London: Pan, p. 174.

Texts

1. *Die Liebe hat gelogen.* Two quatrains.

    (1) Love has lied. Sorrow oppresses me. I am betrayed by all around me.

    (2) Hot tears flow ceaselessly down from my cheeks. Poor heart, beat no more, beat no more.

2. *Ich treibe auf des Lebens Meer.* Two quatrains.

    (1) I drift on the sea of life, I sit comfortably in my boat without destination or tiller, moving to and fro as the current takes me, as the winds blow.

    (2) It is folly to seek a blessed isle for none exists. Have faith, and make your landing wherever the water breaks on the shore.

3. *Wie klag ich's aus, das Sterbefühl.* A quatrain followed by a cinquain.

    (1) 'How can I lament the presentiment of death, the dissolution that flows through my limbs? How shall I sing of the feeling of new life, of the prospect of deliverance that breathes on my spirit?'

    (2) So it lamented, so it sang, fearful of annihilation, glad of transfiguration, until life fled. That is the meaning of the swan's song.

4. *In tiefster Erde ruht ein alt Gesetz.* Two quatrains and two tercets.

    (1) In the depths of the earth there sleeps an ancient law which I am driven relentlessly to track down. I can accomplish nothing else as I dig. Even though the world spreads its golden net to lure me away –

    (2) even though the shallow prattle of the worldly-wise rings in my ears: 'You are wasting your time and your strength to no avail.' This shall not distract me from my labour; I go on digging furiously, now as always.

    (3) And even though I may never be rewarded by the joy of discovery, even though I am digging my own grave with this hope, I will gladly climb down into it, for then my longing will be stilled.

    (4) So leave me in peace with my obsession! Surely a grave is gladly given to every one; so don't refuse me one, my friends.

Music

Schubert reverses his usual procedure by ending rather than beginning with the song involving the most change and development. *Schatzgräbers Begehr* summarizes the harmonic uncertainties, particularly the frequent oscillations between major and minor, which characterize the first three, shorter songs. More significantly, it is the only song that ends in a passage where the key is firmly settled. The Treasure Hunter asks to be left in peace and, during the course of the 13 bars in which he expresses his desire, the music goes into D major.

1. *Die Liebe hat gelogen*

C minor. Slow 4/4.

Schubert repeats the first stanza at the end to make an ABA structure, altering the repetition to give more emphasis to the phrase 'Sorrow oppresses me' and the word 'all' in the phrase 'deceived by all around me'. The A section is in C minor for the first two lines of the first stanza, and in C major for the remaining two. But the song is harmonically more uncertain in the central section. Schubert repeats the lines 'hot tears run ceaselessly down my cheeks'. On the first occasion he modulates from C minor to Ab major, on the second he uses the same music but transposes it a semitone higher.

2. *Selige Welt*

Ab major. Not too fast 4/4.

As in the previous song, Schubert creates an ABA structure out of a two-stanza poem. But in this case when the A section returns he uses only the last two lines of the poem: 'Have faith, make your landing wherever the water breaks on the shore.' The vigour and sense of conviction the music conveys seems to be at odds with what the poem appears to be about. Drifting, going where the current takes you, only finds expression in the central section. Dietrich Fischer-Dieskau believes that like *Mut* in *Winterreise*, the musical exuberance of *Selige Welt* is only a mask 'hiding a profound inner sorrow' (DF-D, p. 157).

3. *Schwanengesang*

Ab major. Very slow 2/2.

A binary structure in which the alternation between major and minor to convey the swan's contradictory feelings is immediately established in the piano's introduction.

One of the most effective shifts from minor to major occurs when Schubert modulates to Cb major, the key which has its root on Ab minor's third, for the words 'the dissolution that flows through my limbs', and then immediately goes into Ab major for the words 'how shall I sing of the feeling of new life?'.

4. *Schatzgräbers Begehr*

D minor – major. At a walking pace 2/2.

The song is through-composed, but the sections into which it falls cut across Schober's stanzaic divisions. Schubert's main concern is to constantly alternate between minor and major. When in the minor, the music tends to be chromatic; when in the major diatonic. It is only in the last D major section that the key and the mode become stabilized. However, Schubert ends the song not with a major triad, but with bare fifths. In music this could be construed as conforming to an 'ancient law' on the grounds that this was the rule in medieval music. The original manuscript has not survived, but a copy of it, in private hands, shows that he originally preceded these fifths with a return to the minor for one bar.

In the version he prepared for publication, Schubert transposed the penultimate bar to the major, softened the dynamics and removed the accents, including the *fortepiano* in the last bar which emphasized the emptiness of the fifths. In his second version the music simply appears to be drifting away.

Opus 24

Published by Sauer & Leidesdorf, 27 October 1823.

1. *Gruppe aus dem Tartarus* (Group from Hades) Friedrich von Schiller, D583 (September 1817)
2. *Schlaflied* (Slumber Song) Johann Mayrhofer, D527 (version b, January 1817)

In the early summer of 1823, when Schubert compiled this set, *Gruppe aus dem Tartarus* was his only song successfully performed in public but not yet published. In style it has the intensity, restlessness and drama associated with *Sturm und Drang*. The range of the song and the nature of the piano part tempted Brahms to score it for orchestra. In the opinion of Dietrich Fischer-Dieskau 'the total effect is frightening; even today an interpreter will find that, if it is placed at the end of a programme, the listener will be left stunned and terrified' (DF-D, p. 99). It therefore seems strange that Schubert should want to follow it with a lullaby.

Schiller's poem concerns a group of tormented souls from the deepest region of Hades asking each other when their suffering will end; Mayrhofer's a boy who has responded to the call of the woods and the river and has been healed of all pain. Schubert may have selected the songs because they contrast those outside nature with someone immersed in it. His point may have been that only nature had the power to heal. But he may also be referring to Schiller's essay on the naive and the sentimental, a work which would have been of considerable interest to Schubert's literary friends because it contrasts those literary figures who are spontaneous, unselfconscious, realistic, objective and essentially classical in outlook like Goethe, with those whom Schiller thought were like himself – reflective, speculative, idealistic, subjective and essentially romantic in outlook.

Schiller maintained that the naive represents the vanished paradise of childhood, the lost state of innocence when we felt at one with nature. In the process of growing up we become reflective, self-conscious and consequently divided from nature. It is then that we become sentimental, yearn to experience the sense of oneness again. With the poems he had at his disposal, Schubert could not indicate how Schiller removed the opposition between the naive and the sentimental, and therefore between Goethe and himself, all he could do was to present extreme examples of yearning self-consciousness and innocence.

Texts

1. *Horch – wie Murmeln des empörten Meeres.* Three stanzas of respectively four, six and four lines of unequal length.

   (1) Hark! Like the angry murmuring of the sea, like a brook sobbing through hollow places in the rocks, there rises a low groan, heavy, empty, tortured.
   (2) Pain distorts their features, their mouths are open and cursing, their eyes are hollow, their frightened gaze strains towards the bridge over the Cocytus, scanning the river's mournful course as they weep.
   (3) Anxiously, softly, they ask each other whether the end is in sight. Eternity spreads its encircling wings about them, breaking Saturn's scythe in two.[8]

2. *Es mahnt der Wald, es ruft der Strom.* Three quatrains.

   (1) The forest calls, the river cries: 'Sweet child, come to us.' The boy approaches, full of wonder, stays and is cured of every pain.
   (2) The quail's song floats out of the bushes, the day makes play with shimmering colours; on flowers red and blue the moist dew of heaven glistens.
   (3) He lies down in the cool grass and watches the clouds sail by; nestling close to his mother he is lulled to sleep by the god of dreams.

Music

1. *Gruppe aus dem Tartarus*

There are no sharps or flats in the key signature. Schubert marks the tempo of the first stanza *Etwas geschwind* (rather fast), the voice being in 4/4, the piano in 12/8, and the tempo of the rest of the song Allegro 4/4.

The song is through-composed and unusual on two counts, one being the declamatory nature of the vocal line, which at no time is allowed to linger over a phrase or be lyrical, the other the constant use of rising chromatic scales. These are initially introduced to depict the low groans rising from

---

[8] The bridge over the Cocytus (the river of wailing) was used to take the dead to Hades: Saturn is the Roman god of time.

the depths, but they persist right up to the point when the word 'Ewigkeit' ('eternity') occurs at the climax of the song. As a result the music creates very little sense of key. It pounds forward searching for a point of rest, but fails to find one even when 'Ewigkeit' dramatically blazes forth in C major. In that moment the harmony may find its tonic, but not its destined mode because, within seconds, the key changes to C minor. The rising chromatic scales are transformed into a descending diatonic one falling down over two octaves, the final gesture being a spread C minor chord across the middle to upper registers of the piano to represent the last sweep of Saturn's scythe.

2. Schlaflied

F major. Moderato 12/8.

A strophic song with a lilting rhythm apparently totally different from what has gone before. But Schubert would never have selected it had it not had some connection with the previous song. It becomes apparent as soon as the voice enters. The octave Cs in the vocal line and the alternation of the chords of F major and C major on the piano relate unmistakably to the octave Cs and the alternation of C major and F minor for the line 'Ewigkeit schwingt über ihnen Kreise' ('Eternity spreads its encircling wings around them') in *Gruppe aus dem Tartarus*.

Opus 36

Two songs to poems by Johann Mayrhofer. Published by Cappi & Co., 11 February 1825. Dedicated to Katharina Lászny von Folkusfálva.

1. *Der zürnenden Diana* (To the Angry Diana), D707 (version b, December 1820)
2. *Nachtstück* (Nocturne), D672 (version b, *c.* 1819)

After Schubert's agreement with Sauer & Leidesdorf concluded at the end of 1824, he made use of several publishers, but only on an ad hoc basis. Cappi & Co., the publishers of this set, were established after the breakup of Cappi and Diabelli, also in 1824. Before bringing out these songs they had published as *Dances for the Carnival of 1825* the German Dances and Ecossaises D781 and D783. The firm's notice in the official *Wiener Zeitung* for the songs ran as follows:

> The excellence of Schubert's songs is already so generally acknowledged that they no longer require any recommendation. The publishers have chosen, from the numerous works by this composer of genius, the present two songs, which have already gained full recognition and merited distinction in several of the choicest private circles with their classic performances by the retired I. & R. Court Opera singer, Herr Vogl, that coryphaeus of German vocal art. The publishers therefore flatter themselves that they are offering a welcome gift to all friends of indigenous art. (Doc. 527)

The claim that Cappi & Co. had themselves chosen the songs for publication has no foundation whatsoever, and has helped to promote the myth that Schubert's publishers compiled his song sets and not the composer. But only Schubert had the intimate knowledge of what he had written five or six years earlier, only he would have had the skill to select from the hundreds of unpublished songs that were available two which went so well together both poetically and musically, and only he could have known what his friend and admirer Katharina von Lászny would have liked to have dedicated to her.

She was the wife of a Hungarian aristocrat and suffered from tuberculosis. When she was well enough she held Schubertiads in her house. It may have been at one of these that Vogl sang the songs. Both are operatic in style. The first is an extended cantabile aria for a young man who has just seen the goddess Diana bathing naked with her nymphs, and who also derives sensual pleasure from her anger and the mortal wound he has received from her arrow. The other is a scena about an old man who also sings as death approaches, but in his case calmly rather than ecstatically.

In all probability Schubert chose these particular songs because Katharina von Lászny had been an opera singer. Between 1809 and 1817 she was a member of the Court Opera and made her name singing the roles of Susanna in *Le nozze di Figaro* and the Princess in Boieldieu's opéra comique *Jean de Paris*. She had been married twice, and had the reputation of being something of a temptress. In 1814 she was said to be involved in love affairs with two princes at the same time. When Schubert's 19-year-old friend, the painter Moritz von Schwind, visited her shortly after the publication of Op. 36, he wrote a letter to Franz von Schober describing the impact she made on him. 'What a woman!', he said.

> If she were not nearly twice as old as I and unhappily always ill, I should have to leave Vienna, for it would be more than I could stand. Schubert has known her a long time, but I met her only recently. She is pleased with my things and with myself, more than anybody else except you; I had quite a shock the first time, the way she spoke to me and went on with me, as though there were nothing about me she didn't know. Immediately afterwards she was taken ill again and spat blood. I have not seen her for some time; but we eat there tomorrow. So I now know what a person looks like who is in ill repute all over the city, and what she does. (Doc. 528)

Schubert dedicated two works to her, the other being the *Divertissement à la hongroise* for piano four hands, Op. 54. The fact that Schubert chose songs about people who welcome rather than fear death suggests that she might have told him at some stage that she would like to go to her death singing. She died in 1828 at the age of 39.

Texts

1. *Ja, spanne nur den Bogen, mich zu töten*. A single stanza of 13 lines, the first seven containing 11 syllables, the last six containing 9.

Yes, draw your bow to slay me, you divine woman; flushed with anger you are even more enchanting. I shall never regret that I saw you on the flowering bank outshining your nymphs as they bathed, spreading beauty throughout the wilderness like rays of light. Your image will gladden me even as I die.

He who has beheld your unveiled radiance will breathe more purely, more freely. Your arrow hit its mark, yet warm waves flow gently from the wound. My failing senses still tremble at the vision of this last sweet hour.

2. *Wenn über Berge sich der Nebel breitet.* Four quatrains.

(1) When the mist spreads over the mountains, and the moon battles with the clouds, the old man takes his harp and walks towards the wood, singing softly.

(2) 'Holy night, soon it will be accomplished. Soon I shall sleep the long sleep which will release me from all care.'

(3) Then the green trees rustle: 'Sleep sweetly, good old man'; and the swaying grasses whisper: 'We will cover his resting place.'

(4) And many a sweet bird calls: 'Let him rest in his grassy grave.' The old man listens, the old man falls silent. Death has beckoned to him.

Music

1. *Der zürnenden Diana*

A♭ major. Risoluto 2/2.

In the first draft the song was marked *Entschlossen* (resolute), in the fair copy *Feurig* (impassioned). By using the Italian word for resolute when the song was published, Schubert might have wanted to instruct singers to perform it as if it were an Italian operatic aria with German words. The poem may be only 13 lines long, but by repeating phrases in the Italian opera manner, he was able to fashion an aria on a grand scale. Although through-composed, it divides into four sections. When one section is completed he moves to a key a major third lower so that the key sequence is A♭ major, E major, C major and finally A♭ major again. At the end of the song when the young man (Endymion) is about to expire, Schubert includes in his final phrase an appoggiatura on the key's flattened sixth (F♭), a gesture usually associated with grief or anxiety. Here, however, the phrasing softens it, changing its usual 'meaning'. In this context it has the sensuality later associated with Wagner's *Tristan und Isolde*.

The piano's postlude brings the song to a conclusion with the same texture as here, the right hand echoing in thirds the voice's Fb-Eb.

2. Nachtstück

C minor. Very slow 4/4.

The song opens with a prelude in which the pianist's left hand takes up the thirds at the end of *Der zürnenden Diana* and extends them to form Schubert's death motif (a slowly descending chromatic scale).

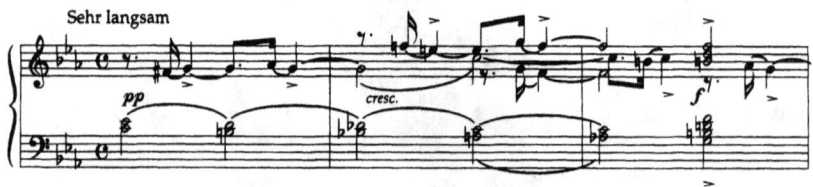

Once the scene has been established in what Graham Johnson calls a 'bipartite upbeat'[9] (stanza 1), Schubert has an aria for the old man (stanza 2) and then another aria in which nature welcomes him (stanzas 3 and 4). In the first, a harp-like accompaniment has to be played with the sustaining pedal held down to evoke the undampened resonances of a harp. Then, when nature prepares the old man's grave and he dies, the accompaniment changes to a rocking motion not unlike a gentle lullaby. Like its beginning, the song ends with a reference to the closing bars of *Der zürnenden Diana*. As in the previous song, the man's dying words are accompanied by harmonies containing Fb then Eb, but in this instance Eb eventually moves up to E natural, Fb's enharmonic equivalent, so that the song can end in C major.

---

9   Sleeve note for the Hyperion recording on CDJ 33004.

Opus 37

Two songs to poems by Friedrich von Schiller. Published by Cappi & Co., 28 February 1825. Dedicated to Ludwig Ferdinand Schnorr von Carolsfeld 'out of friendship'.

1. *Der Pilgrim* (The Pilgrim), D794 (version b, *c.* 1823)
2. *Der Alpenjäger* (The Alpine Huntsman), D588 (version b, *c.* 1817)

Both poems relate to aspects of Schiller's philosophy which influenced the German Romantic movement, namely the relationship between the ideal and the real, man's responsibility for nature, and the relationship between inclination and duty. Both are about young men who leave home to search for something that ultimately eludes them. *Der Pilgrim* concerns Schiller's belief, expounded in his philosophical poem *Das Ideal und das Leben* (The Ideal and Life), that there is an unbridgeable gap between the ideal and the real. When this was applied to art Friedrich von Schlegel called it 'romantic irony', the artist's consciousness of the unbridgeable gap between the ideal artistic goal and the limited possibilities of achieving it. *Der Alpenjäger*, on the other hand, condenses one of the ideas Schiller developed in his 1793 essay *Über Anmut und Würde* (Concerning Grace and Dignity). In this he argued that human beings are not only capable of performing moral acts, they were also intended to be moral in all aspects of their behaviour. If they exert their will against nature, for example, if they set out to exploit it, then nature becomes their responsibility. This, in effect, is what the spirit of the mountains tells the youth who has been hunting the gazelle. Until then the boy has just been following his inclination, but Schiller held that inclination should always be balanced by duty, freedom by moral restraint. Essentially man should be able to commune with nature, and this would be impossible if he abused it. For the Romantics this was a fundamental tenet, and it led among other things to Friedrich von Schlegel's belief that nature was the mediator between man and God.

Schnorr von Carolsfeld, the set's dedicatee, was a friend of Schlegel, and a leading figure in the Romantic school of painters.

Texts

1. *Noch in meines Lebens Lenze*. Nine quatrains.

(1) I was still in the springtime of my life when I journeyed forth, leaving the merry dances of youth in my father's house.

(2) I cast aside all my inheritance, all my possessions. Happy in my faith, I innocently set out with my light pilgrim's staff.

(3) A great hope spurred me on, a dark-hued word of faith. 'Walk on', a voice cried, 'the way is open. Follow the path that ascends.

(4) Go on until you reach a golden gate; then enter it, for there earthly things become celestial, immortal.'

(5) Evening came, morning came, never, never did I stop; but what I seek, what I want always remains hidden.

(6) Mountains blocked my path, rivers flowed across my route. I built bridges across yawning chasms, crossings over turbulent rivers.

(7) Then I came to the bank of a river that flowed east, so trusting its course I cast myself on its bosom.

(8) Its swirling waves bore me to a great ocean. In its vast emptiness it lies before me now, and I am no nearer my goal.

(9) Ah, no way can take me beyond it, the sky above will never touch the earth, and the There is never Here (und das Dort ist niemals Hier!).

2. *Willst du nicht das Lämmlein hüten?* Eight sixains.

(1) Won't you look after the little lamb, the little lamb so meek and mild? It feeds on blades of grass and frolics on the banks of the stream. 'Mother, mother, let me go hunting in the high mountains.'

(2) Won't you summon the herd with the merry sound of your horn? The cow-bells mingle sweetly with the joyful song of the forest. 'Mother, mother, let me go and roam in the wild heights.'

(3) Won't you tend the little flowers that grow so charmingly in their beds? No garden will welcome you out there on those bare mountain tops. 'Forget the little flowers, let them bloom. Mother, mother, let me go.'

(4) And the youth went hunting, driven blindly onwards with daring to the remote parts of the mountains. Before him the trembling gazelle flees like the wind.

(5) It bounds effortlessly up the bare crags, leaps bravely across the chasms. But close on its heels the hunter follows with his deadly bow.

(6) Now it clings to the jagged ridge above the gorge where the path ends and the drop below is sheer. Behind it, the enemy approaches.

(7) With a mute gaze of misery it pleads with the cruel hunter. But its pleas are in vain, for his bow is already drawn to shoot. Suddenly from a crevice in the rocks the spirit of the mountains appears.

(8) With his godlike hands he protects the tormented beast. 'Must you bring death and destruction to my kingdom?' he cries. 'The earth has room for all; why do you persecute my flock?'

Music

Although these songs have no distinctive melodic, harmonic or rhythmic features in common, they are structurally similar. Both are scenas containing set pieces, a dramatic section in which the young man fails to gain his quest, and a slow coda containing the moral of the story. In addition, both end in a key a minor third lower than the one in which they begin.

1. *Der Pilgrim*

D major – F major. Moderate 2/2 – B minor. Very slow 3/4.

The young man begins with a confident, marching song in D major (stanzas 1–4). When the way becomes difficult and he cannot find what he is looking for, Schubert embarks on a section in which the vocal line becomes increasingly distorted and the harmony emphasizes F rather than F♯ (stanzas 5 and 6). Having crossed the turbulent river the young man follows it with renewed enthusiasm. He consequently goes back to his marching song, but sings it a minor third higher in F major (stanza 7). When he reaches the ocean and finds nothing but a vast emptiness, the music for stanza 5 returns. Not only does the melody change its character, so too does the marching rhythm (stanza 8). F♯ is restored, but now its purpose is to be the dominant of 'black' B minor. Ultimately the marching rhythm is dropped, and the music becomes reflective (stanza 9). The most dramatic stroke, however, is reserved for the sudden change of dynamics from *pianissimo* to *fortissimo* for the last 'ist niemals Hier'. Schubert harmonizes the word 'Hier' with a B major chord, but peremptorily changes the mode back to B minor for two strongly accented chords on the piano.

2. *Der Alpenjäger*

C major. Moderate (the mother), fast (the son) 2/4 – A♭ major. Fast 6/8 – A major. Slow 2/2.

The song contains two set pieces. The first is a duet for the mother and her son in strophic verse/refrain form (stanzas 1–3). The other, also in strophic form, deals with the events of the hunt (stanzas 4–7). Two-thirds through the last section of this, when the hunter is about to release his arrow, there is a melodramatic pause. For the unexpected appearance of the spirit of the mountains the music is suddenly lifted up a semitone from Gb major to G major. Gradually the music makes its way through E major to C# minor for the first part of the homily, then to A major for the song's tranquil conclusion (stanza 8).

Opus 43

Published by Anton Pennauer, 25 July 1825.

1. *Die junge Nonne* (The Young Nun) Jakob Nikolaus Craigher de Jache-lutta, D828 (early 1825)
2. *Nacht und Träume* (Night and Dreams) Matthäus von Collin, D827 (version b, by June 1823)

Matthäus von Collin died on 23 November 1824, and circumstantial evidence suggests that this set was intended to be a valediction to him. He was one of Schubert's most enthusiastic admirers and the poet of three of his finest songs. In 1810 at the age of 31 he was appointed professor of philosophy at Cracow University. Two years later he took up the same position at Vienna University. When his name as a poet, playwright and editor became firmly established, he was asked to be the tutor to the young Duke of Reichstadt, the son of Napoleon and the Empress Marie Louise. He first met Schubert in 1820. Shortly afterwards he gave the first of several musical parties specifically designed to promote the composer and his music. At the first he introduced the composer to Count Moritz von Dietrichstein, the administrative head of music at the imperial court, Josef von Hammer-Purgstall, the orientalist, Franz von Mosel, a leading figure in the Gesellschaft der Musik, Karoline Pichler, who ran a literary salon frequented by all the literary celebrities of Vienna, and Johann Ladislaus Pyrker, who had just been appointed Patriarch of Venice.

Collin was also a leading figure in Romantic circles. John Reed suggested he was the link between the Schubert circle and a group of writers and thinkers who acknowledged August and Friedrich von Schlegel as leaders. He points out that the five Collin poems Schubert set all belong to the years 1822–23 when Schubert was closest to Romantic ideas (SSC, p. 463). Of these, none reflects the spirit of Romanticism more effectively than *Nacht und Träume*. 'The discovery of the unconscious, and the preoccupation with night, with mystery and with dreams to which it led', said Reed,

> is here celebrated in the most Romantic song Schubert wrote. Here is the musical equivalent of the gibbous moons and moon-haunted landscapes which permeated the imagination of Samuel Palmer and Caspar Friedrich, the first deeply felt expression in music of that sense of mystery and the infinite which *heilige Nacht* conjured up in the breast of every Romantic. (SSC, p. 339)

Collin died on 23 November 1824, and although no precise date can be assigned to the composition of *Die junge Nonne*, it is generally assumed it was written a few weeks later. Since it makes a perfect companion for *Nacht und Träume*, both poetically and musically, it must also be assumed that Schubert planned it to be the first song in this set. Craigher's poem begins by observing that the night is as dark as the grave. But when the storm subsides and, as the bride of Christ, the young nun awaits her groom, it becomes 'holy night'. In other words *Die junge Nonne* involves a transition which leads directly into the first words of Collin's poem.

Two years earlier Schubert had dedicated Op. 22 to Collin, and in any case his dedicatees were always living people. Yet if he intended Op. 43 to be a valediction for the poet then he must have had a shock when the set was issued, for instead of attributing *Nacht und Träume* to Collin the publishers placed Schiller's name on the title page.

Texts

1. *Wie braust durch die Wipfel der heulende Sturm!* Four stanzas of respectively four, five, five, and seven lines.

   (1) How the howling storm rages through the tree-tops. The rafters creak, the whole house trembles. Thunder rolls, lightning flashes, and the night is as dark as the grave.

   (2) No matter, no matter; not long ago a storm raged in me. Life roared as the storm does now; my limbs trembled, as the house now trembles; love flared as the lightning now flashes; and my heart was as dark as the grave.

   (3) Rage on, wild and mighty storm, in my heart there is peace and repose. The loving bride awaits the bridegroom – she is purified in the testing fire and betrothed to eternal love.

   (4) I await you with longing, my Saviour. Heavenly bridegroom, come to claim your bride, deliver my soul from its earthly bonds. Listen, the bell tolls peacefully from the tower. Its sweet sound calls me powerfully to the eternal heights. Hallelujah!

2. *Heil'ge Nacht, du sinkest nieder.* An eight-line stanza in the form of a double quatrain.

   Holy night, you sink down upon us; as your moonlight descends through space, so dreams descend into the stilled hearts of men.
       Men joyfully listen to these dreams and call, when days breaks: 'Come back, sweet night! Sweet dreams, come back.'

Music

The songs are constructed on the principle of verse and refrain, the verses being musically varied, the refrains remaining the same. They have certain melodic and harmonic features in common, and in their accompaniments both make use of a *moto perpetuo* in the form of a measured tremolo.

1. *Die junge Nonne*

F minor – major. At a moderate pace 12/8.

The whole song is dominated by the figures the pianist plays in the first three bars: the figure in octaves, the measured tremolo and the repeated note representing the Convent bell.

The first two stanzas dealing with the storm are in the minor. For the lines 'And the night is as dark as the grave' at the end of the first, then 'And my heart was as dark as the grave' at the end of the second, Schubert writes a refrain built from a descending three-note chromatic scale related to his death motif. When the nun calmly awaits her Saviour in the last two stanzas, the refrain changes. It becomes diatonic, 'open' and exultant.

ge - rein-igt in prü - fen-der Glut—— der e - wi-gen, e - wi-gen Lie - be ge - traut.

For the word 'Alleluja' Schubert adds a coda where the features which will be taken up in *Nacht und Träume* occur: the falling minor third in the vocal line, the oscillating chords in the accompaniment (see over).

Al - le - lu - ja!

2. *Nacht und Träume*

B major. Very slow 4/4.

As mentioned when discussing *Am Strome* in Op. 8, Schubert reserved B major for feelings of spiritual transcendence. The relationship between F major and B major is remote, but when *Nacht und Träume* begins, it is as if we are still in the presence of the young nun. The tremolo has now become slow and peaceful, and the two F♯s in the upper line, if at first they seem to be echoing the sound of the bell, flower into one of Schubert's most sonorous cantilenas.

When the voice enters she sings one of several phrases which end with the falling minor third heard in 'Alleluja'.

Heil' - ge Nacht,—— du sin-kest nie - der!

Schubert is true to the poem's structure in that the eight-line stanza finds expression in the continuous musical flow, while the division of it into two quatrains is reflected by the use of the same music to bring each of them to a conclusion.

In his analysis of the song, Carl Schachter draws attention to the F♯-F×-G♯ in bars 2 and 3, and to the reverse progression of G♯-G-F♯ in bar 4. In both instances the second notes are passing notes. But in the second part of the song in bars 15–19 Schubert gives the G a measure of stability by making it the root of a major triad. However in bar 20 it enharmonically changes into F× and becomes a passing note again. 'By combining in a single sonority two different and contrasting orders of musical reality', Schachter writes,

> Schubert gives this song a great central image; the song embodies a musical symbol of dreams. The G major section crystallizes around a most transitory musical event – a chromatic passing tone. Yet, while we are immersed in it, it assumes the guise of that most solid tonal structure, the major triad. Only at 'wenn der Tag erwacht' (when day awakes) does its insubstantiality become manifest; it vanishes, never to return except as an indistinct memory in the Gs of the coda. (Schachter, pp. 216–18)

Ideally *Die junge Nonne* should be sung by a woman, for as John Reed points out, 'everything is heard and seen through the mind of the singer'. So, too, should *Nacht und Träume*, for only a woman's voice can float the vocal cantilena high above the persistently sonorous accompaniment.

Opus 52

Seven songs from Walter Scott's *The Lady of the Lake*. Published with English and German words in two books by Matthias Artaria, 5 April 1826. 'Most respectfully dedicated to Sophie, Countess von Weissenwolff out of high regard.'

Book 1

1. *Ellens Gesang I: Raste Krieger* (Ellen's Song I: Rest, warrior), D837 (April–July 1825)
2. *Ellens Gesang II: Jäger, ruhe* (Ellen's Song II: Huntsman, rest), D838 (April–July 1825)
3. *Bootgesang* (Boat Song), part-song for TTBB and piano, D835 (Spring 1825)
4. *Coronach,* part-song for SSA and piano, D836 (Spring 1825)

Book 2

5. *Normans Gesang* (Norman's Song), D846 (April 1825)
6. *Ellens Gesang III: Ave Maria* (Ellen's Song III: Ave Maria), D839 (April 1825)
7. *Lied des gefangenen Jägers* (Song of the Imprisoned Huntsman), D843 (April 1825)

The Lady of the Lake is a long narrative poem in six cantos set mainly in the vicinity of Loch Katrine in the Trossachs during the first half of the sixteenth century. The story concerns the unwavering devotion of Ellen, the lady of the lake, to her lover Malcolm Graeme and her father Lord James of Douglas, who has been outlawed by King James V. The action centres on a quarrel between the king, who has disguised himself as a knight called James Fitz-James, and Roderick Dhu, a fierce Highland chief and suitor for Ellen's hand. When Ellen tends Fitz-James following a riding accident he too falls in love with her. He withdraws his suit when she tells him she has given her heart to someone else. He then gives her a signet ring which will enable her to obtain from the king anything she requires. In the end the king and Douglas are reconciled after Ellen produces the ring; Roderick dies of the wounds inflicted on him by the king in a fight, and Ellen marries Malcolm.

Scott published the poem in 1810 and the German translation by Adam Storck came out in 1819. It soon became as popular in Austria and

Germany as it was in Britain. In a letter he wrote to his parents on 25 July 1825 when he was visiting Upper Austria, Schubert explained why he had chosen to set Scott, and why he wanted the songs published in English and German:

> I intend to use a very different procedure with the publication of these songs from the usual one, which yields so very little, since they bear the celebrated name of Scott at their head and may in that way arouse greater curiosity, and might also make me better known in England by the addition of the English words. (Doc. 572)

This plan could not be fully realized because Schubert composed the songs in German and Storck's translations do not match the original English very well. Indeed *Normans Gesang* is metrically so different from Scott's poem that only the German version appeared in print.[10]

Scott was regarded as one of the foremost Romantics of the day, and his influence on music as well as literature was far-reaching. In 1819 Rossini based *La donna del lago*, the most Romantic of his Italian operas, on *The Lady of the Lake*. The story, with its romantic heroine innocently caught between warring factions and jealous rivalries, eventually became the prototype for many of the operas of Bellini and Donizetti. Yet Scott's poem was read not only for its story; its greatest appeal lay in its descriptions of the Scottish Highlands. Scott was considered to be second to none for his 'objective scene painting' as it was called. He was particularly admired for his ability to show the effect of light and shade on scenery. The seven lyrical episodes Schubert selected from the 13 in the narrative poem were chosen because their imagery could be conveyed in music. This is undoubtedly why he did not set Blanche of Devan's 'They bid me sleep' in Canto 4 and Allanbane's Lament in Canto 6 even though they supply vital information about the plot. The chosen seven are placed in the order they appear in the poem, but those who are unacquainted with Scott's narrative will find it difficult to construct a story from them. Furthermore, as mentioned in the introduction, those who do know it will have to supply the denouement from their memories.

Texts

1. *Ellens Gesang I: Raste Kreiger*
   Ellen sings 'Soldier rest' to James Fitz-James, who has found shelter in the house where she lives with her parents after his horse had collapsed and died under him during a hunt on the moors above Loch

---

[10] The two part-songs are not included in the Bärenreiter/Henle edition of Schubert's songs. They can be found in vol. IV/3 of the New Schubert Edition.

Katrine. Scott calls it 'an old lay'. The lyric is prefaced with the lines:
'She sung, and still a harp unseen/Filled up the symphony between.'

Soldier rest! thy warfare o'er,
Sleep the sleep that knows not
   breaking;
Dream of battled fields no more,
Days of danger, nights of waking.

In our isle's enchanted hall,
Hands unseen thy couch are
   strewing,
Fairy strains of music fall,
Every sense in slumber dewing.

Soldier rest! thy warfare o'er,
Dream of fighting fields no
   more:
Sleep the sleep that knows not
   breaking,
Morn of toil, nor night of
   waking.

No rude sound shall reach thine
   ear,
Armour's clang, or war steed

champing,
Trump nor pibroch summon
   here
Mustering clan, or squadron
   tramping.

Yet the lark's shrill fife may
   come
At the day-break from the
   follow,
And the bittern sound his drum,
Booming from the sedgy
   shallow.

Ruder sounds shall none be
   near
Guards nor warders challenge
   here,
Here's no war-steed neigh and
   champing,
Shouting clans, or squadrons
   stamping.

2. *Ellens Gesang II: Jäger, ruhe*

Ellen sings 'Huntsman, rest' to the slumbering James Fitz-James immediately after 'Soldier rest'. Scott says she extemporizes a song 'to grace the stranger of the day'.

Huntsman, rest! thy chase is
   done,
While our slumbrous spells
   assail ye,
Dream not, with the rising sun,
Bugles here shall sound reveillé.
Sleep! the deer is in his den;
Sleep! Thy hounds are by thee

lying;
Sleep! not dream in yonder glen,
How thy gallant steed lay dying.
Huntsman, rest! thy chase is
   done,
Think not of the rising sun,
For at dawning to assail ye,
Here no bugles sound reveillé.

3. *Bootgesang*

The Boat Song is sung by clansmen as they row across the lake to greet Roderick Dhu, who is assembling his forces to withstand the supposed threat from the king's troops.

Hail to the Chief who in
 triumph advances!
Honour'd and bless'd be the
 ever-green Pine!
Long may the tree, in his
 banner that glances,
Flourish, the shelter and grace
 of our line!
Heaven send it happy dew,
Earth lend it sap anew,
Gaily to bourgeon, and broadly
 to grow,
While every Highland glen
Sends our shout back agen,
'Roderigh Vich Alpine dhu, ho!
 ieroe!'
[i.e. Black Roderick, the
descendant of Alpine.]

Ours is no sapling, chance-
 sown by the fountain,
Blooming at Beltane, in winter
 to fade;
When the whirlwind has
 stripp'd every leaf on the
 mountain,
The more shall Clan-Alpine
 exult in her shade.
Moor'd in the rifted rock.
Proof to the tempest's shock,
Firmer it roots him the ruder it
 blow;
Menteith and Breadalbane,
 then,
Echo his praise agen,

'Roderigh Vich Alpine dhu, ho!
 ieroe!'

Proudly our pibroch has thrill'd
 in Glen Fruin,
And Bannochar's groans to our
 slogan replied;
Glen Luss and Ross dhu, they
 are smoking in ruin,
And the best of Loch Lomond
 lie dead on her side,
Widow and Saxon maid
Long shall lament our raid,
Think of Clan-Alpine with fear
 and with woe,
Lennox and Leven-glen
Shake when they hear agen,
'Roderigh Vich Alpine dhu, ho!
 ieroe!'

Row, vassals, row, for the pride
 of the Highlands!
Stretch to your oars, for the
 ever-green Pine!
O that the rose-bud that graces
 yon islands
Were wreathed in a garland
 around him to twine!
O that some seedling gem,
Worthy such noble stem,
Honour'd and bless'd in their
 shadow might grow;
Loud should Clan-Alpine then,
Ring from his deepmost glen,
'Roderigh Vich Alpine dhu, ho!
 iereo!'

4. *Coronach*
   Coronach is a funeral lament for Duncan, a dead chieftain.

He is gone on the mountain,
He is lost to the forest,
Like a summer-dried fountain,
When our need was the
 sorest.

The fount, reappearing,
From the rain-drops shall
 borrow,
But to us comes no cheering,
To Duncan no morrow.

The hand of the reaper
Takes the ears that are hoary,
But the voice of the weeper
Wails manhood in glory.
The autumn winds rushing
Waft the leaves that are searest,
But our flower was in flushing,
When blighting was nearest.

Fleet foot on the correi
Sage counsel in cumber,

Red hand in the foray,
How sound is thy slumber!
Like the dew on the mountain,
Like the foam on the river,
Like the bubble on the
    fountain,
Thou art gone, and for ever!
[The correi is the hollow side of
the hill, where game usually
lies.]

5. *Normans Gesang*

Norman, heir of Armandave and one of Roderick's clansmen, leaves
his young bride and sings this song as he marches over the moors to
join his chief.

The heath this night must be my
    bed,
The bracken curtain for my
    head,
My lullaby the warder's tread,
Far, far from love and thee,
    Mary.

To-morrow eve, more stilly
    laid,
My couch may be my bloody
    plaid,
My vesper song, thy wail, sweet
    maid!
It will not waken me, Mary.

I may not, dare not, fancy now
The grief that clouds thy lovely
    brow,
I dare not think upon thy vow
And all it promised me, Mary.

No fond regret must Norman
    know:

When bursts Clan Alpine on the
    foe,
His heart must be like bended
    bow,
His foot like arrow free, Mary.

A time will come with feeling
    fraught,
For if I fall in battle fought,
Thy hapless lover's dying
    thought
Shall be a thought on thee,
    Mary.

And if returned from conquered
    foes,
How blithely will the evening
    close,
How sweet the linnet sing
    repose
To my young bride and me,
    Mary.

6. *Ellens Gesang III: Ave Maria*

Ellen sings this prayer when she and her father are on their way to
Stirling castle, he to surrender himself to the king, she to plead for her
father's life.

Ave Maria! Maiden mild!
Listen to a maiden's prayer!
Thou canst hear though from
the wild,
Thou canst save amid despair.
Safe may we sleep beneath thy
care,
Though banished outcast and
reviled –
Maiden, hear a maiden's
prayer,
Mother, hear a suppliant child.

Ave Maria! undefiled!
The flinty couch we now must
share
Shall seem with down of eider
piled,
If thy protection hover there.
The murky cavern's heavy air

Shall breathe of balm if thou
hast smiled;
Then, Maiden! hear a maiden's
prayer,
Mother list a suppliant child!

Ave Maria! stainless styled!
Foul demons of the earth and
air,
From this their wonted haunt
exiled,
Shall flee before thy presence
fair.
We bow us to our lot of care,
Beneath thy guidance
reconciled;
Hear for a maid a maiden's
prayer,
And for a father hear a child!
Ave Maria!

7. *Lied des gefangenen Jägers*
Ellen overhears her lover, Malcolm, singing this song from a turret of
Stirling castle where he is being held captive. Scott calls the lyric 'a
love-sick lay'.

My hawk is tired of perch and
hood,
My idle greyhound loathes his
food,
My horse is weary of his stall,
And I am sick of captive thrall.
I wish I were, as I have been,
Hunting the hart in forest
green,
With bended bow and
bloodhound free.
For that's the life is meet for me.

I hate to learn the ebb of time,
From yon dull steeple's drowsy
chime,
Or mark it as the sunbeams

crawl,
Inch after inch, along the wall.
The lark was wont my matins
ring;
The sable rook my vespers sing,
Those towers, although a king's
they be,
Have not a hall of joy for me.

No more a dawning morn I rise,
And sun myself in Ellen's eyes,
Drive the fleet deer the forest
through,
And homeward wend with
evening dew;
A blithesome welcome blithely
meet,

And lay my trophies at her feet,   That life is lost to love and me!
While fled the eve on wing of
  glee –

Music

Although Scott calls 'The Song of the Imprisoned Huntsman' a 'love
sick lay' in the poem and has Malcolm end his song saying that life and
love are lost to him, Schubert set it in the style of a dashing polonaise.
John Reed suggests that his purpose was to emphasize Malcolm's
unbroken spirit (SSC, p. 317). But the song had also to comply with the
structural plan Schubert devised for the set. It was based on the way the
central finales of most of Mozart's and Rossini's operas, particularly the
comic ones, are organized. These usually end in a state of confusion
with the plot left in mid-air. The technique involves alternating fast
tempos advancing the action with slow tempos reflecting on it. To give
the structure momentum, the slow tempos tend to get progressively
slower, the fast tempos progressively faster with the result that the act
ends with the slowest, most reflective number being followed by the
fastest, most active one. By this means a strong sense of end accentua-
tion and consequently musical closure is achieved. The prime example is
the second act finale of *Le nozze di Figaro*, where the progression of
slow tempos culminates in the highly suspenseful *Andante*, during
which Figaro gradually reveals that the papers Antonio has found are
Cherubino's commission; the fast tempos accelerate to the *prestissimo*
which brings the curtain down on the Count's party in triumph and the
Countess's party in despair.

In the songs from *The Lady of the Lake* Schubert establishes the
principle that fast tempos will alternate with slow tempos in the first song.
Thereafter songs No. 2 (Ellen's second song), No. 4 (Coronach) and No.
6 (Ellen's third song) provide the sequence of progressively slower tempos,
while songs No. 3 (Boat Song), No. 5 (Norman's Song) and No. 7
(Malcolm's Song) provide the sequence of progressively faster ones. This
was why Malcolm's song had to be vigorous and at odds with the text.

Schubert's sequence of keys also has its roots in Mozart's central
finale. Mozart's keys are all major ones. His first three are Eb, Bb and G.
Then to get back to Eb, he moves through a sequence descending in fifths:
(G)-C-F-Bb-Eb. Schubert uses only flat keys. Ellen's songs are cast in a
sequence of major keys, Db (five flats), Eb (three flats) and Bb (two flats);
the other songs in a sequence of minor keys, C (three flats), F (four flats)
and D (one flat). When these are ordered as they are in the set, the first
three keys go from five flats (Db major) to three flats (Eb major and C

minor). Following Mozart's example, Schubert then introduces a logical sequence, in this case a sequence based on the number of flats each key contains: four flats (F minor), three flats (C minor), two flats (B♭ major), one flat (D minor). The last song is the only one that touches on a sharp key. In this D minor becomes D major whenever Malcolm refers to his life as a huntsman.

1. *Ellens Gesang I: Raste Krieger*

D♭ major. Moderate 3/4 – A major. Slow 2/2 – D♭ major. Moderate 3/4 – A major. Fast, slower, fast, slower, slow 4/4 – D♭ major. Moderate 3/4.

Ellen's first song is appropriately the longest and most varied in the set. Storck must have had difficulty in translating Scott's second stanza, because he made two quatrains out of it. Schubert also made some alterations to the text. He ignored Storck's translation of stanza 3 and replaced it with a repetition of stanza 1. He also brought back stanza 1 at the end of the text. In addition he changed round stanzas 5 and 6.[11] By making these alterations he was able to cast the song as a rondo with two substantial episodes. The harp-like accompaniment suggested by Scott in his introduction to the lyric is reserved for the *Ave Maria* Ellen sings later in the set. Here the rondo theme is accompanied by a figure resembling a half-heard military fanfare. In the first episode the accompaniment becomes more like a lullaby. For this Schubert modulates to B♭♭ major, D♭ major's flat submediant. However, to make it easier to read he writes it in A major, B♭♭ major's enharmonic equivalent. He uses the same key for the second episode where the text refers to the battles the soldier may have experienced. Here the music suggests galloping horses. But since the purpose of the song is to relax the weary soldier, Schubert gradually brings back the lullaby. He does so in stages: fast-slower-fast-slower-slow. By this means, listeners are given a clue as to how the set as a whole will proceed in terms of its sequence of tempos.

2. *Ellens Gesang II: Jäger, ruhe*

E♭ major. Schubert's tempo marking is *Etwas geschwind* (rather fast) 4/4, but it is only a shade faster than the *Mässig* of the previous song.

Scott's single 12-line stanza is divided into three quatrains which Schubert casts in modified strophic form. The song is one of his most

---

[11] In the English version, the words of the second stanza are repeated; Schubert retained Scott's words for the third stanza.

atmospheric for the accompaniment consists of the muffled sound of bugles announcing reveille, and, more persistently, horn calls presented as if they were echoing across empty moors.

3. Bootgesang

C minor. Moderate and powerful 4/4.

Strophic. Schubert conveys the image of men pulling together vigorously on their oars when at the end of each verse they stretch the word 'Held' or the word 'iereo' across the concluding dominant and tonic chords with a strong crescendo from one to the other.

4. Coronach

F minor. Slow 12/8. Strophic.

The pianist's left hand plays a tremolo on the first and third beats of every bar, and the wailing thirds above them suggest a funeral march as well as a lament. The song brings the set's first book to a close.

5. Normans Gesang

C minor. Schubert marks it *Geschwind* 4/4, but the tempo should be no faster than a brisk walking pace.

The strophes are modified, but the marching dotted rhythm persists throughout the song. In the last strophe, when Norman speaks of the possibility of returning home after the battle and greeting his Mary again, the key turns into the major.

6. Ellens Gesang III: Ave Maria

B♭ major. Very slow 4/4. Strophic.

The accompaniment to one of Schubert's most famous songs is the sound of a harp, the instrument Scott suggested was suitable for song No. 1 when Ellen sings to the sleeping Fitz-James after his accident. But as Schubert here proves, its sound is far more suitable for Ellen's religious devotion.

7. Lied des gefangenen Jägers

D minor. Rather fast 3/4.

The actual pulse of this song may be slower than the one required for Norman's Song, but because its rhythm is so vigorous it is bound to sound more lively. Like Norman's Song and Ellen's second song the form is modified strophic. Storck divided the three eight-line stanzas into six quatrains. Schubert casts the first, third and fifth in the minor, the second, fourth and sixth in the major. But for the last lines of stanzas 4 and 6 ('Have not a hall of joy for me' – 'That life is lost to love and me'), the music returns to the minor.

As always Schubert took care to construct the set so that it had a coherent structure, but in this case he went against his normal custom of ending peacefully. The presence of part-songs is also unusual. If these are sung, the set requires a minimum of seven singers to perform. And yet, according to the records, it was the one and only set which did get performed in Schubert's lifetime. This was when Michael Vogl and the composer gave the five solo songs at a private concert at Anton Otten-wald's home in Linz when they were touring Upper Austria in July 1825. As mentioned in the introduction, Vogl was a dominating personality and a man of the theatre. It was almost certainly he who chose to begin with the song most likely to arouse the audience's sympathy and end with the one he could perform in a manner that would prompt the loudest applause. In a letter to Josef von Spaun, this is what Anton Ottenwald had to say about the occasion:

> We heard Vogl three times, and Schubert himself condescended to sing something after breakfast among ourselves, and also played his marches, two- and four-handed variations and an overture on the pianoforte, compositions of such significance that one cannot trust oneself to discuss them. And if I cannot do so worthily with his latest songs on W. Scott, I cannot keep silent about them either. There are five in particular: 1. 'Ave Maria', Ellen's evening song and prayer for her father in the wilderness where they live in hiding. 2. 'Soldier, rest', a captivating slumber song of the kind Arminda might sing for Rinaldo to her magic harp. 3. 'Huntsman, rest', another slumber song, more simple and touching, I feel; in the accompaniment the tune of horns, I should say, like the echoes of a hunting-song in a fair dream. 4. 'Lay of the Imprisoned Huntsman' – 'My idle greyhound loathes his food, My horse is weary of his stall, And I am sick of captive thrall' ... Accompaniment – ah, how shall I describe those angrily throbbing, briefly cut-off chords? I am almost ashamed again at having taken into my head to write about it. And what of the last, 'Norman's song?' The warrior with his sacrificial torch, the summons to arms, sings as he fares across the country. Hurrying without respite, he thinks of his errand, of the bride he has left at the altar, of the morrow's combat, of victory, of reunion. The tune and the accompaniment you will have to imagine. Schubert himself regards this as the best of the Scott songs. Vogl himself interprets it heavily (a syllable, often a word, to each note), but splendidly. (Doc. 574)

Opus 56

Published in two books 'with Italian words printed below' by Anton Pennauer, 14 July 1826. 'Dedicated to Karl Pinterics out of friendship.'

Book 1

1. *Willkommen und Abschied* (Hail and Farewell) Johann Wolfgang von Goethe, D767 (version b, *c.* 1822)

Book 2

2. *An die Leier* (To my Lyre) Anacreon, freely translated by Franz von Bruchmann, D737 (?1822 or 1823)
3. *Im Haine* (In the Wood) Franz von Bruchmann, D738 (?1822 or 1823)

Having just produced a set with German and English words, Schubert decided to follow it with one containing German and Italian words. But now he had the Viennese market in mind rather than a foreign one. The songs were written at a time when all things Italian had become extremely popular in Vienna. In December 1821 the Italian impresario Domenico Barbaia acquired the lease on the Kärntnertor Theatre for several years, and the following year he imported his Neapolitan company and its composer, Rossini, for a three-month Rossini festival between April and July. Six operas were given with extraordinary success. Rossini was followed by crowds virtually wherever he went. 'People wore Rossini hats and Rossini cravats, they ate Rossini dishes and watched Rossini parodies in the popular theatres' (DF-D, p. 200). Three years later, when the lease expired, the theatre was closed. But Barbaia acquired another lease in 1826, and it was in anticipation of a renewed interest in Italian music that Schubert assembled this set. The Italian translations were probably undertaken by his friend Jakob Nikolaus Craigher de Jachelutta, who had been born and brought up in Italy.

There are two possible reasons why the set was issued in two books. One is that the songs required more engraving than was usual for a three-song set, and to make a profit Pennhauer had to break the set up into two parts and charge the standard lower price of 1 florin, 30 kreuzer for each of them rather than the 2 florins he would have had to charge for a single book. Alternatively, or perhaps coincidentally, Schubert may have felt that, if the set were split in two, its structure might be clarified. Usually his three-song sets involve a progression within a topic, the central song acting as a transition between the outer ones. In this set, however, the topic is a musical style, and there is no transition between Goethe's passionate love song and terrifying landscape, and Bruchmann's reluctant love song and peaceful landscape. Looked at from this point of view, the structure is closer to a two-song set than a three-song one.

Texts

1. *Es schlug mein Herz, geschwind zu Pferde!* Four eight-line stanzas.

   (1) My heart pounded. Quick, to horse. No sooner thought than done. Evening was already cradling the earth and night hung upon the mountains. The oak tree stood in its misty raiments, a huge, towering giant, there, where darkness peeped out of the bushes with a hundred jet-black eyes.

   (2) From a bank of cloud the moon gazed plaintively down through the haze. The wind flapped its wings gently, and eerily whistled about my ears. The night created a thousand monsters, yet my mood was bright and cheerful. What fire in my veins; what ardour in my heart!

   (3) I saw you, and from your eyes flowed a gentle joy. My whole heart was with you, my every breath was for you. A rose-tinted springtime framed your dear features, Ye gods, I had hoped for this, your tenderness for me, but I never deserved it!

   (4) But alas, with the morning sun came the farewell. What ecstasy in your kisses, what sorrow in your eyes. I went, you gazed after me, and your eyes were moist. What joy to be loved, and to love, ye gods, what bliss.

2. *Ich will von Atreus' Söhnen.* Two quatrains and a sixain.

   (1) I would like to sing of the sons of Atreus and of Cadmus, but my strings bring forth only sounds of love.

   (2) I have changed the strings, and should have changed the lyre. Then the victorious march of Alcides would have thundered from his mighty heart!

   (3) But these strings too bring forth only sounds of love. So farewell heroes. Instead of producing threats and heroic songs my strings will produce nothing but the sounds of love.

3. *Sonnenstrahlen*. Three seven-line stanzas.

   (1) Sunlight falling through the fir trees dispels our grief and leaves peace in our hearts.

   (2) Every meadow is caressed by balmy breezes and the delicate scents that float down from the branches.

   (3) If only dark trees, shimmering sunlight and the flowers that edge the wood could be about us forever and wipe away all pain.

Music

Each song represents a different aspect of the Italian style, and all make use of the strings of triplets found so often in Rossini's accompaniments.

1. *Willkommen und Abschied*

C major. Fast 4/4.

Apart from three short moments for reflection, the galloping, triplet rhythm in the accompaniment, which represents both the horse's hooves and the pounding heart of the lover, continues right through to the end of the song, and is therefore present even when the couple greet and say farewell to each other. Although the song is through-composed, certain phrases are repeated. One is the bravura passage which brings the second and the fourth stanzas to a close. Originally Schubert wrote the song in D major, but to enable it to be sung by a high baritone as well as a tenor he transposed it to C when he came to publish it. Its operatic conclusion requires a full, powerful, ringing tone to bring it off.

2. *An die Leier*

Eb major. Fast – somewhat slower 4/4.

Schubert divides the song into four sections which he separates from each other by a bar of reflective silence. Those lines of the poem which relate to war (1–2 and 5–8) are cast as strongly dramatic recitatives requiring a voice of great power; those relating to love (3–4 and 9–14) are simple ariosos that never rise above *pianissimo* and need a perfectly controlled *sotto voce*. This juxtaposition creates the impression that the singer has had to withdraw unwillingly from what he wants to do. His passion is roused only by the exploits of heroes: he sings of love reluctantly.

3. *Im Haine*

A major. At a moderate pace 9/8.

The poem reads like an internal monologue, but Schubert treats the use of the first person plural literally, and makes it into a lilting song addressed to the 'other' about the poet's vision of the wood as a heaven on earth. The song is strophic and has a waltz-like accompaniment which could be likened to a slowed-down version of the galloping rhythm accompanying *Willkommen und Abschied*. What makes it more specific-ally Italian are the elaborations of the vocal line. The singer needs a flexible, effortless technique with the ability to float up to top G.

Opus 57

Published by Thaddäus Weigl, 6 April 1826.

1. *Der Schmetterling* (The Butterfly) Friedrich von Schlegel, D633 (*c.* 1819)
2. *Die Berge* (The Mountains) Friedrich von Schlegel, D634 (*c.* 1820)
3. *An den Mond* (To the Moon) Ludwig Hölty, D193 (17 May 1815)

This is the first of Schubert's works to be published by Thaddäus Weigl, who had been in business since 1801 and was to publish six of Schubert's works in the composer's lifetime. He brought out Op. 57 and Op. 58 (a set devoted to poems by Schiller) on the same day. Originally Op. 58 had been designated Op. 56, but since this number had already been allotted to Pennauer for the Goethe/Bruchmann set it had to be changed after publication. Weigl labelled the three songs in this Op. 57 set 4, 5 and 6, songs 1, 2 and 3 being those in the Schiller set. He had the six songs engraved so that they could be sold separately. This meant they could be obtained as two separate sets, as six single songs, or as what was in effect a single set in two books (Doc. 645f).

The decision to publish the sets in this way may have been taken in consultation with Schubert, for there is a link between Opp. 57 and 58 in that both deal with the relationship between imagination and reason or reality. The importance of the imagination to Romantic writers, musicians and painters is one of the first points H.G. Schenk makes in his book, *The Mind of the European Romantics*. As mentioned in the introduction, he chose to quote Schubert's notebook entry for 29 March 1824 as an illustration. This is where Schubert called the imagination 'mankind's greatest treasure' and dubbed the rationalist philosophy of the Enlightenment 'that ugly skeleton without flesh or blood'.

It was one of five notebook jottings Schubert made during the last week of March 1824 during a serious bout of illness in which he attempted to come to grips with what was concerning him at the time. In fact he was probably more concerned with the relationship between imagination and reality than with attacking the Enlightenment's emphasis on reason. Four months later, in a letter to his brother Ferdinand, he revealed what might have been behind his jotting. He said he was going through 'a period of fateful recognition of a miserable reality, which I endeavour to beautify as far as possible by my imagination (thank God)' (Doc. 484). This remark finds musical expression in Op. 60 containing Rückert's *Greisengesang* and Schiller's *Dithyrambe*. The other three sets dealing with the relationship, however, are not so condemnatory of reality or reason. They take a more balanced view of the issue.

Der Schmetterling and *Die Berge*, the first two songs in this Op. 57, both come from Schlegel's *Abendröte* cycle of poems, and were set by Schubert one after the other. Taken by itself *Der Schmetterling* is simply a poem about the way the butterfly can flit from one thing to another without hindrance, but in the company of *Die Berge* it becomes a metaphor for the way the imagination behaves. As the leading philosopher of Romanticism, Schlegel placed the highest value on imagination, but he knew full well that man is 'rooted in reality' and that he has built his 'edifices of thought' on reason. The imagination can only 'jest on the edge of the abyss' if it is aware of the reality of the mountain. This implies that the imagination functions best when it has reality or reason to focus its activities. Consequently Schubert chose to end the set with Hölty's *An den Mond*. Here the bereaved lover wants the moon to dispel 'the fancies and dream-like images' that flit before him so that by its light he can focus his imagination on the actual places where his beloved had once been.

Texts

1. *Wie soll ich nicht tanzen*. Four quatrains with a two-line refrain coming after stanzas 2 and 4.

   (1) Why should I not dance? It costs me no trouble, and enchanting colours shimmer here on the verdure.
   (2) Ever lovelier glisten my gaily coloured wings; ever sweeter is the scent from each tiny blossom.
   (Refrain) I feast on the blossoms. You cannot protect them.
   (3) What joy it is be it late or early to flit so blithely over hill and dale.
   (4) The clouds glow when the evening murmurs; the meadows become radiant when the air is golden.
   (Refrain) I feast on the blossoms. You cannot protect them.

2. *Sieht uns der Blick gehoben*. Three sixains.

   (1) When we look upwards our hearts believe that we can overcome gravity and reach the gods above. Man can imagine he is soaring aloft and passing through the clouds.
   (2) Yet to his astonishment he soon realises that we are rooted in our nature. Then with concentrated effort he devotes himself to tasks

that endure, endeavours not to escape from his roots, builds rock-like edifices of thoughts.

(3) And then with new joy he sees the bold cliffs hang mockingly. Forgetting his sorrows, he feels only the longing to jest on the edge of the abyss, for high courage swells in his noble breast.

3. *Geuss, lieber Mond, geuss deine Silberflimmer.* Four quatrains.

(1) Beloved moon shed your silver radiance through these green beeches, where fancies and dream-like images flit before me.

(2) Unveil yourself so that I can find the place where my sweetheart often sat, where she forgot the gilded town in the swaying branches of the beech and lime.

(3) Unveil yourself so that I can see the whispering bushes that cooled her, so that I can lay a wreath on the meadow where she listened to the brook.

(4) Then beloved moon, veil your face once more and mourn for your friend. Weep down through the haze of the clouds as I, the forsaken one, weep.

Music

It was not Schubert's usual practice to begin with a simple strophic song, but when the set is performed *Der Schmetterling* will probably sound like an introduction to *Die Berge.* Not only is it brief, it also makes use of the same type of arpeggio-based material. Indeed, in this context the opening of *Die Berge* will sound like a more emphatic version of *Der Schmetterling*'s refrain. In fact the whole set is dominated by arpeggios. When in the vocal line they represent the imagination in full flight, when in the accompaniment the imagination contained and focused.

1. *Der Schmetterling*

F major. Rather fast 2/4.

Schubert combines stanzas 1 and 2, and 3 and 4 to make two strophes each ending with the refrain. The flight of the butterfly is captured in the piano's introduction and postlude, but as far as the set is concerned the crucial material lies in the refrain, particularly the three notes of a rising arpeggio in its second bar and its inversion in bars 30 and 32. They may be clichés, but it is by means of such stereotypes that Schubert is able to make connections between songs.

Ich na - sche die Blü - ten, ihr könnt— sie nich hü - ten, ich na - sche die

Blü - ten, ihr könnt— sie nich hü - ten.

2. *Die Berge*

G major. Lively 6/8.

Schubert casts the three stanzas in ternary form (ABA). Since the first and third are concerned with the capacity of the imagination to defy gravity, the arpeggios are exposed in the vocal line.

Sieht uns der Blick ge - ho - ben,

In the central section when Schlegel speaks of the concentrated effort needed to build edifices of thought on reason, the imagination has to be contained, so the arpeggio figures move into the accompaniment.

3. *An den Mond*

F minor. Slow 12/8 – rather fast 2/2 – slow 12/8.

Schubert casts the four stanzas in a binary structure ABBA, the A sections being slow, the B ones rather fast. Since the bereaved lover wants his imagination to be focused on those places where his beloved had been, the arpeggio figures are mostly confined to the accompaniment. As has frequently been noted the opening has a strong resemblance to the first movement of Beethoven's 'Moonlight' Sonata. The only time an arpeggiated figuration moves into the vocal line is when the words speak of 'the fancies and dream-like images' flitting before the bereaved lover.

wo Phan - ta - sien— und Traum - ge - stal - ten

Opus 58

Three songs to poems by Friedrich von Schiller. Published by Thaddäus Weigl, 6 April 1826.

1. *Hektors Abschied* (Hector's Farewell), D312 (version b, *c.* 1815)
2. *An Emma* (To Emma), D113 (version c, *c.* 1814)
3. *Des Mädchens Klage* (The Maiden's Lament), D191 (version b, 1815)

This set concerns those who mourn. Do they get comfort from imagining the departed continue to love them, or should they face reality and accept that the consolation they require lies simply in the act of lamenting? As mentioned when discussing Op. 57, the set was originally designated Op. 56 and the songs were numbered 1, 2 and 3, with 4, 5 and 6 being contained in Op. 57. This was undoubtedly a marketing decision taken by the publisher, but if Schubert was in agreement with it, then he must have felt it could be intellectually justified. Taken by itself Op. 58 is about accepting the fact that the dead do not continue to love the living. Hector knows full well that his longings and thoughts will perish when he crosses the River Lethe. He is merely comforting Andromache when he tells her his love will not die. Taken in conjunction with Op. 57, however, another dimension opens up. Emphasis is placed on the relationship between the imagination and reason. In telling his wife he will continue to love her even in death, Hector is allowing his imagination to take over. He is offering her a palliative reason cannot sustain. The prime concern of Op. 57, however, was to suggest that to be really effective the imagination has to work in harmony with reason, and this is the ultimate message here.

Texts

1. *Will sich Hektor ewig von mir wenden.* Four sixains.

   (1) *Andromache:* Will Hector leave me for ever after Achilles makes his terrible sacrifice for Patroclus with his proud hands? Who will teach your son to throw javelins and revere the gods when the dark underworld engulfs you?
   (2) *Hector:* Dear wife, stem your tears. My ardent heart longs for battle! These arms will protect Troy. I shall fall fighting for the sacred home of the gods and descend to the Stygian river as the saviour of my fatherland.

(3) *Andromache:* Never more will I hear the clang of your armour. Your sword will lie idle in the hall. Priam's heroic race will be destroyed. You will go where no daylight shines, where the Cocytus weeps in the wasteland; your love will die in the waters of the Lethe.

(4) *Hector:* All my longing and all my thoughts will be drowned in the Lethe, but not my love for you. Listen! a wild crowd rages at the wall. Gird my sword. Cease lamenting. Hector's love will not perish in the Lethe.

2. *Weit in nebelgrauer Ferne.* Three sixains.

(1) Far in the grey, misty distance lies my past happiness. My gaze still lingers lovingly on one far star alone. But like the star's splendour it is only an illusion of the night.

(2) Laid out in a long slumber, your eyes closed by death, my grief might still possess you, you would be alive in my heart. But no! you live in the light, you do not live for my love.

(3) Emma, can love's sweet longing fade and pass away? What is over and vanished, can it be love? Can the heavenly ardour of its flame die like worldly goods?

3. *Der Eichwald braust, die Wolken ziehn.* Four cinquains.

(1) The oak trees roar, the clouds scud by, the maiden sits on the grassy shore. The waves break with a mighty force, and she sighs in the darkness of the night, her eyes dimmed by weeping.

(2) 'My heart is dead, the world is empty, and there is nothing left I might wish for. Holy one call back your child. I have enjoyed earthly happiness. I have lived and loved.'

(3) Her tears run their futile course; her lament does not waken the dead. But say, what comfort can heal the heart when the sweet joys of love have vanished? I, the holy one, shall not fail to name it.

(4) 'Let your tears run their futile course; your lament will not waken the dead. When the joys of love have vanished, the sweetest fate for the heart in mourning is the pain, the sorrow of love.'

Music

The outstanding musical feature of this set is the way Schubert co-ordinates it and illustrates its argument by changing the function, and by

implication the meaning, of a particular note; here, as in Op. 6, the note
A♭. It was a technique he brought to perfection in his Heine set. In that
set the songs were intended to go together; here they were not. Yet this
does not mean the result was fortuitous; it simply shows that Schubert
selected the songs so that there was some feature in the the set which
would integrate it.

1. *Hektors Abschied*

Hektors Abschied is one of a number of Schubert's songs involving
progressive tonality. It starts in F minor and reaches A♭ major through A
minor. The song is a through-composed dramatic scene in four sections
corresponding to the four stanzas of Schiller's poem. (1) F minor. Slow 2/
2. In this A♭ is the minor third of a key Schubert frequently used to
express thoughts about death. It appears prominently in the piano's
introduction to Andromache's, 'Will Hector leave me for ever'. Yet F
minor is never stabilized; it remains as uncertain as Andromache's
thoughts. (2) A minor. Fast 2/2. This section is even more unstable, but
here the main purpose is to reflect Hector's anticipation of the forthcoming battle. It moves into A♭ major when he says confidently , 'These
arms shall protect Troy. I shall die fighting for the sacred home of the
gods'. Schubert then goes through the words of the stanza again, this
time in an even more warlike manner. He moves to A major where its
leading note G♯, A♭'s enharmonic equivalent, becomes prominent. (3) G♯
is equally prominent when A minor is finally reached for Andromache's
response. Schubert leans on it over and over again as if he wanted to
draw attention to its highly unstable nature as the leading note of the key.
His ploy becomes apparent in the final section. (4) A♭ major. Not too
quick 4/4. This is the only harmonically stable section in the song. But
Schubert delays the confirmation of A♭ as the tonic of the key for the
poem's last line, when the doomed hero, in absolute confidence, says,
'Hector's love will not perish in the Lethe'.

2. *An Emma*

F major. At a moderate pace 2/4.

In this and the following song, just as the poetry undermines Hector's
confident claim, so the stability of A♭ is undermined. *An Emma*, a
through-composed song, modulates to A♭ major two-thirds of the way
through for the words: 'Yet you do not live for my love. Emma, can love's
sweet longing pass away?' The passage ends with the last two words set
as a musical question mark, a rising minor third (C-E♭) over an A♭ triad

in root position with the second note held as a pause. Schiller's text may not supply the answer, but Schubert's music for the next two lines does. 'That which is over and past, Emma, can that be love?', modulates to the dominant of D minor. The same musical question mark brings this passage to an end, but now the two notes and the triad lie a semitone higher. From here the music can slip quickly back to the home key. In other words the song does not progress from F to a highly stable Ab as the first song did. Ab 'passes away'.

3. Des Mädchens Klage

C minor. Very slow 2/4.

In fact the chord of Ab major has not quite 'passed away'. It makes an appearance in the piano's refrain which introduces each verse and brings the song to a conclusion. In C minor Ab has become the sixth degree of a minor scale, and when it functions as an appoggiatura resolving on to G, the key's dominant, it traditionally expresses grief.

Although the sense of grief comes from the clash of the Ab against the G on the third beat of these bars, the notes are placed in an unobtrusive inner voice. Ab is prominent only in the piano's refrain. It makes its mark in the first bar where Schubert has it as the bass of an accented Ab triad. In the context of the set, listeners may well associate this with the way it sounded at the end of *Hektors Abschied*. But in fact its function, as in the passage quoted above, is not to be assertive. Its authority is denied. It is simply a member of a sequence: Eb-Ab, C-Fm; Bb-Eb, G-Cm.

Opus 59

Published by Sauer & Leidesdorf, 21 September 1826.

1. *Du liebst mich nicht* (You love me not) August von Platen-Haller-münde, D756 (version b, July 1822)
2. *Dass sie hier gewesen* (That she was here) Friedrich Rückert, D775 (?1823)
3. *Du bist die Ruh* (You are repose) Friedrich Rückert, D776 (1823)
4. *Lachen und Weinen* (Laughter and tears) Friedrich Rückert, D777 (?1823)

Schubert came across the poetry of Platen and Rückert through Franz von Bruchmann who had befriended the poets. Like Goethe and Friedrich von Schlegel, they took a deep interest in oriental verse. Platen's poem comes from a volume called *Ghaselen* (Ghazals) published in 1821, Rückert's from *Östliche Rosen* (Oriental Roses), which came out shortly afterwards. As mentioned when discussing Op. 14, a ghazal consists of couplets with a strict metre and a strict rhyme scheme in the pattern AA BA CA DA etc. Platen's *Du Liebst mich nicht* differs from the model in that, instead of simply repeating the last vowel, he repeats the whole line, the line being: '*du liebst mich nicht*'. It consequently becomes a refrain occurring obsessively six times in the ten-line poem. Rückert's poems are equally strict, and apart from *Du bist der Ruh* they too make unusual use of a refrain. However, when he composed *Du bist der Ruh* Schubert added a musical refrain in that he set the last lines of stanzas 2, 4 and 5 to the same music. The main feature of the set is, therefore, the way different types of refrains are ordered.

As usual in his four-song sets, Schubert groups the songs into related pairs. They can be tabulated as follows:

I 1. Refrain confined to the text; music through-composed.
   2. Refrain occurs at the end of each stanza, but it changes its pronoun. The reader has to decide why 'you' is used in the first stanza and 'she' in the last.
   Is the poet (the 'I') referring to two different people, or does he feel he can no longer address the 'she' as 'you'.

II 3. Refrain confined to the music; text through-composed.
   4. Refrain occurs at the beginning of each stanza.

Texts

1. *Mein Herz ist zerrissen, du liebst mich nicht!* Five couplets.

   (1) My heart is broken: you do not love me. You have shown me plainly you do not love me.
   (2) Though I came to you begging, wooing, zealously loving, you do not love me.
   (3) You told me so, you said it all too explicitly in words: you do not love me.
   (4) I must forgo the stars, the moon, the sun. You do not love me.
   (5) It no longer matters that the rose, the jasmine, the narcissus bloom. You do not love me.

2. *Dass der Ostwind Düfte.* Three quatrains.

   (1) The east wind blows gently, scenting the air; and so it tells me that you have been here.
   (2) Since tears fall here, you will know, even though you were not told, that I have been here.
   (3) Can beauty and love remain concealed? The breezes and the tears reveal that she has been here.

3. *Du bist die Ruh.* Five short-line quatrains.

   (1) You are repose and gentle peace; you are my longing and yet you still it.
   (2) Full of joy and grief, I consecrate my eyes and heart to you as a dwelling place.
   (3) Come in to me, and softly close the door behind you.
   (4) Drive all grief from my breast. Let my heart be filled with your joy.
   (5) The temple of my eyes is lit by your radiance alone. Fill it wholly.

4. *Lachen und Weinen zu jeglicher Stunde.* Two sixains.

   (1) Laughter and tears arise in love at whatever hour and from so many different causes. In the morning I was laughing with joy, and why I should be weeping in the evening puzzles me.
   (2) Laughter and tears arise in love at whatever hour and from so many different causes. In the evening I was weeping with grief. Why is it, my heart, that I awaken in the morning laughing?

Music

1. *Du liebst mich nicht*

A minor. At a moderate pace 3/4.

A through-composed song, nothing being repeated save the words of the
refrain and the rhythmic figure in the accompaniment which relates to
the way Schubert initially sets the words *Du liebst mich nicht.*

The rhythm would be as obsessive as the refrain had not Schubert varied
it and added unexpected cross-accents. Equally disturbing are the unexpected switches of key. He ends the second couplet in A♭ major, the third
in G♭ major, and during the rest of the song oscillates continuously
between A minor and A major. Originally the song was cast in the rare
key of G♯ minor, a key the theorists of the time regarded as being the 'key
of misery, of the depressed heart, of a heart squeezed until it suffocates'
(Steblin, p. 286). The song still has something of these qualities in A
minor, the much 'easier' key Schubert transposed it to for publication.
However the qualities are not fully revealed until the last repetition of the
refrain. At the beginning of the song the refrain sounds flat and matter of
fact, but on each repetition it becomes increasingly more rhetorical and
impassioned until eventually it borders on the hysterical.

2. *Dass sie hier gewesen*

C major. Very slow 2/4.

Schubert's song is as ambiguous as Rückert's poem. But whereas Rückert seems to be suggesting that 'you' and 'she' are different people, Schubert gives the impression the pronouns apply to the same person. His music suggests that in the first two stanzas the 'I' addresses the woman as if the wind had evoked her physical presence; in the last she becomes the woman he has lost. To convey this, two types of music are involved: chromatic, tonally ambiguous music laden with appoggiaturas, representing the east wind and his awakening memories, and diatonic, matter-of-fact music devoid of appoggiaturas, representing what has been recalled. The chromatic music holds back the key of the song for 13 bars, but even when C major arrives for the refrain, the resolution into it is suspended. The ensuing silence after the repetition of 'Dass du hier gewesen' suggests that more memories are coming to mind.

Schubert structures the song in rounded bar form (AAB), a form harking back to the Minnesingers. B is longer than A, contains new material, but ends with the same C major refrain. It is in this B section that the man's memories become less vague. Schubert sets all the words of the last stanza twice, on each occasion repeating 'Dass sie hier gewesen' (that she was here). He modulates to F minor for the man's remembrance of the tears that were shed, and then to Ab major for his first version of the line containing 'she' rather than 'you'. But this has a warmth and expressivity the recurring C major refrain lacks (see previous page, bar 51ff).

After this the plain C major version of the refrain, which rounds the song off, is bound to sound even plainer than it did after the first two strophes. The music may be the same, but what it implies has changed. A sense of presence has been replaced by a sense of loss.

3. *Du bist die Ruh*

Eb major. Slow 3/8.

Schubert structures *Du bist die Ruh* in rounded binary form, AABB. The first A sets stanzas 1 and 2, the second stanzas 3 and 4. The two Bs are both settings of stanza 5. A four-bar musical refrain rounds each section off first appearing in bars 22-5 (see below). In the A sections it is seamlessly attached to the music preceding it.

In the B sections this concluding four-bar refrain is separated from what has gone before by a bar's silence. It now represents the essence of the song. Not only is the sense of peace enhanced but, with the additional imitative counterpoint in the piano, so too is the sense of fullness and intimacy.

4. *Lachen und Weinen*

A♭ major. Rather fast 2/4.

Although Rückert's poem places laughter and tears on an equal footing, Schubert's lively song gives greater emphasis to laughter. The two stanzas are cast in modified strophic form. Both set Rückert's opening two-line refrain in the same way; they differ in the settings of lines 3, 4 and 5 simply because one proceeds from laughter to tears (major to minor), the other from tears to laughter (minor to major). However, the song has three refrains. In addition to the vocal refrain at the beginning of the stro-phes, there are two for the piano to round them off. One is a pianistic version of the music for the sixth line, the other a repetition of the piano's introduction. The song makes an ideal ending for the set, not only in its use of refrains, but also because, in conjunction with *Du bist die Ruh*, it emphasizes the pleasurable as opposed to the dolorous side of love.

Opus 60

Two songs for bass voice published by Cappi and Czerny, 10 June 1826.

1. *Greisengesang* (Song of Old Age) Friedrich Rückert, D778 (version b, by June 1823)
2. *Dithyrambe* (Dithyramb) Friedrich von Schiller, D801 (by June 1826)

Although this set was published three months before Op. 59, it was probably assembled at about the same time, that is to say some time in January or early February 1826. In both sets the first song is modelled on the Persian ghazal. *Greisengesang* comes after *Lachen und Weinen* in order of composition, and the set as a whole also swings between 'laughing and weeping'. In this case, 'weeping' arises from being old, 'laughter' from the ability to dream, to live in one's imagination. As mentioned when discussing Op. 57, this is the first of two sets in which the imagination is seen as a consolation for 'miserable reality'. 'Shut out the harshness of reality, and give house room only to the fragrance of dreams', says the first old man. As if on cue, the second old man provides us with an uproarious specimen of what such dreams might be.

Texts

1. *Der Frost hat mir bereifet des Hauses Dach*. Eight long-line couplets.

    (1) The frost has covered the roof of my house, but I have kept warm in the living room.
    (2) Winter has whitened the top of my head, but the blood flows red in my heart.
    (3) On my cheeks the flush of youth has gone, the roses have disappeared one by one.
    (4) Where have they gone? Down into my heart where they bloom whenever I want them to.
    (5) Have all the rivers of joy in the world run dry? In my heart a quiet stream still flows.
    (6) Have the nightingales in the meadow fallen silent? In the silence within me one stirs.
    (7) She sings: 'Master of the house, bolt your door, lest the world's chill wind should invade the parlour.
    (8) Shut out the harsh breath of reality, and give shelter only to the fragrance of dreams.'

2. *Nimmer, das glaubt mir, erscheinen die Götter.* Three seven-line stanzas.

(1) Believe me, the gods never appear alone. No sooner is jolly Bacchus with me than in comes Cupid, the smiling boy, and then glorious Phoebus. They approach, they come in, all the deities – this earthly abode is filled with gods!

(2) Tell me how can I, being earth-born, entertain this heavenly choir? What can a mere mortal give you? Grant me your immortal life, ye gods. Lift me up to Olympus. Give me the cup filled with nectar, for only joy dwells in the hall of Jupiter.

(3) Pass him the cup, Hebe, just one more drink for the poet. Moisten his eyes so that he might not behold the hateful Styx, so that he might think of himself as one of us. The heavenly spring gushes and foams, the heart grows tranquil, the eye grows bright.

Music

According to Walther Dürr in the *Neue Schubert Ausgabe* and his preface to Volume 7 of the Bärenreiter/Henle edition of Schubert's songs there are three versions of *Greisengesang* and two of *Dithyrambe*.[12] He claims that the first version of *Greisengesang* together with the original version of *Dithyrambe*, exists in an autographed fair copy dating from 1826. Although he does not mention it, the musical evidence suggests that *Dithyrambe* was written to complement *Greisengesang*. The other versions of both songs must have been revisions of those in the fair copy. This suggests that Schubert took great trouble in preparing the set for the publisher.

1. *Greisengesang*

B minor – major. At a moderate pace 2/2.

Schubert divides the song into two strophes, the second differing from the first in the setting of the first line of the last couplet ('Shut out the harsh breath of reality'). The principal feature of the song is the constant alternation between B minor and B major, B minor being the key he usually used for deeply troubled states of mind, B major for when suffering is transcended in some way. In his first 1823 version the song is surprisingly austere even in the B major sections (see over).

---

[12] The compiler of the catalogue of Schubert's songs in the second edition of *The New Grove Dictionary of Music and Musicians*, however, lists only one version of *Dithyrambe*.

In the two versions he made in 1826 these bare notes are ornamented, presumably to convey the increased animation of the old man at the prospect of indulging in the world of the imagination. In this Schubert was probably influenced by the way Vogl ornamented the song when he sang it to Schubert's accompaniment at St Florian in June 1823.

The severity of the chords in the piano's introduction to the two strophes suggests that Schubert wanted to establish a note of defiance in the old man's comments about his age, a mood not present in Rückert's text. This is probably why he chose to preserve the austerity even when the song moves into the major in his original version. The chords are the same in all the versions, the only difference being that this, the third version, has no staccato markings.

2. Dithyrambe

A major. Fast, ardently 6/8.

A strophic song in which the piano's introduction and postlude are linked to the introduction of *Greisengesang* through having in common the chords of B minor, F♯ major, C♯ major, and a diminished seventh on A♯. But whereas in *Greisengesang* they were in 'black' B minor, here they are in the traditionally cheerful key of A major (Steblin, p. 288). From time to time the song creates the impression that Schubert had the Vivace in

Beethoven's A major Seventh Symphony in mind when he composed the song.

Opus 62

Songs from Goethe's *Wilhelm Meister's Apprenticeship*. Published by Anton Diabelli and Co., 2 March 1827. 'Reverentially dedicated to Mathilde, Princess of Schwarzenberg.'

1. *Nur wer die Sehnsucht kennt* (Only he who knows longing), D877, No. 1 (January 1826) (Duet for soprano and tenor or high baritone)
2. *Heiss mich nicht reden* (Ask me not to speak), D877, No. 2 (January 1826)
3. *So lasst mich scheinen* (Such let me seem), D877, No. 3 (January 1826)
4. *Nur wer die Sehnsucht kennt* (Only he who knows longing), D877, No. 4 (January 1826) (Version for single voice)

The first three numbers of this set are on an autographed manuscript of five pages dated January 1826 now in the Sächsische Landesbibliothek, Dresden; the fourth is on a separate sheet now in the Stadt-und-Landes-bibliothek, Vienna. Opinion is divided as to whether the second version of *Nur wer die Sehnsucht kennt* was composed a little later than the other three songs (perhaps at the request of Diabelli), or whether Schubert conceived it as an alternative to the duet from the start, for it is possible the original manuscript contained six sheets, the last becoming separated from the first five at some later date.

The songs are three of the four the 13-year-old dancer, Mignon, sings in Goethe's novel, the other being *Kennst du das Land?* Wilhelm Meister comes across Mignon in a travelling circus, and buys her freedom from a troupe of tight-rope dancers. Together with the equally mysterious Harper, she becomes Wilhelm's companion during his apprenticeship. They represent the 'sterile Romanticism' which Wilhelm has to overcome if he is to be a useful member of society. Unlike the Harper, who finds a measure of peace near the end of the novel, Mignon never achieves the inner harmony Goethe regarded as being the essential prerequisite for a useful and fulfilled life. Her secret love for Wilhelm causes her intense suffering and ultimately breaks her heart.

Georg Lukács believed 'the seductive romantic beauty of these figures' distracted the majority of romantics from seeing that Goethe was condemning what they represent.[13] Among these he might have

---

[13] Lukács, Georg (1968), *Goethe and his Age*, trans. R. Anchor, London: Merlin Press, p. 59.

numbered Schubert, for Schubert's numerous settings of the Harper and Mignon lyrics suggest that he was totally captivated by the pair. Over a period of 11 years he made six settings of *Nur wer die Sehnsucht kennt*, two of *Heiss mich nicht reden* and four of *So lasst mich scheinen*. His prime purpose seems to have been to find a way of expressing to his satisfaction Mignon's elusive combination of innocence and pathos. He must have felt he had eventually achieved his goal in this set, for with these songs he said farewell to both Mignon and Goethe.

Texts

1. *Nur wer die Sehnsucht kennt*. A single 12-line stanza, the first two lines being repeated at the end.
   (Wilhelm falls into a reverie full of longing for the woman he loves. His feelings are mirrored by the 'irregular duet' Mignon and the Harper are singing at that moment 'with profound expression'. Schubert would not have known that in Goethe's first draft of the novel, *Wilhelm Meister's Theatrical Mission* of 1785, Mignon sings the song by herself, so that by including a solo version he was being equally true to Goethe.)

   'Only those who know longing know what I suffer. Alone, cut off from every joy, I gaze at the sky in yonder direction. Ah, he who loves and knows me is far away. I feel giddy, my vitals burn. Only those who know longing know what I suffer.'

2. *Heiss mich nicht reden, heiss mich schweigen*. Three quatrains.
   Mignon sings this to herself at the end of Book 5 of the novel just before Wilhelm leaves on a journey.

   (1) Do not ask me to speak, bid me to be silent, for my duty is to guard my secret. I long to reveal my whole soul to you, but fate does not permit it.
   (2) The sun in its appointed course drives away the dark, and night turns to day. The hard rock opens its bosom, and ungrudgingly bestows on the earth its deepest springs.
   (3) Everyone seeks peace in the arms of a friend, for there the heart can pour out its sorrow. But my lips are sealed by a vow, and only a god can open them.

3. *So lasst mich scheinen, bis ich werde*. Four quatrains.
   Mignon sings this just before she dies of a broken heart. She has

dressed up as an angel to entertain children at a party, and begs to be allowed to keep the costume on.

(1) Let me look like this, until I become like this. Do not take off my white dress. Soon I shall leave the fair earth for a safe dwelling below.
(2) There for a brief silence I shall rest; then I shall see with fresh eyes. I shall leave behind this pure raiment, this girdle and garland.
(3) Heavenly beings do not ask who is man or who is woman, and no garments will enclose this transfigured body.
(4) True, I have lived without toil or trouble, yet I have known deep suffering. Sorrow aged me too early; make me young again for ever.

Music

The Harper and Mignon both experience intense emotions but need to keep them under control: he, because he fears he may go mad if he does not repress them; she, because she does not want to expose her feelings for Wilhelm. Schubert conveys the Harper's control in Op. 12 by using the key of A minor as a containing frame. We are given only glimpses of his repressed feelings in the sudden shifts from *piano* to *fortissimo* and back again in his first two songs. Mignon's songs are also soft or very soft, and they too contain quickly controlled dynamic outbursts. Schubert indicates her surface coolness and latent passion by starting each vocal line in a subdued manner with phrases lying within a narrow orbit, then expanding them so that they cover a wider range and involve larger leaps.

The set conforms to Schubert's usual procedure in that it involves a progression from the most varied song to the simplest, from the one with the greatest internal tension to the one with the least. The last song is the only one in a major key, and the only one in a tempo faster than slow.

Although the duet version of *Nur wer die Sehnsucht kennt* is rarely performed, the layout of the set suggests that Schubert considered it to be his preferred choice for the first song.

1. *Nur wer die Sehnsucht kennt* (duet for soprano and tenor or high baritone)

B minor. Slow 2/2.

Schubert interprets Goethe's 'irregular duet' as one in which the material changes every two lines, and in which the voices overlap irregularly.

Apart from when the first two lines come back at the end, Mignon leads. The two sing only in rhythmic unison for lines 5 to 8: 'I gaze at the sky in yonder direction. Ah, he who loves and knows me is far away.' When they speak of feeling giddy the musical flow is interrupted by a short recitative-like section with dramatic tremolos in the bass. These continue to the end of the song so that when the opening section comes back, Schubert is able to indicate the feelings that lie beneath their controlled delivery.

2. *Heiss mich nicht reden*

E minor. Slow 2/2.

The contents of Goethe's three stanzas suggests that the song should be in ternary form (ABA). But when Schubert comes back to the first section, he transposes the key to the major for the first two lines of the quatrain, and then for the lines 'But my lips are sealed by a vow, and only a god can open them' he writes music much closer to dramatic recitative than song. It contrasts vividly with the simple, hymn-like nature of the rest of the song and functions as a transition to the final song.

3. *So lasst mich scheinen*

B major. Not too slow 3/4.

Schubert casts this, the simplest of the three songs, in the form ABAB. The key is the one Schubert inevitably uses for transcendence. But when Mignon speaks of her deep suffering she gives way to her feelings in a phrase which quickly rises from *pianissimo* to *fortissimo*. At its peak Schubert flattens B major's third by suddenly going to D minor. He then restores it so that for her words 'macht auf ewig wieder jung' ('make me young again for ever') the end of the song sounds radiant.

4. *Nur wer die Sehnsucht kennt* (for single voice)

A minor. Slow 6/8.

The solo version of *Nur wer die Sehnsucht kennt* is based on a song Schubert composed in 1816 to words by Salis-Seewis, *Ins stille Land* (To the Land of Peace). This captures the combination of innocence and pathos needed for Mignon. In the middle section, when the words speak of her giddiness, the music becomes agitated. Unlike the tremolos in the duet version, this agitated texture is not sustained. He returns to the music for lines 1 and 2 without it. This means he cannot convey the dichotomy between what she says and what she feels. However, he gives greater emphasis to the words 'Sehnsucht kennt' ('knows longing') than previously.

Opus 65

Published by Cappi and Czerny, 24 November 1826.

1. *Lied eines Schiffers an die Dioskuren* (A Sailor's Song to the Dioscuri)
   Johann Mayrhofer, D360 (1816)
2. *Der Wanderer* (The Wanderer) Friedrich von Schlegel, D649
   (February 1819)
3. *Heliopolis I* (Heliopolis I) Johann Mayrhofer, D753 (April 1822)

Heliopolis (The City of the Sun) is a sequence of six epigrams and 20
poems Mayrhofer worked on over a number of years and completed in
the autumn of 1821. Schubert set four of the poems as *Heliopolis I*,
Heliopolis II, *Lied eines Schiffers an die Dioskuren* and *Nachtviolen*.
Heliopolis I comes fifth in the sequence, and *Lied eines Schiffers an die
Dioskuren* is the twentieth.[14] The ancient Syrian city of Heliopolis was
the seat of worship of Baal, one of whose symbols was the sun. Hence the
Greek name for the city. The Greeks, who worshipped Helios, described
him as the god who sees and hears everything. Mayrhofer's Heliopolis
probably had its origins in Plato's ideas about the need for religious
reform in the *Laws*. As E.R. Dodds puts it:[15]

> The great novelty in Plato's project for religious reform was the
> emphasis he laid, not merely on the divinity of sun, moon, and stars
> (for that was nothing new), but on their cult. In the *Laws*, not only
> are the stars described as 'the gods in heaven', the sun and moon as
> 'great gods', but Plato insists that prayer and sacrifice shall be made
> to them by all; and the focal point of his new State Church is to be a
> joint cult of Apollo and the sun-god Helios, to which the High Priest
> will be attached and the highest political officers will be solemnly
> dedicated. This joint cult – in place of the expected cult of Zeus –
> expresses the union of old and new, Apollo standing for the tradition-
> alism of the masses, and Helios for the new 'natural religion' of the
> philosophers; it is Plato's last desperate attempt to build a bridge
> between the intellectuals and the people, and thereby save the unity of
> Greek belief and of Greek culture.

In his short preface to his sequence Mayrhofer wrote: 'We will vary an
ancient theme, recited in the dim past. Though we stumble and lose our

---

[14] For more information see Gramit, D. (1993), 'Schubert and the Biedermeier: the
aesthetics of Johann Mayrhofer's *Heliopolis*', *Music and Letters*, 74, 3, pp. 355–82.
[15] Dodds, E.R. (1951), *The Greeks and the Irrational*, Berkeley, CA: University of California Press, pp. 220–21.

way we may still dare to look towards the sun.' His own particular religious reform is based on the worship of art. The sun is art, and Heliopolis the place where artistic values and insights hold sway, where artists can find refuge from 'a world of limitation and suppression' (Youens, p. 176).

Although the relationship between Mayrhofer and Schubert had become cool when Mayrhofer completed the poems, Schubert must have been familiar with what lay behind the poet's ideas, for the sequence he selected for this set concerns a sailor, a wanderer and a pilgrim being guided to their destinations by what Plato called 'the visible gods' arranged in the reverse order of their brightness – stars, moon and sun.

Texts

1. *Dioskuren, Zwillingssterne.* Three quatrains.
   The Dioscuri, Castor and Pollux, lie close together and are two of the brightest stars in the sky.

   (1) Dioscuri, twin stars, shining on my boat, your gentleness and watchfulness comfort me on the ocean.
   (2) Although a man may be confident in himself and able to face the storm fearlessly, he feels doubly valiant and blessed in your light.
   (3) When I have landed I shall hang this oar with which I ply the waves on your temple.

2. *Wie deutlich des Mondes Licht.* Two ten-line stanzas.

   (1) How clearly the moon's light speaks to me, cheering me on my journey: 'Follow faithfully the old way; lest harder times bring endless trouble. Choose nowhere for your home. Move on to other places lightly, casting off all your grief.'
   (2) So with a gentle ebb and flow deep within me, I make my way in the darkness climbing boldly and singing cheerfully. The world seems good. I see all things clearly, nothing is blurred in the heat of the day. All around there is joy, and yet I am alone.

3. *Im kalten, rauhen Norden.* A single 18-line stanza.

   In the cold, harsh north I heard tell of a city of the sun. But where is the ship or the path which will take me to its courts? Men could not tell me for they were entangled in conflicts. I then turned to the flower chosen by Helios, which always gazes into his face – and I was enchanted. 'Turn your eyes to the sun like me. There is bliss, there is life. Make your pilgrimage in true devotion and have no doubts. In its light you will find peace. Light kindles ardour, sows the seeds of hope, promotes noble deeds.'

Music

Although written in the treble clef, the songs are more suitable for a bass or bass-baritone than a tenor or high baritone. This is because, quite frequently, the voice lies in a register lower than the piano's, and has to function as the bass of the harmony. Kristina Muxfeldt, in her article 'Schubert's songs: the transformation of a genre', regards the positioning of the voice within a texture as one of Schubert's technical innovations in song writing, and she cites *Der Wanderer* as a prime example of it (Companion, pp. 126–7). Here, as well as supplying the functional bass, the voice also carries the melody. This is also the case in the first part of *Heliopolis I*. In fact the whole set is governed by the way the voice is positioned in relation to the piano. It is by this means that Schubert can illustrate, among other things, the progression from darkness to light.

1. *Lied eines Schiffers an die Dioskuren*

Ab major. Slow 3/4.

The song is a solemn hymn to the Dioscuri in ABA form, sung on an otherwise dark night. The piano's spread chords at the opening represent the slight swell of the sea; later when they are articulated in semiquavers the plying of the oar. Throughout the song the piano's low, very full texture is written in the bass clef, its upper voice being doubled by the singer. At the end of the song the melodic line descends in stages from Eb to Ab, and the song is brought to a close by the piano becoming lower and darker than ever. Its descending four-note scale (Db-C-Bb-Ab) will be echoed a semitone higher in the third bar of the next song, and perhaps even more significantly in the closing bars of the third.

2. *Der Wanderer*

D major. Slow 4/4.

Schubert casts the song in two strophes, the second being a modification of the first. The piano's hymn-like introduction relates it to the previous song and, after the darkness of that song, suggests, through its relatively high tessitura, the clarity of the moonlight. The voice, doubled by the pianist's left hand, provides both the melody and the bass line, the harmony being supplied lightly by the pianist's right hand lying above it.

This texture continues throughout the first strophe. It could also be taken to represent the moon's advice to 'choose nowhere as your home', for the bass of the harmony, its 'roots', are carried by the Wanderer, and go wherever he goes. In the first seven bars of the second strophe the piano supplies the bass line by itself. This enables Schubert to bring back the role of the voice as simultaneous provider of melody and bass more vividly at the end of the song. (The voice's last five notes will be echoed a minor third lower at the beginning of the next song.)

nichts ver-wor-ren in des Ta-ges Glut ver-dor-ren: froh un-be-gen, doch al-lei - ne.

3. Heliopolis I

E minor – major. At a moderate pace 4/4.

Schubert divides *Heliopolis I* into two parts. The first deals with the pilgrim's inability to find any information about the city of the sun. Here the music is in the minor, through-composed, and begins with the voice doubling the piano's single bass line; the sparsity of the music illustrating the 'cold, harsh north'. Schubert gradually fills out the texture until at the end of the second part it becomes as full as it could possibly be. The second part starts as soon the pilgrim notices the sunflower. The key turns to the major, the music becomes more structured, especially when the sunflower speaks, and the voice dips below the piano only rarely. Maximum fullness is reached in bar 62. The piano's descending four-note scale, C♯-B-A-G♯, in the last two bars, echoes at a distance the scale D♭-C-B♭-A♭ at the end of the first song, the notes C♯/D♭ and G♯/A♭ being enharmonically equivalent. But the new harmonic context, the faster tempo and the shorter durations make this ending much lighter, much more in keeping with the transformation that has taken place across the set.

Hoff - nungs - pflan - zen,—— Ta - ten - flu - ten!"

Opus 79

Two songs to poems by Ladislaus von Pyrker. Published by Tobias Haslinger, 16 May 1827. 'Dedicated to the poet out of profound respect.'

1. *Das Heimweh* (Homesickness), D851 (version b, August 1825)
2. *Die Allmacht* (The Almighty), D852 (version b, August 1825)

Pyrker was appointed Patriarch of Venice in 1820 and Archbishop of Erlau in 1827. Schubert first met him in 1820 at the house of Matthäus von Collin, and the following year he dedicated his Op. 4 set to him. They met again when he visited Bad Gastein in August 1825. Pyrker had established a convalescent home there for soldiers wounded in the Napoleonic War. According to Anton Schindler, Schubert treasured his meeting with the Archbishop as one of the most inspiring moments in his life (Mems, p. 318). It was then that he composed these songs. In all probability Pyrker had a hand in selecting the poems. Both involve the process of looking upwards, *Das Heimweh* to the majesty of the mountain peaks, *Die Allmacht* to the majesty of the Almighty One.

   Pyrker's verse is totally out of keeping with the folk-like poetry his contemporaries liked to emulate. His model was the classical hexameter which consists of five dactyls (long-short-short), which may be substituted by a spondee (long-long), followed by usually a trochee (long-short) or perhaps another spondee. But since German is stress-timed rather than syllabic, only the German equivalent of the dactyl (lift-dip-dip) and trochee (lift-dip) are used in hexameters. Pyrker ends both poems with one, the first having the pattern I / x I / x x I / x I / x x I / x x I / x ('Ach, es zieht ihn dahin mit unwiderstehlicher Sehnsucht'), the second with the pattern I / x I / x x I / x I / x I / x x I / x ('Blickst du flehend empor und hoffst auf Huld und Erbarmen'). The lines leading up to these hexameters are equally long, but are governed by neither a rhyming nor metric scheme, nor by any regular stanzaic grouping. In many ways they are like rolling prose.

Texts

1. *Ach, der Gebirgssohn hängt*. Twenty-three lines divided into four stanzas containing respectively four, eight, seven and four lines.

   (1) The son of the mountains clings to his homeland with a

childlike love; as the Alpine flower wilts when plucked from the Alpine meadow, so too does he wither when torn from his native soil.

(2) He sees always the cosy cottage among the fragrant green meadows where he was born; he sees the dark pinewoods, the towering cliff above, mountain upon mountain looming in fearful majesty and glowing in the rosy light of evening. The image always hovers before his eyes, obscuring everything else around him.

(3) He listens anxiously; he thinks he hears the lowing of cattle in the nearby woods, or bells tinkling from high in the Alps; he thinks he hears the call of shepherds or the song of the dairymaid, her yodelling voice echoing through the mountains. It rings in his ears all the time.

(4) The charm of the smiling plains cannot hold him; alone he flees from the constricting walls of the town, and with moist eyes looks upwards from the foothills to his native peaks. Ah, he is drawn to them with irresistible longing!

2. *Gross ist Jehova, der Herr! Denn Himmel.* A single stanza of 13 lines.

Great is Jehovah, the Lord! For heaven and earth proclaim His might. You hear it in the roaring storm, in the loud, surging cry of the forest stream, in the murmur of the greenwood; you hear it in the golden, waving corn, in the radiant glow of lovely flowers, in the splendour of the star-strewn sky. It echoes awesomely in the rolling thunder, it flares in the quivering flight of the lightening. But your beating heart will feel more readily the power of Jehovah, the eternal God, if you look upwards in prayer and hope for grace and mercy.

Music

The nature of Pyrker's versification means that neither song could be given a regular structure; they had to be through-composed.

1. *Das Heimweh*

A scena in five sections: (1) G minor. Rather slow 4/4 (the son of the mountain's homesickness), (2) Bb major. Same tempo (his remembrance of his home), (3) B major. Same tempo (the majesty of the mountains), (4) G major. Fast 3/4 (the call of the shepherds and the song of the milkmaid), (5) G minor. Tempo I (his intensified longing for home).

2. *Die Allmacht*

C major. Slow – solemn 2/2.

This too is divided into sections, but these are less clearly defined because throughout the song the piano plays a *moto perpetuo* of repeated triplets, which drive the music forward to new, powerful music for the repetition of the first two lines at the end: 'Great is Jehovah, the Lord. For heaven and earth proclaim His might.'

Schubert must have decided these songs were worthy of publication shortly after leaving Bad Gastein and returning to Vienna, for it was then that he made structural alterations to his original version of *Das Heimweh*.[16] Originally the fast 3/4 tempo used for section 4 continued to the end of the song. Later, when he found a publisher for the set, he transposed the two songs. Originally they were in A minor and A major. Presumably he felt the differences between the two songs required more than just a change of mode. The transpositions mean that the second song is now preceded by its dominant minor rather than its tonic minor. They also give greater strength to the opening of *Die Allmacht*. Throughout the two songs great use is made of German and French sixths, and chords of the diminished seventh. At the end of *Das Heimweh* the German sixth, which has characterized the music in G minor, is suddenly changed into a diminished seventh to convey a stab of homesickness.

In A minor, of course, that passage would be a tone higher. Had the next song been in A major, the powerful diminished seventh in its second bar would have been the stabbing chord redistributed. This would have reduced the powerful impact it now has in the transposed key.

---

[16] On the evidence of his paper studies, Robert Winter believes the date of these alterations was September 1825 (Studies 1, pp. 231–2).

The transposition of the songs, however, poses problems for the singer. In A minor and A major the range of both songs is A-g', which is that of a high baritone. When transposed the range of the first song becomes G-f' (that of a bass baritone) and the second song c-bb' (that of a high tenor). Schubert was obviously aware of this and, to allow the two songs to be sung by a single voice, he made the three lowest notes in *Das Heimweh* (G, A and B) and the high Bb in bar 77 of *Das Allmacht* optional. Even so, the tessitura is still high. However, a good high baritone such as Michael Vogl may have welcomed the challenge of singing top A in the song's closing passage.

Opus 80

Three songs to poems by Johann Gabriel Seidl. Published by Tobias Haslinger, 25 May 1827. 'Dedicated to Josef Wilhem Witteczek out of friendship.'

1. *Der Wanderer an den Mond* (The Wanderer's Address to the Moon), D870 (1826)
2. *Das Zügenglöcklein* (The Passing Bell), D871 (version b, 1826)
3. *Im Freien* (In the Open), D880 (March 1826)

This is the first of three sets devoted to poems by Seidl (1804–75), whose poetry became extremely popular in Vienna after the publication of his first collection of verse in 1826. Two years earlier Schubert had promised to write incidental music for his play *Der kurze Mantel* (The Short Coat), based on a popular folk tale, but since he did not receive the text in time through the negligence of his publisher, Leidesdorf, nothing came of it. In a letter from the 20-year-old playwright to the composer asking for the music as quickly as possible, Seidl addressed Schubert as 'Valued Sir and Friend'. The friendship waned after Schubert failed to produce music for the play, and was not restored until January 1826. In that year Schubert set eight of Seidl's poems as six solo songs and two part-songs for male voices. These three come from the sequence in the collection entitled *Lieder der Nacht* (Songs of the Night). Their regular rhyming and metric patterns, lilting rhythms and conventional sentiments stand in direct contrast to Pyrker's verse in Op. 79. It is as if Schubert had wanted to follow his Pyrker set with something much more homely. Indeed home is the set's topic.

In that the three poems also refer to the stars, moon and sun, Schubert was looking back at Op. 65. There these heavenly bodies were the guides for three travellers, the last having the utopian city of the sun as his destination. Here only the first and third poems concern travellers, the second refers to the sun as the light under which a dying man wants to tarry. In all probability Schubert chose to begin with *Der Wanderer an dem Mond* because it relates to Schlegel's *Der Wanderer* in Op. 65. Schlegel's moon tells the traveller to choose nowhere as his home, 'lest bad times bring endless cares', but Seidl's wanderer laments his lack of a home, and wishes he could be like the moon, at home wherever he goes. Thus the desire to be at home replaces the idealism, the quest for the beyond, which Op. 65 pursued.

Texts

1. *Ich auf der Erd', am Himmel du*

In his translations of Schubert's complete song texts Richard Wigmore,[17] like Seidl presumably, prints the poem in three stanzas – two cinquains and a sixain. But the poem falls more naturally into four quatrains, and this is how Schubert viewed it.

(1) I on earth, you in the sky, both of us moving steadily on; I solemn and gloomy, you gentle and pure, what can be the real difference between us?

(2) I wander as a stranger from land to land so homeless, so unknown, uphill and downhill, in and out of forests, but alas I am at home nowhere.

(3) You wander up and down from your cradle in the west to your grave in the east, travel in and out of every land, and yet you are at home wherever you are.

(4) The sky, endlessly extended, is your beloved homeland. O happy is he who, wherever he goes, always stands on his native soil.

2. *Kling' die Nacht durch, klinge.* Five sixains.

Das Zügenglöcklein is a small tolling bell rung in Austrian churches as a call to prayer when a parishioner is dying.

(1) Ring, ring the night through, bring sweet peace to him you toll for. Ring out into the far distance for in this way you reconcile the pilgrim and the world.

(2) But who would follow in the steps of dear loved ones gone before? Though he may ring the door bell gladly, when a voice cries 'enter', he trembles on the threshold.

(3) Does it ring for the erring son who curses its sound because it is sacred? No, it rings more loudly when a man who trusts in God concludes his life's journey.

(4) But if it is for some weary man deserted by his kin, whose faith in the world has been saved only by some faithful animal, call him to You, O God.

(5) If it is for one of the blessed who enjoys love and friendship, allow him still the bliss of life under the sun where he gladly tarries!

---

[17] Wigmore, R. (1988), *Schubert: The Complete Song Texts with English Translations*, London: Gollancz; New York: Schirmer Books.

3. *Draussen in der weiten Nacht.* Eight quatrains.

   (1) Once again I stand outside in the vastness of the night; its bright
        starry splendour gives my heart no peace.
   (2) A thousand arms beckon me, sweetly enticing; a thousand voices
        call: 'Greetings, dear friend!'
   (3) I know what draws me, what calls me like a friend's song and
        greeting floating through the air.
   (4) Do you see the cottage there on which the moonlight lingers?
        From its shining windows loving eyes look out.
   (5) Do you see the house there by the stream, lit by the moon?
        Beneath its snug roof my dearest friend sleeps.
   (6) Do you see that tree gleaming with silvery leaves? Oh, how often
        did my heart swell there in happier days.
   (7) Every tiny place that beckons to me is dear to my heart, and
        wherever the moonlight falls a treasured memory is recalled.
   (8) So everything here commands my affection, and draws me like
        the sounds of true love.

Music

The autographed first draft of *Im Freien* is dated March 1826. The
manuscript containing the drafts of *Der Wanderer an den Mond* and *Das
Zügenglöcklein*, on the other hand, lacks a date. It is usually assigned to
some time between January and September 1826. But the set's reference
to Op. 65, which was probably compiled about four or five months
before it was published in November 1826, means that the two songs
were probably composed after June or July 1826. This claim is made on
the grounds that the set is so highly integrated it seems unbelievable it
was not conceived as a unit. The use of a *moto perpetuo* in all three songs
may not be unusual, but the set's progression from the first song's folk-
song style to songs becoming increasingly more sophisticated, especially
in their accompaniments and in the way they develop, suggests delibera-
tion.

1. *Der Wanderer an den Mond*

G minor – major. 'Moving steadily on' (*Etwas bewegt*) 2/4.

The song is in two closely related parts. The first sets the initial two
quatrains in strophic form, the diatonic simplicity of the vocal line and
the guitar-like accompaniment giving the impression it is meant to be a

folk song. The second part marks the first step in the process of increasing sophistication. Schubert separates quatrains 3 and 4, but here he abandons simple strophic form in favour of a rounded binary structure. The guitar-like accompaniment is also jettisoned and becomes more characteristically pianistic. The features which persist throughout the song are the marching rhythm and the almost continuous reference to the D below middle C which functions as an inner pedal in quaver motion.

2. *Das Zügenglöcklein*

Ab major. Slow 2/2.

The song is a prime example of Schubert's use of varied strophic form. All five strophes are the same length, contain seven one-bar phrases (most of them starting with a dotted rhythm) and end with a slightly longer phrase resembling yodelling. Yet no two strophes are the same. Superimposed on highly repetitive strophic form is the principle of continuous development.

This is also the principle governing the highly pianistic accompaniment. Between an Eb pedal representing the softly tolling bell in the right hand, and a regular quaver motion in the left, lies a slowly developing melody shared alternatively by instrument and voice.

On two occasions the pitch of the tolling bell ascends to Gb, and the dynamics rise from *piano* to *forte*. The first occurs when the words speak of the bell ringing more loudly when the man who trusts in God concludes his life's journey, the second when they speak of the bliss granted to the person who is allowed to 'tarry beneath the sun'.

3. *Im Freien*

Eb major. At a moderate pace, with fervour 2/4.

On the grounds that Schubert separates his music for the eight stanzas, and seems to be making use of similar melodic and rhythmic patterns, the song might be said to be another example of varied strophic form. But if it is, the principle has been taken to the extreme, for the continuous development suggests the song could equally well be deemed through-composed. In addition, the accompaniment, which for the most part doubles the vocal line, could be performed separately. It could make a perfectly satisfactory impromptu. The constant rhythmic motion and pitch repetitions featured in the previous songs now characterize each bar.

Opus 81

Three songs to poems by Johann Friedrich Rochlitz. Published by Tobias Haslinger, 28 May 1827.

1. *Alinde* (Alinde), D904 (January 1827)
2. *An die Laute* (To the Lute), D905 (January 1827)
3. *Zur guten Nacht* (For Good Night), for baritone solo and chorus of TTBB, D903 (January 1827)

Rochlitz was the founder of the *Allgemeine Musikalische Zeitung* in Leipzig, its editor between 1798 and 1818, and a well respected contributor to it until 1836. He was therefore a man of considerable influence in the musical world. Since composing Rochlitz's *Klagelied* in 1812, Schubert had shown no interest in his poetry. He was probably encouraged to compose this set by Tobias Haslinger, who could see the advantages it might gain for the composer. It was Haslinger who appended the dedication of the set to Rochlitz, calling him 'that author deserving so well of music and the polite sciences'. Haslinger had in his possession the complete works of Rochlitz which included novels, plays and musical articles as well as poetry. It was undoubtedly these volumes Schubert consulted when choosing these poems. That he selected the most light-hearted may have been his response to the poet's pomposity, a characteristic verified by the letter he received from him in November 1827. In it Rochlitz asked him if he would like to set his lengthy poem *Der erste Ton* (The First Sound), which Weber had already set in 1808 for reciter, chorus and orchestra. But instead of giving Schubert his head, he told him how it should be done. Schubert's reply was polite but cool.

The poems Schubert selected are all 'poems of the night', as were Seidl's in Op. 80.

Texts

1. *Die Sonne sinkt ins tiefe Meer.* Eight quatrains with the addition of the refrain 'Alinde, Alinde!' placed between the first two lines of stanzas two, four, six and eight.

   (1) The sun sinks into the deep ocean. She said she would come. Quietly the reaper goes by. My heart aches.
   (2) 'Reaper, have you seen my love?' Alinde, Alinde! 'I must go home

to my wife and children. I cannot look for other girls. They are waiting for me under the lime tree.'

(3) The moon enters its heavenly course, and still she does not come. A fisherman lands his boat. My heart aches.

(4) 'Fisherman, have you seen my love?' Alinde, Alinde! 'I must see to my oyster creels. I have no time for chasing girls. See what a catch I've made.'

(5) The bright stars appear, and still she does not come. A huntsman rides swiftly along. My heart aches.

(6) 'Huntsman, have you seen my love?' Alinde, Alinde! 'I must go after the brown roebuck. I never care to look for girls. There he goes in the evening breeze.'

(7) Here stands the grove in darkest night, and still she does not come. Alone and lonely, I wander anxious and afraid.

(8) 'To you echo, I confess my sorrow'. Alinde, Alinde! 'Alinde' came in soft reply. Then I saw her by my side. 'You searched so faithfully. Now you have found me.'

2. *Leiser, leiser, kleine Laute.* Two sixains.

(1) Play more softly, little lute, whisper my secret to that window up there. Send your message to my mistress like a ripple of gentle breezes, like moonlight and the scent of flowers.

(2) A solitary light gleams from my beauty's window, and the neighbours' sons are jealous. So play yet more softly, little lute, so that my love can hear you, but not – oh not – the neighbours!

3. *Horcht auf! Es schlägt die Stunde.* Three cinquains.

(1) *The Spokesman:* Hark! The hour strikes, telling each one at this table to go home when he has emptied his glass, thanked the host and finished singing this rhyme.
The Company: First let us empty this glass, thank the host and finish singing this song.

(2) *The Spokesman:* We should go merrily. No one should regret what we have heard, seen or done, our shared experience, binding us more closely to friends and to art, should gladden us.
The Company: Yes, our shared experience, binding us more closely to friends and to art, should gladden us.

(3) *The Spokesman:* Sleep well and dream like brides! Come again gladly as we did today, and think on many a new song. And if, one day, one of us should go to his rest in the grave, sing to him with love, 'Good Night'.

The Company: Yes, if one day one of us should go to his rest in the grave, sing to him, with love, 'Good Night'.

Music

The previous set progressed from folk art to high art. This one reverses the procedure: a song in modified strophic form with a charmingly 'graced' accompaniment is followed by two songs in simple strophic form, the last having a singularly plain accompaniment. Schubert may also have had his 1812 setting of Rochlitz's *Klagelied* in mind when he composed the set. This is considered to be his first strophic song, but he took only the first stanza into account when he wrote it. The musical images he found for a rustling breeze and a murmuring brook are totally inappropriate for the rest of the poem. He should have composed a modified strophic song, varying each strophe to suit the words. *Alinde* makes up for his former inexperience because he varies the strophes with great subtlety. The cry 'Alinde, Alinde', for example, is never the same twice.

1. *Alinde*

A major. At a moderate pace 6/8.

Schubert arranges the eight stanzas in pairs to make four modified strophes divided into two contrasting parts, the first being concerned with the lover's waiting, the second with the prospect that the reaper, fisherman or huntsman might have seen Alinde. The rhythm is that of a barcarole, which means that Schubert thought of the song as a serenade. As in the Op. 80 set, he made a feature of the repetition of a single note. In the first part it occurs on a pedal A in the bass, in the second on E in the piano's upper voice.

2. *An die Laute*

D major. Rather fast 6/8.

In *Alinde* the lover addresses his sweetheart as if she were some distance away. Here he must be silent because the neighbours might hear him, so he addresses her through his lute. Schubert has no need to modify the second strophe since his music for the first stanza suits the second admirably. The rapidly spread chords suggesting a lute are clearly related to the grace notes which ornamented the first song.

3. *Zur guten Nacht*

D major. Rather slow 4/4.

Schubert has the chorus repeat in a slightly modified form the soloist's music for the last three lines in each cinquain and then echoing the final two words *pianissimo*.

Opus 83

Three Italian Songs for a Bass Voice. Published by Tobias Haslinger, 12 September 1827. Dedicated to Luigi Lablache.

1. *L'incanto degli occhi* (The Magic of Eyes) Pietro Metastasio, D902, No. 1 (1827)
2. *Il traditor deluso* (The Traitor Deceived) Pietro Metastasio, D902, No. 3 (1827)
3. *Il modo di prender moglie* (How to Choose a Wife) Poet unknown, D902, No. 3 (1827)

Luigi Lablache (1794–1858) was the principal bass in Barbaia's Italian company at the Kärntnertor Theatre, and one of the most famous singers of his generation. In April 1827 he sang the bass solos in Mozart's Requiem given at the memorial service for Beethoven. Later he created the roles of Sir George Walton in Bellini's *I Puritani* and the title roles in Donizetti's *Marino Faliero* and *Don Pasquale*. He was thus at home in comic as well as tragic roles. Schubert made Lablache's acquaintance through his friends the Kiesewetters. These songs were written to show off the singer's versatility. The Leipzig *Allgemeine Musikalische Zeitung* of 30 January 1828 thought that Lablache 'was sure to make a furore with them'. Although there is no record of any performance by him, the set must have been near the top of his concert repertoire list because it is doubtful whether any other group of songs could demonstrate his skills so well.

The texts are drawn from the three principal types of Italian dramatic music: opera seria, oratorio and opera buffa. Lablache may have had a hand in selecting them. Under the Italian words, Schubert appended a German translation probably made by his friend, Jakob Nikolaus Craigher. In its review of the songs, the *Allgemeine Musikalische Zeitung* noted that, although it was designated a single work, Haslinger had published the songs separately. Perhaps he realized that only an exceptional singer would have the range of styles to tackle all three, and it was therefore wiser to offer them individually. There is, however, an autographed simplified version of the vocal part which Schubert must have written for a German singer who lacked Lablache's depth. Cast in the treble clef, it contains only the German words. It is reproduced as an ossia in the *Neue Schubert Ausgabe* and Volume 17 of the Bärenreiter/Henle softback edition of Schubert's songs.

Texts

1. *Da voi, cari lumi.* Three stanzas: a quatrain, a couplet and another quatrain.

   From *Attilio Regolo*, an opera seria Metastasio wrote for Johann Hasse in 1740.

   (1) On you, beloved eyes, depends my whole life. You are my gods and my destiny.
   (2) At your bidding my mood changes.
   (3) If you shine with happiness you inspire me with daring; if you are overcast you make me tremble.

2. *Aimè, io tremo!* A ten-line recitative and ten-line aria.

   From *Gioas, rè di Giuda*, an oratorio Metastasio wrote for Johann Reutter in 1735.

   Recitative: What unknown power inspires these voices? I tremble. I feel a cold sweat upon my brow. I must flee. But where? Who will show me the way? Oh God, what do I hear? What has happened? Where am I?

   Aria: The air sparkles and flashes! The perfidious earth shakes and trembles! Deep night surrounds me with horror. What fearful creatures surround me. What furies are these? What wild terror I feel in my breast!

3. *Or sù ! non ci pensiamo.* Although the text is not divided into stanzas, the rhyming scheme indicates that it consists of three quatrains, a sixain and two more quatrains.

   From an unidentified opera buffa.

   (1) Well then, let's not think about it. Courage, let's get it over with. If I have to take a wife, I know very well why I do it.
   (2) I do it to pay my debts. I'll take her for her money. I don't hesitate to say so, again and again.
   (3) Of all the ways in the world of choosing a wife, I know no happier way than mine.
   (4) Some choose a wife for love, others out of respect, another because he's advised to, another from a sense of duty, another on a whim. That's the truth, isn't it?

(5) Well, why shouldn't I take a wife as a remedy for all my troubles?
     I've said it.
(6) And I'll say it again. I do it for the money. Many people do it, and
     so do I.

Music

These are the last and most brilliant pieces Schubert composed in the
Italian style. However, not everyone thought them a success. The
composer Heinrich Marschner, writing in the Berlin *Allgemeine
Musikalische Zeitung* of 19 March 1828 said:

> As an Italian composer Herr S. gives too little scope to song and
> still too much to the accompaniment. The flow of his melodies is
> too intermittent, too heavy handed; it is no glowing lava stream,
> but only a somewhat cold, murmuring northern brooklet, whose
> merry splashing even is often drowned by the seriously dolorous
> rustlings of neighbouring oak forests (in the accompaniment). In
> short, these are not genuine, light-winged Italian song-tunes as the
> Italians of today in particular demand them ... Herr Schubert has
> thus not yet succeeded with these songs in bringing about an alli-
> ance, however desirable, between German and Italian music. (Doc.
> 1060)

In fact Schubert's accompaniments, compared with what he normally
provided, are relatively lightweight. They are a perfect parody of the
Italian style in that, for the most part, all they do is provide the necessary harmonic support and rhythmic impetus. Schubert's model is
Rossini, and he even manages to reflect what Philip Gossett calls the
Italian composer's 'harmonic games' – sudden, unexpected changes of
key. In the first song, which is in C major, he prepares for the return to
the home key by modulating boldly from Ab major to B minor and then
slipping into C major as if by sleight of hand. The second song makes a
feature of shifting suddenly from one minor key to another minor key
lying a major third away. It is true that his melodic lines might not
appear to be as lyrical as most Italian vocal lines, but he was testing the
skill of Lablache to make a beautiful line out of phrases which do not
appear to be lyrical on paper as, for example, this passage from the first
song.

voi sie - te i miei Nu-mi,___ voi sie-te, voi sie - te il mio fa - - - to.

1. *L'incanto degli occhi*

C major. Allegretto 2/4.

Hasse would have set this as a da capo aria, ABA. The first four lines would have been used for the first and last sections, the remaining six for the contrasting middle section. The singer would have demonstrated his vocal prowess by elaborating the da capo with brilliant *fioriture*. Schubert has a different plan. This central section contrasts with the outer sections only in its harmony, not its texture or tempo. Also he supplies his own *fioriture* for the da capo. Throughout the song the piano is confined to supplying a chordal *moto perpetuo* in quavers so that the difference between the lover being inspired to daring by his beloved's eyes or being made to tremble by them has to be conveyed in the vocal line. It is achieved mainly by alternating boldly assertive passages in quavers with semiquaver roulades.

2. *Il traditor deluso*

E minor. Allegro assai 4/4 – Allegro molto 2/2.

Schubert casts the Allegro molto aria in the form of exposition, development, recapitulation and coda. The preceding recitative anticipates the tremolandos, augmented chords and key shifts in it. In the development section these shifts are to keys a major third lower, in the coda to keys a major third higher. Lablache's range is said to have been the two octaves from E♭ to E♭', and in the development section Schubert takes the vocal line to the top of it for the word 'horror'.

3. *Il modo di prender moglie*

C major. Allegro ma non troppo 6/8 – Allegro vivace 4/4.

Schubert must have had Figaro's *Largo al factotum* in Rossini's *Barbiere* in mind when he composed this. But whereas Rossini's aria is allegro vivace 6/8 throughout, Schubert reserves this tempo for a brilliant *cabaletta*.

Opus 85

Two songs to poems in Novels by Sir Walter Scott. Published by Anton Diabelli and Co., 14 March 1828.

1. *Lied der Anne Lyle* (Anne Lyle's Song) Andrew MacDonald, quoted by Scott without acknowledgement in *A Legend of Montrose*, D830 (?early 1825)
2. *Gesang der Norna* (Norna's Song) from Scott's novel *The Pirate*, D831 (early 1825)

This was published on the same day as Op. 86, a setting of *Romanze des Richard Löwenherz* (The Romance of Richard the Lionheart) from Scott's *Ivanhoe*. It is possible the two works were intended to complement each other. The songs in Op. 85 are for women who are forced to keep their feelings secret, whereas Op. 86 is for a man who can speak of his exploits and his love openly. Andrew MacDonald's poem comes from his comedy *Love and Loyalty*, and Scott quotes it in *A Legend of Montrose* in reference to Annot (Anne) Lyle, who loves the Earl of Mentieth. He returns her love, but is prevented from pressing his suit by the obscurity of her birth. When it is eventually revealed that she is the daughter of a baronet and that her social standing is high enough for him to marry her, a rival stabs him to death. Norna is a half-crazy relative of Magnus Troil, a rich Shetlander of Norse descent. She believes she has supernatural powers, but because of a curse she can only reveal her woes for one hour in each year. The curse has been invoked on account of her betrayal to the authorities of Clement Cleveland, the pirate in the novel. Minna, one of Magnus's daughters, becomes betrothed to the pirate, but after he has been betrayed the two are prevented from seeing each other again. Later Norna discovers that Clement is her son.

Schubert set the songs in German, and made no request to have them published with the English words as he had done with his other Scott set, Op. 52. The translator of *Lied der Anne Lyle* is unknown, that of *Gesang der Norna* is S.H. Spiker.

Texts

1. *Lied der Anne Lyle*

Wert thou, like me, in life's low
   vale,
With thee how blest, that lot I
   share;
With thee I'd fly wherever gale
Could waft, or bounding galley
   bear.
But parted by severe decree,
Far different must our fortunes
   prove;
May thine be joy – enough for
   me
To weep and pray for him I
   love.

The pangs this foolish heart
   must feel,
When hope shall be forever
   flown,
No sullen murmur shall reveal,
No selfish murmurs ever own.
Nor will through life's weary
   years,
Like a pale drooping mourner
   move,
While I can think my secret
   tears
May wound the heart of him I
   love.

2. *Gesang der Norna*

For leagues along the watery
   way,
Through gulf and stream my
   course has been;
The hollows know my Runic
   lay,
And smooth their crests to
   silent green.

The hollows know my Runic
   lay –
The gulf grows smooth, the
   stream is still;
The human hearts, more wild
   than they,
Know but the rule of wayward
   will.

One hour is mine, in all the
   year,
To tell my woes – and one
   alone;
When gleams this magic lamp,
   'tis here –
When dies the mystic light, 'tis
   gone.

Daughters of northern Magnus,
   hail!
The lamp is lit, the flame is
   clear –
To you I come to tell my tale,
Awake, arise, my tale to hear!

Music

The pitch of the songs suggests that Schubert wrote them for a mezzo-
soprano or high contralto. Like most of his Scott settings they are based

on rhythmic ostinatos. The clue to the difference between these two can be found in the second stanza of *Gesang der Norna*, where Norna speaks of the waywardness of human hearts and the smoothness and stillness of the waves that know her Runic lay.

1. *Lied der Anne Lyle*

C minor. At a moderate pace 4/4.

To convey waywardness the ostinato is a lilting dance disturbed by strange, irrational cross accents. The strophes are long, the second differing from the first only in details.

2. *Gesang der Norna*

F minor. Not too slow 6/8.

In this the ostinato represents the regular thrust of the oars as Norna is carried across the sea. The regularity of the rhythm, together with the dark harmony, becomes almost hypnotic; the unusual octave doublings suggest that something archaic is being evoked. The only modification to the strophic design occurs in the third stanza, when the words speak of the mystic light. Schubert drops the insistent iambic rhythm in the vocal line, and has the voice sing 'ihr Schein verlischt' on a single, sustained high note. It is a simple change, but it encapsulates the arcane atmosphere which haunts the song.

Opus 87

Published by Anton Pennauer, 6 August 1827.

1. *Der Unglückliche* (The Unhappy Man) Karoline Pichler, D713 (January 1821)
2. *Hoffnung* (Hope) Friedrich von Schiller, D637 (*c.* 1819)
3. *Der Jüngling am Bache* (The Youth by the Stream) Friedrich von Schiller, D638 (version b, *c.* 1819)

Although Op. 85, the previous set, was not published until 14 March 1828, Schubert must have decided to submit it to a publisher early in 1827 shortly after compiling this one. Originally this one was assigned Op. 84. It had to be changed when it was remembered that Thaddäus Weigl had been given this number for the *Andantino varié and Rondeau brillant* for piano, four hands. The stories behind the Op. 85 songs involve lovers who are prevented from fulfilling their love. In the case of Annot Lyle and the Earl of Mentieth the barrier was their social standing. This is also the issue in Karoline Pichler's poem *Der Unglückliche*. The poem comes from her novel *Olivier* telling of a love affair between a singer and a princess, who are forbidden to see each other after their attachment has been discovered because of their social differences. Schubert uses the poem as the starting point for a set about love across social barriers. *Hoffnung* puts forward the belief that we are born for better things, and can dream of better days to come, while *Der Jüngling am Bache* speaks of a youth who manifests hope by calling up to his beloved in her proud castle to join him in his humble cottage.

Walther Dürr, in his preface to Volume 4 of the Bärenreiter/Henle edition of Schubert's songs containing the set, believes that Schubert's motive in selecting this topic was his love for the Countess Caroline Esterházy. In recent years Schubert has been seen as someone who feigned love for women in order to disguise his homosexual proclivities.[18] Rita Steblin in her essay 'Schubert's relationship with women' (Studies, 1998, pp. 220–38) considers this view reveals only the current *Zeitgeist* and should not be confused with history. All the evidence, she claims, shows that Schubert's love for women, notably for Therese Grob

---

[18] See Solomon, M., 'Franz Schubert's "Mein Traum"', *American Imago*, 38, pp. 137–54; 'Franz Schubert and the peacocks of Benvenuto Cellini', *Nineteenth-Century Music*, 12, pp. 193–206; and 'Schubert: some consequences of nostalgia', *Nineteenth-Century Music*, 17, pp. 34–46.

between 1814 and 1817, and then for Caroline Esterházy from 1824 onwards, was passionate and genuine.

He first met Caroline in 1818 when she was nearly 13. He had been engaged by Count Esterházy to teach his daughters Marie and Caroline at his residence in Zseliz in Hungary during the summer months of that year. He returned there in 1824 to perform the same task, but by then Caroline was nearly 19 and had become 'the certain attractive star' of the place. During the winter months of the years between 1818 and 1824 he taught the sisters at their home in Vienna. It is not known whether this was continued after 1824, but he must have certainly had Caroline in mind when he assembled this Op. 87 set early in 1827.

He may also have been thinking of her when he composed his Fantasia in C for violin and piano, D934 in December that year. In the third section he composed variations on his Rückert song, *Sei mir gegrüsst*. The words of the third stanza read: 'In spite of the distance that has imposed itself like an enemy between us, and in defiance of the envious power of fate, I greet you, I kiss you.' The following month he began composition on his Fantasia in F minor for piano, four hands, which he dedicated to Caroline. A month later his close friend Eduard von Bauernfeld wrote in his diary: 'Schubert appears seriously in love with the Countess E. This pleases me about him. He's giving her lessons.'[19] Rita Steblin thinks that what pleased Bauernfeld was that by early 1828 it was clear 'the composer had recovered from letting himself go to pieces in the summer of 1827, roaming around the outskirts of Vienna as Schober reported'. The following months before his death in November were some of the most productive of his life. As well as dedicating the F minor Fantasia to Caroline, he gave her the autograph copy of his E♭ Piano Trio, and told her when she reproached him in fun for not having dedicated something to her previously: 'What's the point? Everything is dedicated to you anyway.' In Moritz von Schwind's famous sepia drawing, *Ein Schubert-Abend bei Joseph v. Spaun* (1868), a portrait of Caroline features prominently on the back wall of the room, as if it were commonly agreed by all Schubert's friends gathered there that she was the inspiration behind what he is playing on the piano.

Texts

1. *Die Nacht bricht an, mit leisen Lüften sinket*. Pichler's poem contains eight quatrains, but Schubert omitted the last six lines to make six quatrains and a couplet.

---

[19] Litschauer, Walburga (ed.) (1986), *Neue Dokumente zum Schubert-Kreis. Aus Briefen und Tagebüchern seiner Freunde*, Vienna: Musikwissenschaftlicher, p. 68.

(1) Night falls with light breezes on weary mortals; gentle sleep, brother of death, beckons and lays them kindly in their daily graves.

(2) Now only malice and pain keep watch over the earth, bereft of light. And now, since there is nothing to disturb them, let your wounds bleed, poor heart.

(3) Sink into the depths of your misery, and if half forgotten sorrows have been sleeping in your anguished heart, rouse them with bitter-sweet delight.

(4) Consider your lost happiness, count all the flowers in paradise from which, in the golden days of youth, the harsh hand of fate banished you.

(5) You have loved, you have experienced a happiness which eclipses all earthly bliss. You have found a heart that understands you, and your wildest hopes have been fulfilled.

(6) Then the cruel decree of authority dashed you down from your heaven and destroyed your peace of mind. Your all-too-lovely vision returned to the better world from where it came.

(7) Now all the sweet bonds are torn asunder. Now no heart beats for me in all the world.

2. *Es reden und träumen die Menschen viel.* Three sixains.

(1) Men talk and dream of happy days to come. They run and chase after a golden goal. The world grows old and young again, but man forever hopes for better things.

(2) Hope leads us into life, it hovers around the carefree boy, its magic radiance inspires the youth. Nor is it buried with the old man in the grave. For although he ends his life there, yet in his grave he plants the seeds of hope.

(3) It is no empty, flattering illusion born in the mind of a fool. Loudly it proclaims itself in men's hearts. We are born for better things, and the inner voice does not deceive the hopeful soul.

3. *An der Quelle sass der Knabe.* Four eight-line stanzas.

(1) By the stream sat a youth, weaving flowers to make a wreath; he saw them carried off and swept along by the dancing waves. 'So too my days fly away like the stream without stay. So too my youth fades away and quickly withers like the wreath.

(2) 'Do not ask why I mourn in the blossom time of youth. All things are filled with joy and hope when spring returns. But in the depths of my heart the thousand voices of awakening nature awake only deep sorrow.

(3) 'What good to me is the joy that the fair spring offers me? There is only one I seek. She is near yet eternally distant. Yearningly, I open my arms to grasp her shadowy image. But I cannot reach her, and my heart is still troubled.

(4) 'Come down, gracious beauty, and leave your proud castle. I will scatter on your lap flowers born of the spring. Listen! The grove resounds with song and the rippling stream flows clear. There is room in the tiniest cottage for a happy, loving pair.'

Music

In his book *Classic Music*, Leonard G. Ratner points out that each era in western music treats dissonance in a characteristic way. As an important resource for achieving expressive emphasis, it provides a significant clue to the nature of a musical style. In classical music, he says, 'the most striking dissonance is the appoggiatura ... Classic period structure, with its strong accents spaced regularly within a slowly moving harmony and a rather transparent texture, invites appoggiaturas frequently.' As an example he refers to Mozart's music. Its high saturation of appoggiaturas, he maintains, 'constitute one of the chief ingredients of his musical speech'.[20] In many instances Schubert's music contains an even higher degree of saturation and can be looked on as being a transition between Mozart's use of the appoggiatura and Wagner's. This set is particularly interesting in this respect, for, like Wagner, Schubert contrasts one type of appoggiatura with another, and vividly illustrates how their expressivity can vary according to context.

1. *Der Unglückliche*

B minor 6/8. A through-composed scena in five sections. (1) A formal, antecedent-consequent section in a slow tempo (stanza 1), (2) a three-stage development section in a faster tempo (stanzas 2, 3 and 4), (3) a second antecedent-consequent section this time in B major and fast (stanza 5), (4) a short recitative leading to the return of B minor and the opening slow tempo (stanza 6), (5) a short coda in an alla breve, moderato tempo (the couplet).

Schubert does not make significant use of appoggiaturas until the development section when the protagonist considers his lost happiness. In the phrase setting the words 'Plunge to the depths of your grief', he uses a double appoggiatura over the bass note in bar 49 and a triple one in bar 51.

---

[20] Ratner, L.G. (1980), *Classic Music – Expression, Form, and Style*, New York: Schirmer, pp. 61–4.

Later the listener has the opportunity to compare the appoggiaturas there with those in the third section when the protagonist speaks of having experienced love and happiness. Here the regularly spaced appoggiaturas in the second and fourth bars of this example are single and expressive of positive feelings.

Near the end of the song, for the words 'Now all the sweet bonds are torn asunder', when the feelings have to be negative, Schubert alludes to that positive passage. But now the key is minor rather than major, the tempo slower, the lilting rhythm has been replaced by a tightly dotted one, the accompaniment is lower in tessitura, and the single appoggiatura has been changed to double ones.

2. *Hoffnung*

B♭ major. Rather fast 6/8. Strophic.

The lilting rhythm is similar to the one in the third section of the previous song. Also reminiscent of it are the relatively simple harmonies and the appoggiaturas expressive of pleasurable longing. The music for the piano's prelude and postlude, however, provides something else. The harmony is chromatic, the texture heavy with appoggiaturas, and the tessitura concentrated in the low middle register of the instrument. The only explanation for this is that Schubert wanted to illustrate what Schiller had to say in the second stanza. Hope may hover around the happy boy, and inspire the youth, but it is also present in the weary old man.

3. *Der Jüngling am Bache*

C minor. At a moderate pace 3/4.

Schubert set this poem four times. In his quasi-operatic first version of 1812, he altered each strophe to suit the words. In the next he added horn calls to suggest that the young man's hope might be on the point of being fulfilled. In the subsequent strophic settings the same music has to serve for the expressions of grief in the first three stanzas and the hopeful call to the beloved in the last. In this final version Schubert chose to emphasize the ambiguity of the young man's feelings. He achieves this principally in the piano's prelude and postlude. In the first two bars there is a single appoggiatura on the first beat, in the next two a double one. But in each case they are under a slur, and it is the upbeat to them that has the accent. This means that, although they fall on the first beat of the bar, the appoggiaturas lack the emphasis they would normally have; their poignancy is weakened. Perhaps Schubert wanted to suggest that the young man was attempting to suppress his grief (see over).

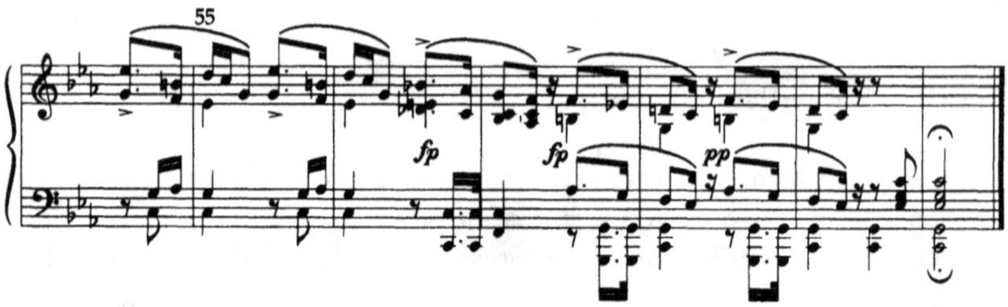
55
fp
fp
pp

Opus 88

Published by Thaddäus Weigl, 12 December 1827.

1. *Abendlied für die Entfernte* (Evening Song for the Distant Beloved) August Wilhelm von Schlegel, D856 (September 1825)
2. *Thekla (eine Geisterstimme)* (Thekla: A Phantom Voice) Friedrich von Schiller, D595 (version b, *c.* 1817)
3. *Um Mitternacht* (At Midnight) Ernst Schulze, D862 (version b, ?March 1826)
4. *An die Musik* (To Music) Franz von Schober, D547 (version b, *c.* 1817)

This is the last of the four sets devoted to the imagination. In Op. 60, the previous one, we were given a specimen of what old men might dream about when they can no longer cope with reality. In that case it was to imagine making contact with a world lying beyond reality, namely the world of the Olympian gods. In this fourth set Schubert selected songs describing contact with other worlds through the medium of sound: distant sounds, ghostly voices and, finally, music.

As usual with four-song sets, the items are grouped in pairs. The first pair considers situations we can imagine as being possible. Reality for Schlegel is the misery he feels at being parted from his beloved. But when his imagination is stirred by distant sounds he can dream of her return. In a stanza omitted by Schubert, he then goes on to discuss the conflict between reality and dreams. But his main point is that life is made bearable by what can be imagined, that life would be the poorer if reality and dreams could not be interwoven.

Schiller's poem looks at the topic from another angle. Thekla is the daughter of Wallenstein, the commander-in-chief of the Catholic forces during the Thirty Years War (1618–48), whose downfall is plotted by Schiller in his dramatic trilogy *Wallenstein*. Nothing is heard of her after she leaves her father's headquarters to search near one of the enemy's outposts for the grave of her lover Max Piccolomini. Schiller wrote this poem to answer queries about her fate. Wallenstein had been murdered because his dreams of becoming king and bringing the war to an end, fostered by his faith in astrology, had led him to ignore reality and allow the enemies in his own camp to gain the upper hand. Thekla's injunction to 'dare to err, and to dream' is a defence of her father's position. She sees him as a man whose dreams were noble and entirely justified.

The other two songs lack the philosophical flavour of the first pair and are more personal. Schulze's love for Adelheid Tychsen, the woman who comes to him during the night, was obsessional and totally unrequited. In Susan Youens' opinion

> the poem epitomizes the machinations of obsession: the fact that Schulze, devoid of any real affirmation of reciprocated love, could continually call up poetic hallucinations and persuade himself of their possible transformation into future reality is precisely why the miserable matter dragged on as long as it did. Like a child who seeks its mother's presence at bedtime as a bulwark against fears of abandonment and death, the poetic persona feels his inner darkness most acutely at midnight, with a long stretch of blackest night left to endure, and calls up a vision of his beloved to comfort him. When he does so, her image transforms into star-spangled clarity, and he can then fall asleep and dream of her, dreams in which she says what *he* would have her say. This is a fantasy with roots in infantile distress, and it seems only fitting that Schulze chose a folk-like form and meter for this lullaby in which he is both mother and child and must sing himself to sleep. (Youens, p. 285)

In the verbal and visual arts the products of the imagination can be specified; in music they cannot. Schulze held that music was too mystical for rational contemplation (DF-D, p. 226). In his play *Die bezauberte Rose* (The Enchanted Rose), he wrote a poetic stanza in which he addresses music as 'Du holde Kunst', the same phrase with which Schober begins his poem. But since Schober's poem was written before Schulze's play won a literary prize in 1817 and became available, Schober cannot be accused of plagiarism. However, neither man could find words for what music conveyed. All Schulze could say is that music makes life bearable, and all Schober could do was to fall back on clichés. It was up to Schubert to demonstrate the power of music to take listeners beyond the confines of reality.

Texts

1. *Hinaus mein Blick! hinaus ins Tal!* Five eight-line stanzas (double quatrains).

    (1) Gaze out, eyes, gaze out towards the valley. There abundant life still dwells. Refresh yourself in the moonlight and the sacred peace. Listen, heart, listen to the soft sounds that press on you for joy or sorrow from far away.

    (2) They crowd in so wondrously, they arouse all my longing. Is this intimation real, or is it a vain illusion? Will my eyes that are now

filled with tears one day smile in unalloyed pleasure? Will my heart so often inflamed with anger one day find blessed peace to caress it?

(3) When presentiment and memory are joined before our eyes, then at dusk the shadows on our soul grow softer. Ah, if we could not interweave reality with dreams, how colourless and dull human life would be.

(4) Thus the heart moves to the grave in unfailing and faithful hope. It invests the moment with love, and counts itself rich in possessions. Fate cannot plunder the possessions it has created for itself. It lives and works in warmth and strength, in faith and trust.

(5) And even when all lie dead in mist and darkness, the heart has won a shield for itself for every battle. In times of trouble it endures its fate in proud defiance. And so I fall asleep, and so I wake up – if not in joy then in peace.

2. *Wo ich sei, und wo mich hingewendet*. Six quatrains.

(1) Where am I, you ask, and where did I go when my fleeting shadow disappeared? I have not finished, have I not reached my end? Have I not loved and lived?

(2) Would you ask after the nightingale whose soulful melodies delighted you in spring? They lived only so long as they loved.

(3) Did I find the one I had lost? Believe me, I am united with him where those who have exchanged vows are never parted, where no tears are shed.

(4) There you will find us again when your love is as our love. There too is my father, cleansed of sin, whom bloody murder can no longer strike.

(5) And he feels he was not deluded when he looked up at the stars; for as man judges so is he judged, and whoever believes this is close to holiness.

(6) There, up in space every fine, deeply-felt belief will be fulfilled; often a higher meaning lies behind child-like play.

3. *Keine Stimme hör' ich schallen*. Seven quatrains.

(1) I hear no voice, no footstep on the dark path; even heaven has closed its beautiful bright eyes.

(2) I alone am awake, sweet life, gazing longingly into the night until your star in the barren distance arouses me with its lovely radiance.

(3) Ah, if only I could see your dear form just once, in secret, I would gladly stand all night in storm and tempest.

(4) Is it you I see shining in the distance? Is it you who gradually approaches? I hear your whispered welcome: 'See, your friend is still awake.'

(5) Sweet words, beloved voice, at which my heart beats. Your whisper has called up a thousand blissful images of love.

(6) I see all the stars glittering on their deep-blue course; the sky has cleared up in the heavens and in my heart.

(7) Sweet echo, come now and rock me gently to sleep. May her beloved words whisper often to me in my dreams.

4. *Du holde Kunst, in wieviel grauen Stunden.* Two quatrains.

(1) You lovely art, how often in dark hours, when I am surrounded by life's tumultuous round, have you kindled in my heart the warmth of love and transported me to a better world.

(2) Often a sigh, a sweet touch of celestial harmony, escaping from your harp, has revealed to me a heaven of happier times. You lovely art, I thank you for this.

Music

The set is unusual in that all four songs are strophic. The first may modify the third and fifth strophe by going into the minor, but it lacks the variety and tension found in most first songs. In fact its lilting pastoral rhythm suggests that Schlegel's speculations are simply a means of consoling himself as he falls asleep. Thekla's music also offers consolation as does the music of *Um Mitternacht* which Youens describes as 'a quietly fraught, strophic hymn-cum-lullaby' (Youens, p. 287). All three songs are characterized by their restricted range of expression, and this throws into relief the expansive qualities which make *An die Musik* such a memorable song.

1. *Abendlied für die Entfernte*

F major. Moderately moving forward 6/8.

Key and rhythm recall the Pastoral Symphony in Handel's *Messiah* except that here the rhythm, being a constant stream of iambs rather than trochees, has much more lilt to it. Schubert divides the five strophes into four periods each devoted to two lines of text and separated by short piano interludes which may be intended to convey 'the soft sounds pressing upon the poet'. He varies the third strophe by, among other things, transposing it into the minor and eliminating the interlude between the last two periods. This means that the crucial last four lines become a single unit: 'Ah, if we could not interweave reality and dreams, how colourless and dull life would be.' The fifth strophe is also cast in the minor for its first period. But here, instead of lengthening the line, he breaks it up so that the word 'Frieden' (peace) is emphasized. And with peace comes sleep.

2. Thekla (eine Geisterstimme)

C minor – major. Very slow 3/4.

Schubert combines Schiller's six stanzas to make three strophes. The first two lines are written in the minor, the remaining six in the major. The purpose of oscillating between minor and major is presumably to convey the difference between earthly cares and heavenly joy. But since Thekla also refers to earthly cares in the major section, Schubert has to incorporate into one passage the 'depressed' notes associated with the minor. The piano is muted throughout the song, the dynamics are mostly confined to *pp* or *ppp*, and the voice is restricted to the notes lying within an augmented fourth. The sense of consolation is created by the gently oscillating quavers on the piano and the sameness of the eight four-bar phrases in the vocal line.

3. Um Mitternacht

B♭ major. At a very moderate pace 2/4.

Schubert combines Schulze's first six stanzas to make three strophes divided into symmetrical halves. The seventh stanza uses only the first of the halves so the fourth strophe is left incomplete, as is appropriate for someone whose thoughts are being interrupted by sleep. All the material derives from the piano's introduction consisting of two ideas: a figure based on a tight, double-dotted rhythm and a more relaxed, flowing figure. There are four variants of these. Two make up the first half of each strophe, the other two the second half. This means that the basic material occurs 18 times in the course of the song. If the source of the material, the piano's introduction, represents the poet's inner tension followed by his more relaxed frame of mind when he imagines the woman has come to soothe him to sleep, then the repetitions of it must surely represent his obsessiveness.

4. *An die Musik*

D major. At a moderate pace, alla breve.

An die Musik supplies what has been missing from the previous songs, notably rhythmic variety and a broad sweep of melody. Of particular significance is the strength of the bass line, which appears to be in dialogue with the voice. In the previous songs the 'other' has been the distant beloved, a phantom voice, a figment of the imagination. In this one it is something palpably 'here' in the pianist's left hand.

Edward T. Cone believes the song's two strophes create 'an indissoluble whole' (Studies, 1998, pp. 118–20). He bases his argument on the way the piano brings the two strophes to a close. At the end of the first it fails to complete the pattern of appoggiaturas or suspensions which has been established in the previous four bars and goes straight back to the simple tonic chord with which the song began.

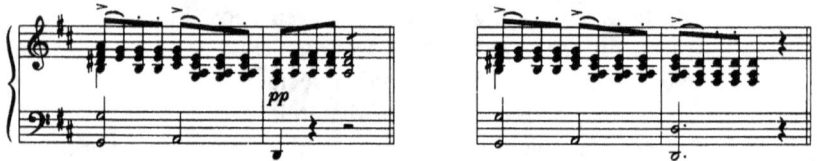

Cone contends that, unlike the ending of the second stanza which completes the pattern of appoggiaturas, the first does not 'effect the necessary discharge of momentum' to bring the song to a satisfactory conclusion, so we are encouraged to hear the song not as A+A, but as an antecedent (the first strophe) followed by a consequent (the second). He considers this is also justified by the way Schubert sets the phrase 'du holde Kunst' when it comes back at the end of the second strophe. The music's fall from D to F♯ refers back to the moment when the phrase originally occurred and has the effect of rounding the song off. 'The coalescence of verbal and musical themes at that point imparts a sense of resolution more satisfying than that of the merely musical reprise at the end of the first stanza' (Studies, 1998, p. 119).

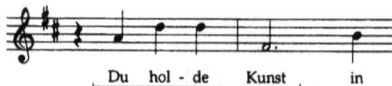

The significance of Cone's analysis for the set as a whole is that *An die Musik* creates a sense of completion the other songs lack. The other three are all open-ended. There is no reason why the first two should not have another verse. The third cannot, nevertheless it breaks off in the middle of a strophe so that although there may be no need to have more words, the listener will certainly want more music. Its inclusion in the set therefore serves as a perfect foil for what Cone calls the 'indissoluable wholeness' of *An die Musik*.

Opus 92

Three songs to poems by Johann Wolfgang von Goethe. Published by
M.J. Leidesdorf, 11 July 1828. Dedicated to Frau Josephine von Franck.

1. *Der Musensohn* (The Son of the Muses), D764 (version b, *c.* 1822)
2. *Auf dem See* (On the Lake), D543 (version b, March 1817)
3. *Geistes-Gruss* (Ghostly Greeting), D142 (version f, revised ?1828)

This was probably compiled in the autumn or early winter of 1827
before Op. 88 was published. Leidesdorf had advertised it at the 1828
Easter Fair of the Leipzig Book Mart, but for some reason withheld
advertising it in Vienna until July. Schubert composed no more Goethe
songs after completing the Mignon set (Op. 62) in 1826. But there were
still well over 30 he had not published; among them were three which
could be united around a topic of fundamental importance to the poet,
namely the relationship between human dynamism and the dynamism of
nature. The unceasing activity and restless search for knowledge which
Goethe identified as the Faustian spirit had its counterpart in the
dynamic change and organic development he found in his botanical and
zoological studies.

In Book 16 of his autobiography *Dichtung und Wahrheit* (Poetry and
Truth), Goethe wrote:

> I have come to look on my indwelling poetic talent altogether as a
> force of Nature; the more so, as I had always been impelled to regard
> outward nature as its proper object. The exercise of this poetic
> faculty might indeed be excited and determined by circumstances;
> but its most joyful and richest action was spontaneous – even invol-
> untary.[21]

He then quotes the first three lines of *Der Musensohn*. In Greek
mythology there is no such god as the Son of the Muses. Goethe invented
him to represent the spirit of restless activity inherent in the world, and to
indicate that everything and everyone dances to the same tune.

Auf dem See was written in 1775 when Goethe was on holiday in
Switzerland, where he had gone without saying a word to his fiancée, Lili
Schönemann. But in this poem it is Nature who holds him to her bosom.
It is here on the lake that he finds love; and life too, life in the restless
motion of waves, wind and twinkling stars.

---

[21]   Goethe, Johann Wolfgang von, trans. Minna Steele Smith (1913), London: Bell, vol.
2, p. 207.

Geistes-Gruss comes from 1774, the year when *Die Leiden des jungen Werthers* (The Sorrows of the Young Werther) was published, and Goethe was halfway through his first version of *Faust*. The 'Storm and Stress' movement which gave rise to *Faust* characterized Goethe's private life as well as his literary style at the time. *Geistes-Gruss* implies that he hopes to find tranquillity as the hero in the poem had done. He discovered it when he moved to Weimar the following year and befriended Charlotte von Stein, who 'calmed his wildness' and 'dropped moderation into his hot blood' (Whitton, p. 51). Faust, however, never finds the tranquillity he yearns for. After his wager with Mephistopheles he finds temporary peace in the company of the Spirit of Nature, but, as the second part of the drama reveals, he never overcomes his restlessness of spirit. Schubert would not have known this since the second part was not published until 1832. He would have assumed that, as Goethe and the ghostly hero in the poem had done, Faust too would find at least a measure of tranquillity some time in his life.

Texts

1. *Durch Feld und Wald zu schweifen.* Five sixains.

   (1) I go from place to place, through field and wood, whistling my song. And all keep time with me, all move in measure with me.
   (2) I can scarcely wait for the first flowers in the garden, the first blossom on the tree. My song welcomes them, and when winter comes again, I shall dream of them in my song.
   (3) I sing it the length and breadth of the ice, far and wide. Then winter blooms in beauty. But this flowering also passes, and on upland farms new joy is discovered.
   (4) For when, by the linden tree, I come across young folk I immediately arouse them. The country lad puffs out his chest, the prim maiden whirls about to my tune.
   (5) Dear kindly Muses, you lend wings to my feet, and drive your darling over hill and dale far from home. When shall I find rest again on the bosom of my beloved?

2. *Und frische Nahrung, neues Blut.* Five quatrains.

   (1) I draw fresh nourishment and new blood from this wide world. How gracious and good is Nature, who holds me to her bosom.
   (2) Our boat is rocked by the waves, and the cloud-capped mountains meet us as we move to the rhythm of the oars.

(3) Why then are my eyes cast down? Golden dreams will you ever return? Begone, dreams, golden though you are. Here too are love and life.

(4) A thousand twinkling stars are mirrored in the waves, soft mists drink up the looming distances.

(5) The morning breeze takes wing across the shaded bay, and the ripening fruit is mirrored on the lake.

3. *Hoch auf dem alten Turme steht*. Three quatrains.

(1) High on the ancient tower stands the spirit of the noble hero; and as the ship passes by, he bids it a safe voyage.

(2) 'Look, these sinews were so strong, this heart so firm and fierce, these bones so full of knightly valour. My cup overflowed.

(3) 'For half my life I tossed like a storm; I let the other half go by in peace. And you, little boat of mankind, sail onward, ever onward.'

Music

Schubert made more changes to these songs when preparing them for publication than to those in any other set. *Der Musensohn* and *Auf dem See* were both transposed down a semitone, from A♭ to G and from E to E♭ respectively. *Auf dem See* had its prelude and postlude extended, and its vocal line substantially altered and improved. *Geistes-Gruss* was transposed up a semitone to end in G rather than G♭. Originally it had begun with a bare recitative. This was changed into a measured, accompanied recitative with tremolos to evoke not only the ghost's presence but the hero's earlier restlessness.

The transpositions were made to allow the set to be sung by one voice. In their original keys *Der Musensohn* and *Auf dem See* needed to be performed by a tenor in order to have the top A♭/G♯s sung with the specified soft dynamic, while the tessitura of *Geistes-Gruss* was best suited to a baritone. But the transpositions also bring about a closer harmonic relationship between the songs, for over the course of the set the most significant harmonic feature is a shift to keys a major third away. Schubert was one of the first composers to make structural use of equal temperament. The enharmonic transpositions which occur over and over again in his songs would never have been used by an older generation of composers brought up to think in terms of mean temperament. They would never have accepted that C♯ major was the same as D♭ major (nor did Beethoven, according to

Schindler[22]). Nor would they have structured a song on descending major thirds as Schubert does in *Der zürnenden Diana* in Op. 36, where he goes from Ab major to E major then C major and finally Ab major again. Mean temperament demanded pure, or very nearly pure, major thirds, and Schubert's song needs the impure but nevertheless perfectly acceptable thirds which equal temperament provides.

Der Musensohn alternates between G major and B major, going from one to the other without any transition: G-B-G-B-G. When G returns it sounds as if the young man is going off on another adventure and his activity will never cease. The same juxtaposition occurs in *Geistes-Gruss*. The opening E major recitative comes to a close on a chord of B major, the key's dominant. The ear expects the return of E, but instead the music plunges into G. Eb major, the key of *Auf dem See* provides a link between these songs, so the overall pattern is: G-B-G-Eb-(E)-B-G.

The advantage of descending in major thirds over the course of the set means that Schubert can end in the key with which he began. Usually this creates a sense of completion, but on this occasion, as Lawrence Kramer observes (Frisch, p. 209), the ending of *Geistes-Gruss* is open-ended, as indeed it has to be to suit the ghost's injunction to 'sail onward, ever onward'.

1. *Der Musensohn*

G major. Rather lively 6/8.

Der Musensohn consists of two alternating strophes, different in their contours, but both underpinned by a dancing rhythmic ostinato. The one in G major moves into B major as if it were the first step in a modulation to E minor, but the shift from B major to G major is abrupt and creates the impression that the music has gone back to the beginning. The only time the dancing ostinato is slowed down is when the young man comes to the word 'Busen' (bosom). But the ritardando only lasts a bar, which means that the young man's plea for peace goes almost unnoticed by the music.

2. *Auf dem See*

Eb major. At a moderate pace 6/8 then 2/4.

Originally Schubert's tempo direction was 'Mässig, ruhig' (moderate, peaceful), but he removed the word 'ruhig' when he came to publish the song. Although the poet feels that gracious Nature is holding him to her

---

[22] Schindler, Anton (1849), *Beethoven as I Knew Him*, ed. Donald W. MacArdie, trans. Constance S. Jolly (1966), Chapel Hill, NC: University of North Carolina Press, p. 368.

breast (Die mich an Busen hält), Schubert's song is calm only during one bar of silence. This occurs between the second and third stanza when the poet asks himself why he should feel cast down. Schubert's musical image relates to the constant motion of the waves, the boat and the oar. The song is through-composed, but when stanza 4 is reached he changes from 6/8 to 2/4 so that the pulse becomes faster. The musical image now suggests twinkling stars as well as dancing over the waves.

That figure in the second and fourth bar will be the one which when changed to B-A-G will bring *Geistes-Gruss* to a conclusion.

3. *Geistes-Gruss*

Geistes-Gruss's opening E major recitative is marked 'not too slow 4/4', the G major arioso 'the same tempo, but strongly and in 3/4'. By moving to E major after Eb major, the ghostly three-bar introduction gives the impression that the scene has changed abruptly. Yet the F✕ and A♯ in the second bar are enharmonically the same as the G and Bb prominent in the last bar of the previous song.

That neighbour-note pattern comes back near the end of the song. But here the purpose is mainly rhythmical. The piano's three-note figure accompanying the word 'du' in bars 26 and 27 has its stress on the dotted quaver. When the same rhythm occurs later, the listener may well feel that the dotted quavers should also be stressed, even though they lie on the third beat of the bar. To make sure that this is how they should be heard Schubert accents them. Without those accents the stress would fall on the first beats of the last two bars, and a strong sense of closure would be obtained. With them, as Lawrence Kramer observes, the song becomes open-ended.

und du,   und du,   du Men - schen - schiff - lein dort,   fahr

im - mer, im - mer zu"

When summarizing this set in the Introduction, it was pointed out that the volte-face in *Geistes-Gruss*, when restlessness is replaced by tranquillity, is mirrored by the volte-face that takes place in the sequence of keys. Since the shift to keys a major third lower is more frequently encountered than the shift to keys a major third higher, listeners may expect that at the end of *Auf dem See* the next key will be B major. That it turns out to be E major may disorientate them. B major does not appear until it is cadenced on at the end of the recitative. But here it is a dominant not a tonic so that the shift down to G major which follows is even more abrupt than the shift from B major to G major in *Der Musensohn*. Its effectiveness in reflecting the text may have been the most important reason why Schubert made so many alterations to the songs.

Opus 93

Two songs to poems by Ernst Konrad Friedrich Schulze. Published by J.A. Kienreich of Graz, 30 May 1828.

1. *Im Walde* (In the Forest), D834 (version b, *c.* 1825)
2. *Auf der Brücke* (On the Bridge), D853 (version b, *c.* 1825)

The ten Schulze poems Schubert set in 1825 and 1826 all come from *Poetisches Tagebuch* (Verse Diary), a collection of 100 poems recording the poet's obsessive but unrequited love for Adelheid Tychsen between 1813 and his death at the age of 28 in 1817. Schulze's title for *Im Walde* was 'Im Walde hinter Falkenhagen. Den. 22. Juli 1814' and for *Auf der Brücke* 'Auf der Bruck. Den. 26 Juli 1814'. Schubert shortened or changed these titles to avoid associating the songs to a specific place or date. (Bruck is a lookout point near Göttingen where both Adelheid and Schulze lived.) In the four days between the first poem and the second, Schulze's mood seems to have become less despairing, for *Auf der Brücke* expresses a measure of hope. This is undoubtedly why Schubert selected it to be the second and concluding song in this set. There is no reason to believe that he intended the two poems to make a set when he composed them, even though they were written one after the other. However, his alteration of *Auf der Brücke*'s final stanza, so that it ends with 'sweet presentiments' rather than with thoughts about love being deceived, seems to suggest that the possibility had occurred to him.

The poems are about men travelling through a forest. One goes in daytime, on foot and believes he will never find rest, the other at night, on horseback and has the conviction he will find both joy and sorrow. We have to take it that the forest symbolizes a mind enclosed by an obsession, and haunted by unrealized desires. In *Im Walde* the images are primarily about unfulfilled sexual desires. Schulze never kissed Adelheid, never played catching games with her, never 'plucked the flower', even though to her doubtless consternation he may have 'often stooped down to it'. In *Auf der Brücke* he deceives himself into believing that the obstacles to his love will be overcome, that the dark night he is going through will end, and that like the migrating birds he will soon find warmer pastures.

Texts

1. *Ich wandre über Berg und Tal.* Six sixains.

(1) I wander over hill and dale, and over the green heather; and my anguish travels with me, never leaving me. And if I were to sail across the wide ocean, it would follow me still.

(2) Though many flowers bloom in the meadow, I have not seen them; for I see but one flower on every path I tread. I have often stooped down towards it, but I have never plucked it.

(3) The bees hum through the grass and linger on the blossoms; this makes my eyes grow clouded and moist, but I cannot help it. Never did I linger so on her sweet lips, so red and soft.

(4) Near and far the birds sing sweetly on the branches; I would like to join them in song, but must keep a mournful silence. The joy and pain of love prefer to remain alone.

(5) I watch the clouds sail across the sky on swift wings; the waves ripple softly and brightly, they must ever come and go. Yet when the wind dies down, cloud catches cloud in play, wave catches wave.

(6) I wander here, I wander there, through weather foul and fair; yet I shall never again find it, never again behold it. O the longing and torment of love – when will the wanderer find rest?

2. *Frisch trabe sonder Ruh und Rast.* Four eight-line stanzas.

(1) Trot briskly on, my good horse, through night and rain without pause for rest. Why do you shy at bush and branch, and stumble on the rough paths? However dark and thick the forest, they must open up at last, and a friendly light from the dark valley will greet us.

(2) On your lithe back I could cheerfully speed over mountain and plain enjoying all the varied delights and charming sights of the world. Many a laughing eye meets mine, promising peace, love and joy. And yet I hurry on restlessly back, back to my sorrow.

(3) For three days now I have been far from her to whom I am eternally bound. For three days the sun and stars, heaven and earth have vanished from my sight. Of the sorrow and joy in my heart which her presence wounds or makes whole again, I have known only the sorrow for three days. The joy I have had to forgo.

(4) So trot on bravely through the night! Though the dark tracks may vanish, the bright eye of longing keeps watch, and sweet presentiments guide me safely on. We watch the birds fly away

across land and water to warmer pastures. How then can love ever be deceived in its course?

(In Schubert's song the fourth stanza is changed to:

(4) We watch the birds fly away across land and water to warmer pastures. How then can love be deceived in its course? So trot on bravely through the night! Though the dark tracks may vanish, the bright eye of longing keeps watch, and sweet presentiments guide me safely on.)

Music

Originally *Im Walde* was in G minor, *Auf der Brücke* in G major. The transpositions to B♭ minor and A♭ major mean that the set can be sung only by a tenor, for it is doubtful whether any high baritone can jump to a high A♭ from the octave below within *piano* as the singer is required to do in *Auf der Brücke*.

To indicate Schulze's obsessive single-mindedness, both songs have a *moto perpetuo* figure running through them, triplets in the first, quavers to represent the horse's trot in the second. Yet they seem to be unnecessarily fast. Nothing in Schulze's poems indicates that the wanderer should be rushing through the forest so restlessly, or that the horse's trot should be so sprightly. It would seem that in selecting these songs for his Schulze set early in 1828, Schubert had deliberately wanted to draw a parallel with the ceaseless activity associated with the Faustian spirit in the songs of his previous set, Op. 92. If so, it is not the first occasion he makes reference to a previous set, nor will it be the last.

1. *Im Walde*

B♭ minor. Not too fast 4/4.

The six stanzas are in highly modified strophic form making up the pattern A^1-B-A^2-A^2-B-A^1, A^1 being entirely in the minor, A^2 a version which starts in the major and returns to the minor, and B a version mainly in the dominant or dominant minor. Each strophe is divided into two more or less equal parts, the first sets the first four lines of the stanza, the second the last two. As well as containing the climax or focal point of each strophe the second part also has its words repeated. One of the features of the song is the sudden switching from diatonic material to chromatic material or vice versa. The piano's introduction, for instance, once the *moto perpetuo* is established, has an open, forthright, diatonic phrase built round a B♭ minor arpeggio, then a confined chromatic phrase marked *forte*, finally another diatonic phrase marked *piano*. In counterpoint with these last two phrases the pianist's left hand plays the chromatically descending scale which Schubert uses as a death motif. Within eight bars he has indicated the obsessiveness of the poet, his mental instability, his vacillation between confidence and doubt, and his latent death wish.

2. *Auf der Brücke*

Ab major. Fast 4/4.

This is also in modified strophic form and, as in the previous song, Schubert divides each strophe into two parts. Here the first part is a setting of the first four lines of the stanza, the second the last four lines. The music for the first part comes back almost note for note, the only marked difference being the move into the minor during the third strophe when the traveller talks about being without sun and stars for three days. The music for the second part, on the other hand, is varied considerably. In this song the alternation between diatonic and chromatic music takes place on a broader scale, for the first parts of each strophe are primarily diatonic, the second parts much more chromatic. The effect is to sharpen the distinction between the traveller's sense of confidence and doubt. Throughout the song the trotting quavers are placed in the pianist's right hand. Schubert devotes the left hand to a single line as often as not in canon with the vocal line. On occasions it falters, a feature which not only suggests the horse's stumbling, but also the poet's sudden uncertainties about himself and the woman he hopes will welcome him.

Opus 95

Four Refrain Songs to poems by Johann Gabriel Seidl. Published by Thaddäus Weigl, 13 August 1828. 'Dedicated most amicably to the poet.'

1. *Die Unterscheidung* (The Distinction), D866, No. 1
2. *Bei dir allein* (With you alone), D866, No. 2
3. *Die Männer sind méchant* (Men are wicked), D866, No. 3
4. *Irdisches Glück* (Earthly happiness), D866, No. 4

The manuscript of these songs is undated, but since a sketch for the first one is contained in the same manuscript as sketches for the opening of the finale of the Piano Sonata in C minor, D958, Robert Winter thinks they were probably composed in the late spring of 1828 (Studies, 1982, p. 255). John Reed believes it may have been Weigl who harnessed 'Schubert's genius to Seidl's light satirical verse' (SSC, p. 172). Weigl brought them out so that they could be purchased as a bound set for 54 Kreuzer or separately (20 Kreuzer for numbers 1, 3 and 4, and 30 Kreuzer for number 2). This suggests he had failed to see that they are more amusing as a set than individually. It also suggests he wanted them to be available to clients who could afford to buy them only one at a time. That he was appealing to popular taste is borne out by his publicity blurb:

> The public has long cherished the wish to have, for once, a composition of a merry, comic nature from this song composer of genius. The wish has been gratified in a surprising manner by Herr Schubert in the present four songs, which in part are truly comic and in part bear in them the character of ingenuousness and humour. (Doc. 1133)

A refrain song (as opposed to a song with a refrain) is one in which each stanza ends with the same line to produce either a dramatic or comic effect according to context. As in most of his four-song sets, Schubert divides the items into two related but contrasting pairs. Each pair has a comic song for a woman, and a more serious song for a man. The women's songs contrast a woman who has total control over her lover with one whose lover is proving unfaithful. The men's songs contrast a man who serenades his woman with passionate ardour with one who has lost interest in women and prefers the company of his own sex.

Texts

1. *Die Mutter hat mich jüngst gescholten.* Four eight-line stanzas.

   (1) Mother recently scolded me, and sternly warned me against love. 'Every woman', she said, 'pays its price, and once you're caught all is lost'. So I think it better if neither of us speaks of it again. Of course I am still yours for ever. But love you, Hans – this I cannot do!

   (2) Above all, Hans, you must never forget that you must cherish only me. Let my smile be always your delight, and smiles from other girls a bore. Yes, to please mother I shall, true to my two-fold duty, still strive to please you. But love you, Hans – this I cannot do!

   (3) Whenever we have a holiday, it will be my greatest joy to have your spray of spring-time offerings adorn my bodice. When the dancing begins, then – as is only fair – it is your duty to dance with Gretchen; I shall even be jealous. But love you, Hans – this I cannot do!

   (4) And when in the cool of the evening we rest filled with tender emotion, keep your hand on my bodice, and feel how my heart beats. And if you intend to teach me with your kisses what your eyes silently tell me, even that I won't deny you. But love you Hans – this I cannot do!

2. *Bei dir allein empfind' ich, dass ich lebe.* Three sixains.

   (1) With you alone I feel I am alive, fired by youthful vigour. A care-free world of love thrills through me; I rejoice in my being with you alone.

   (2) With you alone the breeze is so refreshing, the fields so green, the flowering spring so gentle, the evening so balmy, the grove so cool, with you alone.

   (3) With you alone pain loses its bitterness, every joy is enhanced. In you my heart's natural heritage is fulfilled. I feel I am myself with you alone!

3. *Du sagest mir es, Mutter.* Three eight-line stanzas.

   (1) You warned me, mother – he's a young rogue. I did not believe you until I had tormented myself sick. Yes, I now know he really is; I had simply misjudged him. You warned me, mother – men are wicked!

(2) Yesterday as dusk fell I heard a whisper in the copse outside the village, a whisper saying, 'Good evening', and then a whispered 'Many thanks'. I crept up and listened, then I stood as if spellbound. There he was with someone else – men are wicked!

(3) Oh mother, what torture! I must speak out, I must! It didn't just stop at whispering, it didn't just stop at greetings. It went from greetings to kisses, from kisses to holding hands, from holding hands to ... oh, dear mother – men are wicked!

4. *So mancher sieht mit finst'rer Miene.* Four eight-line stanzas.

(1) So many people look on the wide world with gloomy faces, and grumble. Life's wonderful stage lies open to them in vain. But I know better what to do. Far from being afraid of joy, I relish every moment. And that is happiness for sure.

(2) I have wooed many a heart, though success was short-lived, for my stupidity often ruined what my cheerful spirit had just won. And so I escaped the net. For since no fancy held me prisoner, I had none to flee. And that is happiness for sure.

(3) No laurels have crowned my head, no glorious halo shines about it. Yet my life is not in vain, for quiet thanks are also a halo. He who, far from bold flights, is content with the peaceful pleasures of the valley, need never fear for his neck. And that is happiness for sure.

(4) And when the messenger from the world beyond comes to summon me, as he summons everyone with his grave, hollow voice, then, in parting, I shall bid this lovely world farewell. At the end, maybe true friends will be there to grasp me by the hand and bless me with a kindly smile. And that, brothers, is what true happiness is.

Music

Schubert must have had Viennese light opera or French vaudeville in mind when he composed these songs. His accompaniments, particularly those for the first and third songs, call out for orchestration, and in the three strophic songs (numbers 1, 3 and 4) the extended preludes and postludes resemble the kind of music used for entrances and exits. In each song the essence of the text is captured in the refrain.

1. *Die Unterscheidung*

G major. At a moderate pace 6/8.

The essence of this text is the way the girl affectionately teases poor Hans. Schubert captures it by having the refrain sung twice at the end of each strophe and making the repetition musically different. It is unlikely any singer would sing the varied version strictly in time. To indicate the girl's affection for her boyfriend, she is bound to hold back the leap to top G.

doch lie-ben, Hans!   lie-ben kann ich dich nicht!   doch lie-ben, Hans!   lie-ben kann ich—dich nicht!

2. *Bei dir allein*

Ab major. Not too fast, but with ardour 2/4.

Schubert conveys the man's eagerness by the impetuous nature of the triplet figuration which dominates the accompaniment, and also by the way he pitches the voice in the refrain ending each stanza. The song needs a strong tenor voice to bring it off. It is in ABA form, the second A being a modified version of the first. Schubert's ploy in the first and last parts is to go to Gb major and then to repeat the material in Ab major so that the voice is taken to its highest register.

mich freut mein Sein bei   dir— al - lein, bei   dir— al - lein, bei   dir   al -

lein!————— mich freut mein Sein bei   dir— al - lein, bei— dir— al - lein!

The central section is in E major (that is, Fb major, the home key's flat submediant). Here the rise in pitch affects the harmony rather than the melodic line. Schubert's purpose is to reserve the tenor's most ringing and ardent tone for the end of the last part where, after going up to top Ab again, he gives the voice two sustained notes, the second of which can be held for as long as the singer has breath.

3. *Die Männer sind méchant*

A minor. Rather slow 6/8.

A strophic song closely related to the first song in the set. Although Schubert specifies the tempo should be rather slow, the character of the piano's prelude and postlude with its vigorous cross accents is neverthe-less lively. This must surely be meant to convey the girl's indignation. Her refrain, however, is cast in the minor after a passage in the major, and this captures her sense of humiliation.

4. *Irdisches Glück*

D minor – major. Rather fast 4/4.

A strophic song in which the first half of each strophe is in the minor when the man speaks of people with grim faces, his lack of success and the approach of death, and second half in the major when he talks about escaping the net, finding peace and being consoled by the friendly eyes of his brothers. As if to emphasize the man's leanings to his own sex, the song has a march-like swing to it. It would be rather complacent had not Schubert added acciaccaturas (crushed notes) not only to the accompani-ment but also the vocal line to suggest the man has a twinkle in his eye. It was probably no coincidence that his next set is entirely devoted to bachelors, and that its last song, which is also about a man who thinks he has escaped the net, also contains a humorous twist.

Opus 96

Published privately by the Lithographic Institute of Vienna, July 1828.
'Dedicated in deepest respect to Maria Karolina, Fürstin von Kinsky.'

1. *Die Sterne* (The Stars) Karl Gottfried von Leitner, D939 (January 1828)
2. *Jägers Liebeslied* (Huntsman's Love Song) Franz von Schober, D909 (February 1827)
3. *Wandrers Nachtlied II* (Wanderer's Night Song II) Johann Wolfgang von Goethe, D768 (by July 1824)
4. *Fischerweise* (Fisherman's Ditty) Franz Xaver von Schlechta, D881 (version b, March 1826)

Op. 96 is the second of two sets Schubert had printed privately by the Lithographic Institute in 1828, when it was under the management of his friend Franz von Schober. Schubert himself assigned the opus number, but it was not used until Diabelli issued the set the following year. The first of the two sets, although assigned Op. 106, was actually printed several months earlier. It was intended to be a personal gift for its dedicatee, Marie Pachler, his gracious hostess in Graz. Even though its topic would not have interested her, it was a gift of thanks to someone who had been particularly kind to him.

Charlotte (Maria Karolina) was the widow of Prince Ferdinand von Kinsky, one of Beethoven's patrons. Beethoven admired her singing voice, and dedicated his Six Songs Op. 75, Three Songs Op. 83 and setting of *An die Hoffnung* to her. She frequently held musical soirées for her aristocratic friends in her home, and Schubert was invited to take part in the performance of his songs on at least two occasions with the baritone Baron von Schönstein. Josef von Spaun reported that at one of them

> the enraptured audience surrounded Baron Schönstein with the most ardent appreciation (and with congratulations on his performance). But when no one showed any sign of vouchsafing so much as a look or a word to the composer sitting at the piano, the noble hostess Princess K. tried to make amends for this neglect and greeted Schubert with the highest encomiums, at the same time intimating that he might overlook the fact that the audience, having been absolutely carried away by the singer, paid homage only to him. Schubert replied that he thanked the Princess very much but she was not to bother herself in the least about him, he was quite used to not being noticed, indeed he was really very glad of it, as it caused him less embarrassment. (Mems, p. 135)

The set's four songs, as well as being about bachelors, are also night songs. The first bachelor, gazing at the stars, thinks that some day he might fall in love, the second has fallen in love but with the stars rather than a woman, the third is long past falling in love, the fourth utterly rejects the prospect. In selecting them Schubert's purpose must have been to tease his friend Moritz von Schwind, who in 1825 had fallen head over heels in love with Nettl Hönig, a devoutly religious young woman, who accused Schwind of 'want of religion' and to Schubert's amusement held him at arm's length throughout his courtship of her. He was encouraged to ask for her hand when, in January 1828 Josef von Spaun, at the age of 39, announced his engagement to Franziska von Roner. After hesitating for two months Schwind dressed himself in his best frock coat and sought the permission of her father, who reluctantly agreed to the betrothal but insisted that he could not actually marry his daughter until he had become responsible and successful. Schwind had agreed to meet Schubert and his friend Bauernfeld at a coffee house to celebrate his engagement, but he turned up in despair and with his frock coat torn. Schubert, according to Bauernfeld, 'could not stop tittering good-naturedly' (Doc. 1066). The set could therefore be construed as being his recommendation to stay single.

Texts

1. *Wie blitzen die Sterne so hell durch die Nacht.* Four quatrains.

   (1) How brightly the stars shine through the night. Often they have wakened me. But I do not reproach them for this, because in their stillness they provide much benevolence.

   (2) They wander high above like angels; they light the pilgrim's way through heath and wood; they hover like messengers of love, and often bear kisses across the sea.

   (3) They gaze tenderly into the sufferer's face, and stem his tears with their silvery light; and comfortingly, gently direct us with fingers of gold away from the grave to beyond the blue sky.

   (4) Blessings upon you radiant throng! Long may you shine on me with your clear pleasing light. And if one day I fall in love, then look kindly on the bond; let your twinkling be a blessing upon us.

2. *Ich schiess' den Hirsch im dunklen Forst.* Five eight-line stanzas.

   (1) I shoot the stag in the green forest, the roe in the silent valley, the eagle in its eyrie on the cliffs, the duck on the lake. When my gun

is aimed, no place can give protection. And yet hard as I am, I too have felt love.

(2) Often I have worked in bitter weather and in storms. On winter nights, covered in snow and frost, I have made my bed on stones. I can sleep on stones as on down, immune to the north wind. Yet my rough breast has known love's tender dream.

(3) The fierce hawk was my companion, the wolf my adversary in battle. My day began with the baying of hounds, my night ended in carousing. And yet love flowed in my wild huntsman's blood.

(4) O shepherd on the soft moss playing with flowers, who knows whether you feel the passion of love as hotly and strongly as I do? Every night the great brilliance hovers over the dark forest bathed in moonlight with a regal splendour no master could paint.

(5) When she looks down on me, when her gaze burns through me, I know how the wild animals feel when they flee from my gun. Yet that feeling is united with all the happiness on earth, as if my dearest friend were folding me in his arms.

3. *Über allen Gipfeln*. A single stanza of eight lines.

Over all the peaks there is peace; you can hardly feel a breath of air in the tree tops; the birds in the forest are silent. Only wait! Soon you too will be at peace.

4. *Den Fischer fechten Sorgen*. Six quatrains.

(1) The fisherman is not troubled by cares or sorrows. In the early morning he casts off his boat with a light heart.

(2) All about him, over forest, field and stream, there is peace. With his song, the fisherman bids the golden sun to awake.

(3) With a cheerful heart, he sings as he works. His work gives him strength, his strength exhilarates him.

(4) Soon a colourful throng is seen in the depths, splashing through the sky reflected in the water.

(5) He who casts a net needs good clear eyes, he must be as buoyant as the waves and as free as the tide.

(6) There, on the bridge, the shepherdess is fishing. Sly minx, leave off your tricks. You won't deceive this fish!

Music

Schubert reveals the teasing nature of the set in the last song, but the inclusion of *Wanderers Nachtlied II* places the set on a deeper level, for the horn calls near the end of the song represent a farewell, the wanderer's farewell to life. In the context of the set they could also be construed as being Schubert's farewell to two of his closest friends. When Spaun became engaged he gradually withdrew from the Schubert circle, and, after his marriage on 14 April, he devoted all his spare time to his wife. As a result Schubert saw him only rarely. Schwind was also lost to him, when, to comply with his future father-in-law's demands, he went to study in Munich. In fact, Ludwig Hönig never became his father-in-law because in October 1829 the engagement between Schwind and Nettl was broken off, 'ostensibly on account of her deep religiosity and his inability to tolerate her beliefs' (McKay, p. 308).

In the set, *Wanderers Nachtlied II* functions as the expressive slow movement. Unlike the other songs it is not in modified strophic form, nor does it have a persistent rhythmic figure running throughout its course. Indeed, as Schachter has pointed out, its rhythmic structure, particularly at the metric level, is irregular and 'highly unusual' (Schachter, pp. 89–92).

1. *Die Sterne*

Eb major. Rather fast 2/4.

The crotchet-quaver-quaver rhythm throughout the song derives from Leitner's metre (Wie blitzen die Sterne so hell durch die Nacht) and is used as the musical image for the dancing stars. The other regularities in the song, however, are occasionally broken. The modifications to the four strophes occur mainly in the settings of line 3 which Schubert casts in C major, Cb major, G major then C major again. The effect of these deviations is to throw emphasis on the return of the home key and the words of each stanza's last line, those in the final stanza being 'Let your twinkling be a blessing on us'. On each occasion Schubert repeats the words of the last line and in so doing breaks up the regularity of the phrasing. The other lines are written in five-bar phrases followed by a two-bar gap filled by the piano. The last line, however, is cast in two phrases (4 + 5) followed by a 15-bar gap. This means that there is also regularity in the way the strophes as a whole are organized. But this regularity is broken too. Between the third and fourth lines in the last stanza, Schubert bridges the gap by repeating and consequently drawing attention to 'seid hold dem Verein' (which in the context of the subject matter is best translated as 'look kindly on the bond').

Und wenn ich einst lie-be, seid hold___ dem Ver - ein,_____ seid hold___ dem Ver - ein,____

Since the song was written at the time when Spaun became engaged, it could be that Schubert was using it to send him his best wishes musically.

2. *Jägers Liebeslied*

D major. Moderately fast 6/8.

Now instead of merely gazing at the stars, the protagonist confesses to being in love with them. But here the persistent figure in the accompaniment derives from the rhythm associated with hunting horns. Schubert divides the eight lines of Schober's stanzas into four couplets so that they become the equivalent of the four-line units in *Die Sterne*. As in the previous song his purpose is to place emphasis on their last words – 'And yet though a hard man I have also felt love', etc. He does this in ways similar to those in *Die Sterne*. First, he divides the couplets off from each other. In this case a four-bar phrase is followed by a two-bar gap filled by the piano. He then repeats the words of the last couplet to make an eight-bar period (4 + 4). Secondly, he deviates from the home key in order to make the return to it for the last couplet strong. Thirdly, in the last strophe he breaks up the regularity established in the first four by hastening the return to D major and by cutting out the gap between the third and fourth couplets. As a result he places the greatest emphasis on the last four lines of the poem, in particular the words, 'As if my dearest friend held me in his arms'.

3. *Wandrers Nachtlied II*

Bb major. Slow 4/4.

Since the previous song deviated from D major to Bb major so frequently, the opening of *Wanderers Nachtlied II* sounds inevitable. The 14-bar song is through-composed. Here there is no talk of love, only the desire for peace. The 'horns' are introduced for the line 'Warte nur, balde' ('only wait, soon ...'), and could be interpreted as being not only a farewell (as in Beethoven's 'Les Adieux' Sonata) but also a summons from something in the distance (as near the end of the slow movement of Beethoven's Violin Concerto) (see over).

4. *Fischerweise*

D major. Rather fast 4/4.

Schubert arranges the six stanzas in pairs to make three strophes. As in
the second song, the modification occurs in the last strophe. Once again
he makes the essential point by breaking what he establishes as a norm.
In the first two strophes, the last appearance of the words of the second
and fourth stanzas are set as follows.

In the third strophe, to draw attention to the words 'schlauer Wicht' ('sly
minx') and to make them appear like an aside, the music for the sixth

stanza is altered. Fischer-Dieskau suggests that it sounds as if the fisherman was suppressing his laughter (DF-D, p. 239).

Those bars of quavers are repeated at pitch by the piano two bars later. Einstein described the way the piano and voice echoed one another as being 'a thematic teasing of each other'.[23] But these bars of quavers, passed from voice to piano or from the pianist's left to right hands, have been a feature of the song from the beginning. After a while it becomes clear that they represent a stylized version of 'good-natured tittering'.

---

[23]   Einstein, A. (1951), *Schubert*, trans. David Ascoli, London: Cassell, p. 304.

Opus 98

Published by Diabelli and Co., 10 July 1829.

1. *An die Nachtigall* (To the Nightingale) Matthias Claudius, D497 (November 1816)
2. *Wiegenlied* (Lullaby) Poet unknown, D498 (November 1816)
3. *Iphigenia*, Johann Mayrhofer, D573 (July 1817)

This is so unlike any of Schubert's other sets it is difficult to believe the composer was responsible for it. No other set ends rather than begins with the most dramatic and wide-ranging song. Diabelli brought it out eight months after Schubert's death on the same day as Op. 109, a set he himself compiled. This suggests Diabelli may have devised this one too. But whereas Diabelli tampered with the songs he included in Op. 109, a practice he was to continue in the 50 books of Schubert's songs he brought out between 1830 and 1850 (the *Nachlass*), he left these intact. In fact Schubert must have devised the set, for Diabelli would never have altered songs he had agreed to publish when the composer was alive, nor would Schubert have given the set an opus number before he died had it not been of his own devising.

The set has to be counted among those only his friends, people who were intimate with his ideas and preoccupations, would have comprehended. It has to be seen in relation to the two works Schubert entitled *Glaube, Hoffnung und Liebe* (Faith, Hope and Love), which he composed in August 1828. These are a short choral work (D954) to words by Friedrich Reil, and a song (D955) to words by Christoph Kuffner, which Diabelli published on 6 October 1828 as Op. 97. Both texts are based on the famous passage from the end of the thirteenth chapter of St Paul's First Letter to the Corinthians: 'In a word, there are three things that last for ever: faith, hope and love; but the greatest of them all is love.'

The choral work was commissioned for the dedication of a recast bell in the parish church of the Holy Trinity in Alsergrund, and composed to words specially written for the occasion. The song, however, could be construed as having personal significance for Schubert. It was during this period that the condition of cyclothymia (manic depression) from which he suffered was probably at its most severe. It therefore cannot have been a coincidence that the first stanza of the poem should be: 'Faith, hope, love!/If you remain true to these things/You will never be divided within yourself/And your skies will never be darkened.' These lines are repeated at the end of the poem in the order 3-2-4-1, and to emphasize them Schubert casts them in the solemn tempo they were in at the beginning of the song.

The Op. 98 set is perhaps even more personal. It takes into account the beginning of the fourteenth chapter of St Paul's letter which reads: 'Put love first ...' Whereas the protagonists in his previous Op. 96 set were men, here they are women. The first expresses love for her husband or lover, the second for her child, the third for her homeland. Faith and hope, however, are not so readily confirmed in the set. Iphigenia seems to lack the faith and the hope that she will see her homeland again. Schubert, in a lost notebook of 1824, had said: 'It is with faith that man first comes into the world, and it long precedes intelligence and knowledge; for in order to understand anything, one must first believe in something; that is the higher basis on which feeble understanding first erects the pillars of proof' (Doc. p. 337). Nevertheless Schubert knew only too well that faith is sometimes undermined and that black melancholy can take over just as it took Iphigenia over as she wandered about Tauris. Yet Iphigenia never lost her faith in Artemis just as Schubert never lost his faith in God. Her prayer to the goddess confirms that she still had hope.

Texts

1. *Er liegt und schläft an meinem Herzen*. A single sixain.

> He lies sleeping against my heart; my guardian angel sang him lullabies, and I can be merry and jest, enjoy every flower and leaf. Nightingale, ah, nightingale, do not wake my love with your singing ('Sing mir den Amor nicht wach!').

2. *Schlafe, holder, süsser Knabe*. Three quatrains.

   (1) Sleep, dear boy, your mother's hand rocks you softly, the sway of the cradle strap brings you gentle peace and comfort.
   (2) Sleep in the sweet grave protected by your mother's arms. All her hopes, all her longing she holds lovingly with loving warmth.
   (3) Sleep on her soft lap. Pure notes of love still hover around you. A lily, a rose will be your reward after sleep.

3. *Blüht denn hier, an Tauris Strande*. Three sixains.

   (1) Does no flower from my beloved homeland bloom here on the shore of Tauris? Does no breeze blow from the blessed fields where I played with my sisters? Ah, my life is but smoke!

(2) Sadly I wander through the grove with hesitant steps. I cherish no
     hope of ever seeing my homeland. My soft entreaties are
     drowned by the mighty waves crashing against the cold cliffs.
(3) Goddess who rescued me and imprisoned me in this wilderness,
     save me once more. Have mercy and let me join my own people.
     O goddess grant that I may appear in the hall of the great king.

Music

Although it is not included in the complete edition of Claudius's works,
Schubert and his contemporaries believed he was the author of *Wiegenlied* as well as *An die Nachtigall*. The two were among a group of eight
Claudius settings Schubert made in November 1816. They are thought
to be a pair on the grounds of their subject matter and their musical
relationship to each other. The quasi-improvisatory nature of *An die
Nachtigall*, with its off-key beginning and diversion into G minor, serves
as a kind of prelude to the stable harmony and regular phrasing of
Wiegenlied.

   Iphigenia, a song in progressive tonality, exists in three versions.[24] The
original begins in G♭ major, but Schubert also made versions beginning in
E♭ and F. He chose the one in F for this set. This matches the range of the
other two songs best, and also makes a better link with *Wiegenlied*.

   In the published version he made one or two alterations to Mayrhofer's
text, the most significant being the changes to the second line of the first
stanza. Instead of following *Blüht denn hier, an Tauris Strande* (literally
'Blooms then here on Tauris's shore') with *Keine Blum' aus Hellas Lande*
('No flower from Hellas's land'), he followed it with *Aus dem teuren
Vaterlande keine Blume* ('From the beloved fatherland no flower'). This
spoils Mayrhofer's rhyming pattern, but makes clear that Iphigenia is not
speaking of Greece in general but of her home in Mycenae in particular.
The fact that she is prevented from returning to her home stands in direct
contrast with the strong sense of being at home in *Wiegenlied*.

1. *An die Nachtigall*

G major. At a moderate pace 3/8.

The poem's six lines fall naturally into three couplets. Schubert's song is
through-composed. To create a sense of improvisation he draws on the

---

[24]   For some reason the catalogue in the second edition of *The New Grove Dictionary of
Music and Musicians* fails to note this.

tradition of starting off-key and 'preluding' until the right one is reached. Each of his three short sections starts off-key and moves into G major about halfway through. The first and second begin in C major, the sub-dominant, the third in G minor. This is when the woman asks the nightingale not to wake her lover, and the music smoothes out the lively dotted rhythm (presumably representing the nightingale) heard in the second section.

2. Wiegenlied

Ab major. Slow 4/4. Strophic.

One of the best known of all lullabies. The song has no introduction so that even though it lies a semitone higher than the previous song it creates the impression that *An die Nachtigall* has been its prelude.

3. Iphigenia

F major – C major. Not too slow 4/4.

The piano's short prelude picks up the melodic gestures prominent at the end of the previous song so that a sense of logical continuity is created. This song is a through-composed scena, operatic in nature. Since C major is the tonality's destination then, like *An die Nachtigall*, the song starts in its sub-dominant. Schubert sets the first two stanzas in the style of an accompanied recitative, vividly illustrating in his orchestral-like textures Iphigenia's hesitancy as she walks through the grove, and the sound of the waves crashing against the cliffs. The improvisatory quality of this music is followed, as was *An die Nachtigall*, by music that is mainly diatonic and regular in its phrasing. After the unstable nature of the first section it imparts a strong sense of certainty, nowhere more so than in the piano's postlude where horn-like fanfares are followed by emphatic perfect cadences.

Opus 105

Four songs to poems by Johann Gabriel Seidl. Published by Josef Czerny, 21 November 1828 (the day of Schubert's funeral).

1. *Widerspruch* (Contradiction), D865 (version b, ?1826)
2. *Wiegenlied* (Lullaby), D867 (?1826)
3. *Am Fenster* (At the Window), D878 (March 1826)
4. *Sehnsucht* (Longing), D879 (March 1826)

Schubert compiled this set in early August 1828 for on the 4th he wrote to Seidl asking him to return his settings of *Widerspruch* and *Wiegenlied* so that he could publish them.[25] It was probably Czerny who asked him to produce another set of Seidl songs even though Weigl was about to bring out the Four Refrain Songs, Op. 95. Czerny had just taken over the firm of Cappi and may have wanted to launch the firm on its new footing by publishing another light-hearted set with poems by one of the most popular Viennese authors of the day. But on this occasion Schubert was too preoccupied with major works such as the last three piano sonatas and possibly the string quintet to write something new. He therefore had to put a set together as best he could from material he had available.

As well as the Refrain Songs, Schubert had composed six songs and four part-songs to texts by Seidl, all dating from 1826. Three of the songs had been published as Op. 80. The other three, *Wiegenlied*, *Am Fenster* and *Sehnsucht* were too short to make a set by themselves. Schubert therefore made use of the first tenor line of one of the part-songs. Although *Widerspruch* makes a vigorous and arresting first song, it is inferior to the others in quality. But since the others deal with contradictions, it does fit in with them as far as the topic is concerned. It also links with the second song to create a pair to balance the third and fourth. Its last four lines, 'the sun threatens to crash down on me and the little chamber my heart longs for' suggests that death is on the speaker's mind. The mother also has death in mind in her last four lines. The other two songs reverse this procedure. In these the protagonists overcome gloom. In *Am Fenster* the man's gloomy appearance belies his inner joy; while in *Sehnsucht* the poet gives birth to a song even though he has just said that his inspiration and spontaneity have deserted him.

---

[25] Deutsch, O.E. (1964), *Schubert, Die Documente seines Lebens*, Kassel: Bärenreiter, pp. 529–30.

Texts

1. *Wenn ich durch Busch und Zweig* Three stanzas of four, eight and twelve lines respectively.

   (1) When I strike out on the narrow path, it becomes so open and free for me that my heart almost bursts with joy.
   (2) All around this forest house the walls recede, the leafy chamber seems to be a roof of dizzying height, nearly every leaf weaves itself into a wing for me so that my heart yearns for the open space of eternity.
   (3) Yet when I stand in an open space high in the mountains and gaze over the valley how restricted, how confined I feel in the close atmosphere. The clouds weigh heavily down on my head. The sunset threatens to crash down on me and the little chamber my heart longs for.

2. *Wie sich der Äuglein kindlicher Himmel.* Five quatrains.

   (1) How carelessly the child's heaven shuts itself off from the slumber-laden eyes. When one day the earth tempts you back, close them thus, for heaven lies within you, joy lies outside.
   (2) How your cheeks grow red with sleep! Roses from Eden have breathed on them; your cheeks are roses, your eyes heaven, bright morning, heavenly day.
   (3) How the golden curls of your hair cool the edge of your glowing temple! The golden hair is lovely, even lovelier the garland upon it; dream of the laurel until it blooms for you.
   (4) Dear little mouth, angels hover around you; inside is innocence, inside is love; guard them, my child, guard them faithfully; lips are roses, lips are warmth.
   (5) As an angel has folded your little hands, fold them thus one day when you go to your rest. After prayer dreams are beautiful, and the dream makes up for the awakening.

3. *Ihr lieben Mauren, hold und traut.* Six quatrains.

   (1) Dear friendly walls that keep me cool and safe, you gaze down with a silvery sheen when the full moon shines outside.
   (2) Once, with head sunk in hands, you saw me here so sad, looking only within myself, understood by no one.
   (3) But now a new light has dawned and sadness has fled. Now many keep me company on life's blessed path.

(4) Fortune can never rob me of them; I carry them deep in my soul where fate cannot penetrate.

(5) Walls, you imagine that I am as gloomy as I once was. That is my silent joy. Now when I see the moonlight my heart leaps.

(6) I seem to see at every window a lowered, friendly face that then gazes up to heaven thinking of me.

4. *Die Scheibe friert, der Wind ist rauh*. Five quatrains.

(1) The window pane freezes, the wind is raw, the night clear and blue. I sit in my little room gazing out at it.

(2) Something is missing. I know it all too well. It is my true love. My eyes constantly fill with tears when I look at the stars.

(3) My love, my fair star, so far away, where are you? You know I love and need you. Again tears well up within me.

(4) For many a day I have been tormented because none of my songs has turned out well, because none could be persuaded to blow as freely as the west wind.

(5) But now a gentle flow fills me – a song has appeared! Even though fate has separated me from my darling, I can still sing.

Music

Wiegenlied, *Am Fenster* and *Sehnsucht* are prime examples of Schubert's use of modified strophic form, and in the context of the set *Widerspruch* can be counted as another. Musically the topic of contradiction is reflected in the way sameness and change contrast with each other. Seen in this light the set conforms to Schubert's established method of structuring a four-song set. In both pairs the first song emphasizes sameness, the second change.

1. *Widerspruch*

D major. Rather swiftly 2/4.

Schubert repeats the first two stanzas at the end so that both words and music return to the beginning. This means that instead of ending the song with the poet's longing for 'a little chamber' (this is, a coffin), he returns to the heartiness of the opening. He makes no attempt to disguise the regularity of Seidl's dactylic metre; in fact the song repeats the same two-bar rhythm throughout its course, the alterations being minor and mostly confined to the piano's introduction, interludes and postlude. Change occurs in the central section, but is confined to melody and harmony.

Strictly speaking the song is not strophic but, since the central section is rhythmically so similar to the two outer sections, it sounds in effect like a modification of them.

2. *Wiegenlied*

Ab major. Slow 2/2.

Schubert divides each quatrain into couplets. The first has the soothing regular rhythm of the typical lullaby, and is more or less the same on repetition. The second seems to be more concerned with the mother's thoughts. Although the rocking motion continues in the accompaniment, the vocal line is longer, contains different rhythmic patterns and exists in two versions. They both go from F minor to Ab major, but the first is more chromatically inflected than the second and takes a slightly different route. The overall pattern is: A^1-B^1-A^1-B^2-A^1-B^2-A^1-B^1-A^2-B^2. The slight irregularity of the pattern creates a sense of unpredictability and places the emphasis on change.

3. *Am Fenster*

F major. Slow 2/4.

Schubert's modifications of the strophes create an ABA structure, and thus relate the song to *Widerspruch*.

A – first strophe in F major.
B – second strophe in F minor, third in Db major, fourth in A major, fifth in A minor.
A – sixth in F major (similar to the first).

The A sections reflect the poet's response to the 'dear, familiar walls', the moonlight and the friendly faces he sees at every window; the B sections refer to the gradual transformation of his past gloom to the inner joy he feels as life draws to a close.

The pattern of keys is the one Schubert sometime adopts to create a sense of closure in a song which has to go through several keys in order to reflect the text, but must come 'home' in the end. It simply involves descending enharmonically in major thirds: F-Db-A-F.

4. *Sehnsucht*

D minor – major. Not too fast 4/4.

Schubert divides each quatrain into couplets as he does in the second song, but in this case both are modified on their returns. The first and second strophes are in D minor, the third is in D major modulating to A minor, the fourth in D minor modulating to F major, the fifth remains in D major throughout its course. The song is underpinned by a restless *moto perpetuo* in the pianist's right hand, and opens, rather surprisingly, with a reference to Schubert's death motif, a descending chromatic scale in the bass. Appropriately, at the end of the song when the poet's compositional block has been lifted the bass line pounds out what can only be likened to a triumphant fanfare of timpani strokes.

Opus 106

Printed privately by the Lithographic Institute, Vienna in Spring 1828 without an opus number. Reissued by Diabelli in February 1829 as Op. 106. Dedicated to Marie Pachler.

1. *Heimliches Lieben* (Secret Love) Karoline Louise von Klenke, D922 (version b, September 1827)
2. *Das Weinen* (Tears) Karl Gottfried von Leitner, D926 (autumn 1827 – early 1828)
3. *Vor meiner Wiege* (Before my Cradle) Karl Gottfried von Leitner, D927 (autumn 1827 – early 1828)
4. *An Silvia* (To Sylvia) Shakespeare tr. Eduard von Bauenfeld, D891 (July 1826)

Schubert had this set printed privately by his friend Franz von Schober to thank his hostess Marie Pachler for her hospitality and encouragement when he stayed with her in Graz in September 1827. His original intention was to begin and end the set with the two songs he had composed in her house, *Heimliches Lieben* and *Eine altschottische Ballade* (D923), Herder's translation of the Scottish ballad *Edward* ('Why does your brand sae drop wi' blude'). Both poems had been recommended to him by his hostess, as had the poetry of Leitner, a local poet whose *Drang in die Ferne* he had composed in 1823, and later had published as his Op. 71. *Das Weinen* and *Vor meine Wiege* are two of ten Leitner settings he composed on his return to Vienna. According to Johann Jenger, who went with him to Graz, *Eine altschottische Ballade* was still included in the set when it was sent to the engravers in April 1828 (Doc. 770). At the last minute, however, Schubert substituted it with his setting of Shakespeare's *To Sylvia*. Doubtless he thought, in the circumstances, it was more appropriate to end the set with a song praising rather than cursing a woman.

The self-imposed limitation on his choice of the items meant that the set lacks an overall topic. Nevertheless, like his other four-song sets, they are arranged into two pairs of contrasting songs. The woman in *Heimliches Lieben* immerses herself in her lover, the poet of *Das Weinen* in tears; the son in *Vor meinen Wiege* looks on his mother with love, Edward looks on his mother with hate. He curses her for the 'counsels' she has given him, counsels leading him to murder his father.

Musically the first three songs are linked by a very simple figure which takes on the characteristics of a motif, the last two by the use of a characteristic harmony. Schubert had to sacrifice this connection when he replaced *Eine altschottische Ballade* with *An Silvia*. He wrote three versions of *Eine altschottische Ballade*. The one he composed in Graz is scored for solo voice. The one he prepared for publication came to light in Budapest in 1969 and is available in the *Neue Schubert Ausgabe*. It is longer than the original version and scored for two voices, but, since they never overlap, the song could well be performed by one singer as originally intended.

In a letter to Marie Pachler (Doc. 770), Jenger told her that she would receive copies of the set when Schubert and he returned to Graz in August 1828. But the visit did not take place, and Frau Pachler was never sent a copy. She had to buy one when Diabelli published the set the following year.

Texts

1. *O du, wenn deine Lippen mich berühren.* Five quatrains.

    (1) When your lips touch mine, desire threatens to bear my soul away; I feel a nameless trembling deep within my breast.
    (2) My eyes become enflamed, my cheeks burn, my heart beats with a strange longing, my thoughts, obscured by the stammering of my drunken lips, are scarcely controllable.
    (3) At such a moment, my life hangs on your sweet lips as tender as roses. Enfolded in your beloved arms I almost wish to die.
    (4) And yet though my soul glows within yours, I cannot escape from life. Lips ardent with longing must part.
    (5) Though my lips are pressed so closely to yours, my being cannot dissolve in kisses, and your heart can never dare to beat aloud for me.

2. *Gar tröstlich kommt geronnen.* Four eight-line stanzas.

    (1) The blessed fount of tears flows comfortingly like a healing spring, so bitter, hot and clear. Therefore, wounded heart, so full of grief and silent pain, if you want to recover quickly, immerse yourself in it.
    (2) These waters have a secret, magic power that is gentle balm for wounds, their power increasing with your suffering. They lift from your heart the stone of evil that is crushing you.
    (3) I have felt this myself in my own vale of sorrow when swathed in crepe I have stood by the graves of loved ones. In demented fury I railed against God. Only my tears kept my ship of hope afloat.

(4) And so when you too are ensnared in the darkest night of sorrow, trust the magic power of tears in your anguish. Soon, when your eyes have become red from bitter weeping, a new day will dawn. Already the morning is radiant.

3. *Das also, das ist der enge Schrein.* Five quatrains.

(1) So this is the narrow chest where I once lay as a baby; where I lay frail, helpless and dumb, moving my lips only to cry.

(2) With my tender little hands I could seize nothing, and yet I was tied up like a thief. I possessed small feet, yet lay as if lame until my mother took me to her breast.

(3) Then, as I suckled, I smiled at her, and she sang to me about roses and angels. She sang and with her singing she lulled me to sleep, and lovingly closed my eyes with a kiss.

(4) She spread a cool tent of shady green silk above me. When will I find such a peaceful chamber as that again? Perhaps when the green grass covers me.

(5) O mother, dear mother, stay with me a long time yet. Who else is there to comfort me with songs of angels? Who else is there to close my eyes with a loving kiss for the long, last deepest sleep?

4. *Was ist Silvia, saget an.* Three cinquains.

Who is Sylvia? what is she
That all our swains commend her?
Holy, fair and wise is she;
The heavens such grace did lend her
That she might admired be.

Is she kind as she is fair?
For beauty lives with kindness.
Love doth to her eyes repair,
To help him of his blindness,
And being helped, inhabits there.

Then to Sylvia let us sing,
That Sylvia is excelling:
She excels each mortal thing
Upon the dull earth dwelling:
To her let us garlands bring.

Music

1. *Heimliches Lieben*

Bb major. Moderate 4/4.

The words of the fifth stanza are repeated to produce a song in six sections (A^1-B-A^2-C^1-C^2-D), the texture being unified by a continuous flow of undulating triplets in the accompaniment. On the whole the woman's passion is suggested rather than revealed. The occasions when it comes to the surface are in the fourth and fifth sections (C^1-C^2), where Schubert bases the vocal line on a rising chromatic scale. The motif binding the first three songs occurs in the accompaniment before the voice enters for the first of these passages. It is simply a cadential formula heard over and over again in music, a three-note diatonic scale descending to the tonic, in this case D-C-Bb. Since it immediately becomes an upbeat figure in the vocal line and is then transposed and repeated in different contexts thereafter, it gradually assumes significance.

2. *Das Weinen*

D major. Rather slow 2/2.

A strophic song, simple and vaguely hymn-like in style. The three-note scale is expanded by the addition of an upbeat to make a threefold series of four-note scales, the first standing at the head of most of the phrases which follow. Schubert draws attention to its importance in the piano's introduction.

3. *Vor meiner Wiege*

B minor. Slow 2/2.

Schubert arranges the five stanzas to make a ternary form (A^1-A^2-B-C-A^3), the lyrical, flowing central section (B and C) being in B major. He opens the song with a piano introduction which develops still further the short falling scale. In fact the six-note scale starting on G in the second bar could well be heard as an overlapping continuation of the four-note scale (A-G-F♯-E) which introduced phrases in the previous song.

At the end of the song the key changes from minor to major, but in the penultimate bar Schubert reminds us of the poet's gloomy thoughts about death by stressing a six/four chord over the tonic in which the sixth is flattened. A similar chord stressed and sustained in the same way occurs at crucial moments in *Eine altschottische Ballade*. These are when both mother and son end their lines with the refrain 'O' which Schubert treats as a cry. It first occurs when the mother is completing her line 'And why so sad gang ye? O'.

Eine altschottische Ballade consists of seven stanzas which Schubert sets as a strophic song, so that although the subject matter is grim, the musical structure has the homogeneity a finale requires. However, as a song it lacks the calibre of *An Silvia*, and this is why Schubert's substitution will nearly always be preferred.

4. *An Silvia*

A major. Moderate 4/4.

The relationship between *An Silvia* and the other songs lies in the way it brings together contrasting attitudes. In the previous songs this was mainly confined to the words (closeness/parting – darkness/radiance – life/death), but here Schubert involves the music. He does this by making a strong contrast between the vocal line and the bass line. One is lyrical and features expressive appoggiaturas, the other is devoid of appoggiaturas and consists of a purposeful motion striding upwards in a marching rhythm with every note marked staccato. It may be the song of a man addressing other men about a woman, but his lyrical admiration of her does not preclude his awareness of being a man among men.

Opus 108

Published by M.J. Leidesdorf, 28 January 1829.

1. *Über Wildemann* (Above Wildemann) Ernst Schulze, D884 (March 1826) (Wildemann is a village in the Harz mountains)
2. *Todesmusik* (Death Music) Franz von Schober, D758 (September 1822)
3. *Die Erscheinung* (The Apparition) Ludwig Kosegarten, D229 (7 July 1815)

Although not published until January 1829, this set was advertised by Leidesdorf along with Op. 92 (three Goethe songs) and Op. 94 (the six *Moments Musicaux* for piano) at the 1828 Easter Fair of the Leipzig Book Mart (Doc. 1130). At that stage it was assigned Op. 93, the number later used for the two Schulze songs which Kienreich published in Graz on 30 May 1828. The set's similarity to Op. 92 which immediately preceded it suggests that Schubert may have devised them at more or less the same time, possibly just before the *Moments Musicaux* were completed early in 1828. Both begin in a spirit of intense restlessness, and end with the appearance of a ghostly figure offering the prospect of tranquillity. Whereas Op. 92 reflects the restlessness of spirit Goethe portrayed in *Faust*, this set opens with the tortured restlessness found so frequently in the poetry of Schulze. Schubert set ten poems from Schulze's *Poetisches Tagebuch* (Poetic Diary) in 1826, and his songs bear witness to his deep empathy for the poet. Susan Youens believes that Schubert seems to have understood the delusory erotomania chronicled in Schulze's poetry better than almost anyone else except the poet's friends, and he had the means to make it audible. 'I am not therefore implying', she stresses,

> that Schubert himself was similarly afflicted; great artists can and do re-create human situations not their own, or rather, not precisely their own. The man who told Leopold Kupelwieser in March 1824 that 'his most brilliant hopes' had perished, that the 'felicity of love and friendship' had nothing to offer but pain, who converted his death-haunted despair into artistry, had, I believe, something crucial in common with the poet he set to music so profoundly'. (Youens, p. 302)

Über Wildemann was probably the last Schulze song Schubert composed. In Youens's opinion the poem

is Schulze at his most violent, with its Byronic protagonist striding
from peak to peak in a frenzy. Here indeed was motion to inspire a
bleak, ferocious song, in which everything rushes and shrieks, Nature
and the protagonist alike. One suspects the place name was chosen
with more than geographical location in mind; it is indeed a 'wild
man' who sings in Wildemann. (Youens, p. 298)

One of the few things which brought Schulze a measure of tranquillity
was music. Schubert may not have read the two poems Schulze wrote
after hearing a performance of Bach's Chromatic Fantasia and Fugue,
Musikalische Phantasie and *Sebastian Bach's Apotheosis*, but he was
familiar with what the poet had to say about music in the poetic drama
Die bezauberte Rose. The first line of this was quoted when discussing
Schober's *An die Musik* in Op. 88. The whole text, in Kenneth S.
Whitton's translation, reads:

> O divine art of melodically sweet plaints, O song that is sung out of a
> dark soundless agony, O playful child, who strews scented flowers
> from happy days into our dark nights, without you I could not bear
> what my evil star presages for me! When word and meaning combine
> in song, then all my worries take wing. (DF-D, p. 84)

Schubert never set this text, but, even if he had, it would not have been
suitable as a transition between *Über Wildemann* and *Die Erscheinung*.
To make the transition from earthly anguish to heavenly bliss through the
medium of music, Schubert had to turn to Schober's *Todesmusik* even
though its poetry is hardly the equal of Schulze's – Youens calls it
'gushing claptrap' (Companion, p. 109).

Schulze's *Poetisches Tagebuch* is primarily concerned with the poet's
obsessive love for Adelheid Tychsen from 1813 until his death four years
later. Previously he had been obsessively in love with her sister Cäcilie,
who died in 1812. Susan Youens tells us that in the Poetic Diary's prefa-
tory poem, *Erklärung* (Elucidation), Schulze describes being visited by
the apparition of Cäcilie, who has descended from heaven 'to place the
poet's myrtle garland on his brow' (Youens, p. 257). As the contents of
this are too dense to make a suitable ending for the set, Schubert chose
Kosegarten's much simpler *Die Erscheinung* as an alternative.

Texts

1. *Die Winde sausen.* Five eight-line stanzas.

   (1) The wind whistles across the pine-slopes, the streams rush along
       the valley; for many a long mile I hasten through forest and snow,
       from peak to peak.

(2) And though life down in the open valley is astir to meet the sun's rays, I must pass on with a troubled mind, preferring to look towards winter.

(3) In the green fields and flowering meadows, I would suffer continuously, aware that from the very stones life springs, and that only one creature, alas, closes her heart to me.

(4) O, love, O love, O breath of May! You force the shoots from tree and bush, the birds to sing on the green tree-tops, the springs to gush forth at your touch.

(5) Yet you leave me alone to wander along the rough track in the roar of the wind beset by dark thoughts. O gleam of spring, O blossoms bright, shall I never again delight in you?

2. *In des Todes Feierstunde*. Schober divides the poem into three stanzas consisting of respectively twelve, eight and thirteen lines. Schubert ignores this stanzaic division. He structures his song on the poem's seven sentences. For convenience this is how the text is laid out here.

(1) In the solemn hour of death when I suffer the last battle and pass on, grant, sacred muse, that your tranquil songs, your pure tones, may shed their healing power one last time on the deep wound of parting in my heart.

(2) Release my anguished soul from earthly strife, and bear it aloft on your wings to be united with the light.

(3) Then harmonies will enfold me with sweet bliss, and I will cast off my chains with tranquil ease.

(4) I shall see all the greatness that gave me joy in life; all the beauty that once flowered for me will appear before me even more glorified.

(5) The music will bring to mind every star that shed its friendly light on me through my short journey through the darkness, every flower that adorned my way.

(6) And in those terrible moments when I might have bled to death in agony, I will be enveloped in joyous sounds and see all things bathed in glorious light.

(7) I shall go down under in bliss, sweetly engulfed by waves of joy.

3. *Ich lag auf grünen Matten*. Five eight-line stanzas.

(1) I lay in green meadows by the edge of the clear spring. The shade of alders cooled my burning cheeks. I thought of this and that, and dreamed with gentle melancholy of many of the good and lovely things which this world cannot give.

(2) When from the grove there arose a maiden as bright as the sun. A white veil was wound around her nut-brown hair. Her shining eyes were heavenly blue, and tears of sadness glistened like pearls of dew on her eyelashes.

(3) A mournful smile hovered around her sweet lips. She shuddered and trembled. I thought her tearful eyes and lovelorn gaze were seeking me out. Who could have been so happy as I, and so deluded?

(4) I stood up to embrace her, but alas she drew back. I saw her quickly pale and become more sorrowful. She looked at me fervently. With her hand she gestured solemnly and pensively towards heaven and vanished.

(5) Farewell, vision, farewell! I know you well and understand the meaning of your sign. Though we are parted now, we are united by a fairer bond. Love has its home up above, not here below.

Music

The contrast between the demonic drive in *Über Wildemann* and the simple, folk-like style of *Die Erscheinung* is extreme, but perhaps no more so than the contrasts found in many of Schubert's late works. Although Youens condemns Schober's *Todesmusik*, she acknowledges that nonetheless Schubert made something extremely fine out of it. Its vehemence relates to *Über Wildemann*, its lyricism to *Die Erscheinung*.

This is another set with a motif binding it into a whole. Although the songs were written at different times and were never intended to go together, they all make significant use of a five-note pattern, a rise from the tonic through the supertonic to the mediant and back again. The first two songs begin with a statement of this five-note motif. Thereafter the first song focuses on its first three notes, the second on the last two. The third song presents it intact and at its simplest.

1. *Über Wildemann*

D minor. Fast 4/4.

The form of the song is A^1-B^1-B^2-C-A^2. Schubert conveys the protagonist's restlessness by means of an undeviating galloping rhythm in the accompaniment, and his feelings of estrangement and emptiness by a texture consisting mostly of stark octaves. The motif (D-E-F-E-D) occurs prominently in the piano's introduction and the first two bars of the vocal line (see over).

Die Win - de sau - sen am Tan - nen-hang,   die Quel - len brau - sen das Tal ent - lang;

When the words speak of life rising in the open valley to meet the sun's rays in the first B section, and of the green fields and many coloured meadows in the second, Schubert takes the music into the major, so that the first three notes of the motif change from D-E-F to D-E-F♯. But as soon as the protagonist turns to darker thoughts it reverts to D-E-F.

Auf   grü - nen Hei - den, auf bun - ten Au'n, müsst ich mein Lei - den nur im - mer schaun,

Ultimately it is this minor version which is pounded out *fortissimo* in the piano's postlude. Here the melodic line moves up to A (D-E-F-G-A-E-D), but the basic motif (D-E-F-E-D) receives prominence by being played in unharmonized octaves.

2. *Todesmusik*

G major. Slow, solemnly 2/2.

Schubert originally wrote this song in G♭ major, a rare key he used, according to John Reed, to express 'a profound sense of peace and harmony' (SSC, p. 494). He transposed it to G major when preparing the set for publication. Although G major is an easier key for pianists, the strongest reason for the transposition is that it provides a smoother transition between the opening and closing items. D minor is G major's dominant minor, so the relationship between them is fairly close. The first four bars of *Todesmusik* contain a major version of the basic motif.

When the voice enters, the first three notes of the basic motif are used to generate a melody that will prove to be the most expressive in the song. Its most telling features are the appoggiaturas which terminate each phrase. Melodically they derive from the basic motif's last two notes.

In des To - des Fei - er - stun - de,   wenn ich einst— von hin - nen— schei - de,

As soon as that melody has run its course, Schubert brings back the first three notes of the basic motif in G minor so that it becomes G-A-B♭ rather than G-A-B. This provides the clue to how the song is structured. Schubert divides the song into seven sections each devoted to one of the poem's seven sentences: (1) a lyrical section in G major, (2) a rhetorical recitative-like section in E♭ major, (3) a new lyrical section in G♭ major (which Schubert writes as F♯ major), (4) a modulating recitative-like section similar in texture to the second, (5) a varied repeat of the first lyrical section in B♭ major, (6) a modulating section which continues the texture of the fifth, (7) a closing lyrical section in G major. It may be noted that all the sections between those in G major are in keys containing the note B♭ (G's flattened third): B♭ is E♭ major's fifth, G♭ major's third, and B♭ major's tonic. By giving so much emphasis to B♭, Schubert's strategy was surely to throw into the strongest possible relief, not only the note B when the key returns to G major, but also the first three notes of the basic motif in its major version (G-A-B) when they bring the song to a close.

Since *Die Erscheinung* opens with the voice singing B unaccompanied at the same pitch, it can follow without any need for a break.

3. *Die Erscheinung*

E major. Lovingly 2/2.

Apart from *An die untergehende Sonne*, all Schubert's Kosegarten settings are simple strophic songs. Within a few bars it becomes apparent that in *Die Erscheinung* the set's basic motif is now of prime importance.

Ultimately the rhythm is smoothed out so that the set ends with the motif reduced to its simplest possible form.

PART TWO

The Heine set

The Heine set

Six songs to poems by Heinrich Heine. Published by Tobias Haslinger in *Schwanengesang*, Easter 1829.

1. *Der Atlas* (The Atlas), D957, No. 8
2. *Ihr Bild* (Her Portrait), D957, No. 9
3. *Das Fischermädchen* (The Fisher Girl), D957, No. 10
4. *Die Stadt* (The Town), D957, No. 11
5. *Am Meer* (By the Sea), D957, No. 12
6. *Der Doppelgänger* (The Ghostly Double), D957, No. 13

The genesis of the poems

Heine was born in Düsseldorf in 1797, and was therefore the same age as Schubert. After attending schools organized on French models, he tried to become a businessman, first in Frankfurt am Main (1815), then in Hamburg (1816–19). From 1819 to 1825 he studied law at the universities of Bonn, Göttingen and Berlin. In 1830, unable to find suitable employment in Germany, he went to Paris, and remained there until his death in 1856. His contemporary, Théophile Gautier, said of him, 'Never was nature composed of more diverse elements than those of Henri Heine. He was at the same time gay and sad, skeptic and believer, tender and cruel, sentimentalist and jester, classic and romantic, German and French, sensitive and cynical, enthusiast and *sang-froid*; everything except boring' (Chusid, p. 23). To these contrasting elements S.S. Prawer added, 'a Jew among Germans, a "Hellene" among Jews, a rebel among the bourgeois and a conservative among the revolutionaries'.[1] The melodious sweetness and gentle irony of *Junge Leiden* (1817–21), his first collection of poems, reveal his indebtedness to Wilhelm Müller. In a letter to Müller he said that with the exception of Goethe there was no lyric poet he admired so much, and he thanked him for demonstrating how new wine could be put into the old bottles of folk-song forms.[2] These characteristics are even more in evidence in *Lyrisches Intermezzo* (1821–23), which Schumann drew on for *Dichterliebe*. Heine's model

---

[1] S.S. Prawer (1971), 'Heinrich Heine', in A. Thorlby (ed.), *The Penguin Companion to Literature*, vol. 2, Harmondsworth: Penguin Books, p. 358.

[2] Susan Youens (1992), *Schubert: Die schöne Müllerin*, Cambridge: Cambridge University Press, pp. 2 and 112.

was clearly *Die schöne Müllerin*, except that in his version the characters are unnamed and the narrative is much looser. It starts with the awakening of love, proceeds to the point when a successful rival appears and ends in despair. However, instead of drowning himself in the brook, Heine's lover places his love and pain in a huge coffin and has it thrown into the depths of the sea.

Parody, particularly self-parody, comes to the fore in *Die Heimkehr* (The Homecoming), 88 lyrical and five narrative poems written when he was staying with relatives in Hamburg and on holiday in the North Sea resort of Cuxhaven during 1823 and 1824. Unlike those in *Lyrisches Intermezzo* these were not conceived as a sequence. Order was imposed on them when they were published. Thirty of them, plus three he later rejected, came out in 1824 in one arrangement; the complete collection, issued in the first volume of his *Reisebilder* (Travel Pictures), appeared two years later in a different arrangement. In this the 88 lyrical poems are divided into three unequal sections: the first six poems establish the tone of the collection, the opening one saying he is writing them to stem his tears; the next eight present an outline (with interpolations) of an unhappy affair with a fisher girl in Cuxhaven; the rest look back at events in the affair and express his feelings of loss and despair at its outcome. In the last poem he tells us the flame of his love has gone out and that his anthology is the urn containing its ashes.

One or two of the poems seem to refer to Heine's love for his cousin, Amelia, and her rejection of him during his first period in Hamburg in 1817 (notably No. 6: *Als ich, auf der Reise zufällig*). His letters from the period show that he was absolutely distraught at her refusal of him. Later, during his second stay in Hamburg in 1823, he fell for her sister, Therese, who also rejected him. Since most romantic lyrics are about lost or unrequited love, his experiences had probably only an oblique bearing on the affair with the fisher girl (and she may have been a fiction).

The other three volumes of *Reisebilder* came out between 1827 and 1831. These contain mainly prose works of various kinds, including landscape descriptions and satirical comment on contemporary institutions and figures of prominence. But it was the *Buch der Lieder* (1827) which made Heine's reputation. This brought together all his early poems including those in the first volume of *Reisebilder*. Within a comparatively short time it was being read and discussed in literary circles throughout the German-speaking world. According to Prawer, even statesmen such as Metternich and Friedrich von Gentz, who were fundamentally opposed to everything Heine stood for politically, counted it among their favourite reading (Prawer, p. 9).

The genesis of the music

Schubert came across Heine's work in January 1828, when his friend Franz von Schober reinstated his reading parties. Franz von Hartmann, who recorded most of the day-to-day activities of the Schubert circle, noted in his diary for 12 January: 'To Schober's where the splendid *Story of the Marquise von O* by Kleist was read to the end, and a book of "Travel Notions" by Heine begun – some pleasant things. Much wit. False tendencies. What pleased me most so far were the youthful recollections of Düsseldorf' (Doc. 1000). The book was undoubtedly Heine's second volume of *Reisebilder*, which contains an amusing account of his origins, and unstinting praise for Napoleon, who led his army into Düsseldorf when Heine was a boy. Years later, at the end of his long life, the singer Baron von Schönstein remembered that Schubert had given him a copy of *Buch der Lieder* with the pages on which the six poems appeared ear-marked (Mems, pp. 332–34). This suggests that Schubert must have read through the whole of *Junge Leiden* and *Lyrisches Intermezzo*, containing some of the most settable lyrics in the German language, in order to find poems that interested him. In all likelihood his source was the first volume of *Reisebilder*, which opens with *Die Heimkehr*. In this he would have found the poems he selected almost at once.

No sketches for the songs are extant, nor is it known when Schubert composed them. In August 1828 he made a fair copy of them preceded by seven of the Rellstab songs he had composed that year. Two months later, on 2 October, he offered the Heine songs, the String Quintet and the last three Piano Sonatas to the Leipzig publisher, Heinrich Probst, saying that the songs had been well received in Vienna (Doc. 1152). They were probably given at a concert in the home of Dr Ignaz Menz on 27 September, when Baron von Schönstein sang and Schubert played piano sonatas as well as acting as accompanist. In his prompt reply Probst expressed no interest in the instrumental music, but asked to see the songs. By then Schubert was well known as a song writer, and the popularity of Heine must have been an added advantage. However, Schubert never sent them; presumably by that time he was too ill to do so.

Shortly after his death, his brother Ferdinand sold the fair copy of the Rellstab and Heine songs to the Viennese publisher Tobias Haslinger. Before receiving the manuscript Haslinger had planned to issue the Rellstab songs in two books and the Heine songs in another two. When the manuscript arrived he discovered that attached to the end of it in Schubert's own hand was the composer's last song, his setting of Seidl's *Die Taubenpost*. Haslinger therefore changed his mind. Having just completed the publication of *Winterreise* in two books, he decided to print the 14 songs in the manuscript under the title *Schwanengesang,* 'the last blossomings' of Schubert's noble art', also in two books. The first book contained the first six Rellstab songs, the second book the last of them, the Heine songs and the Seidl.

The Rellstab songs are settings of ten poems the poet had sent to Beethoven. Anton Schindler, Beethoven's amanuesis, found the poems in Beethoven's estate after his death, and said he handed them to Schubert in the summer of 1827 (Mems, p. 319), a report confirmed by Rellstab himself (Mems, p. 303). Schubert may have considered the poems as a legacy he had inherited from Beethoven, and that in setting them he was fulfilling what Beethoven would have done had he lived. The seven in *Schwanengesang* are placed in an order which ends as *Winterreise* begins, with a song of farewell. In Rellstab's *Abschied,* however, the rejected lover says farewell not only to the girl but to everything he has come to love in the town, as he sets out on his journey at night. Yet, although the sequence of events leading up to this proceeds fairly logically from one to the other, the group is much too loose to be counted as a song cycle or among the sets. It simple reflects Schubert's innate desire for good continuity.

The six poems Schubert chose to set in Heine's *Die Heimkehr* are numbers 8, 14, 16, 20, 23 and 24. As well as supplying them with titles, Schubert also changed their order. His sequence is 24 (*Der Atlas*), 23 (*Ihr Bild*), 8 (*Das Fischermädchen*), 16 (*Die Stadt*), 14 (*Am Meer*) and 20 (*Der Doppelgänger*). Only numbers 8 and 14 come from the section outlining the love affair: *Das Fischermädchen* refers to its beginning, *Am Meer* to its end. The others are concerned with the poet's feelings after the affair is over. By beginning with *Der Atlas* and *Ihr Bild* it could be said that, like Heine in the first six poems of *Die Heimkehr,* he is establishing that his theme is loss and despair; but by inserting between *Das Fischermädchen* and *Am Meer* the poem telling how he was rowed across the sea to gaze at the place where the affair ended (*Die Stadt*), the events are no longer in chronological order. Maurice Brown, Harry Goldschmidt and Richard Kramer advocated the restoration of Heine's order. According to Brown this would turn the songs into 'a miniature song cycle'.[3] Later Goldschmidt and Kramer supplied arguements to support this view.[4] However, their remarks make it clear they had no knowledge of Schubert's song sets, and were consequently unaware that the Heine set was a continuation of earlier procedures.

---

[3]   Brown, Maurice J.E. (1967), *Schubert's Songs,* London: BBC Publications, p. 61.

[4]   Goldschmidt, Harry (1974), 'Welches war die ursprüngliche Reihenfolge in Schuberts Heine Liedern', *Deutsches Jahrbuch der Musikwissenschaft für 1972,* pp. 52–62; Kramer, Richard (1985), 'Schubert's Heine', *Nineteenth-Century Music VIII,* pp. 213–25, reprinted with additions in R. Kramer (1994), *Distant Cycles: Schubert and the Conceiving of Song,* Chicago: Chicago University Press, pp. 125–47.

Heine's dual nature

The sets discussed in this present study bear witness to the fact that, even though their integrity was ignored by his contemporaries, Schubert was at pains to make them as meaningful as possible. It would have been totally out of character for him to publish anything lacking coherence. To suggest otherwise is to misjudge him entirely. His ordering of the poems makes sense only if it is seen as a character study of Heine himself. From his reading of *Die Heimkehr* and knowledge gained from the second volume of *Reisebilder* he would have discovered that Heine's personality was as complex as the characters of the Harper, Johann Senn and Mignon that he had dealt with in Opp. 12, 23 and 62. As in the Harper and Mignon sets, the poems are drawn from a literary narrative, but only hint at the story lying behind them. The interest lies in the person's capacity to suffer, and ultimately to find a measure of inner peace.

The key poem of *Die Heimkehr* and indeed the whole of *Buch der Lieder*, according to Prawer, is *Der Doppelgänger*. It is here that Heine's character is most succinctly revealed (Prawer, p. 2). The poem concerns an encounter with the ghostly representative of his other self and dramatically encapsulates the dual nature of his personality. Schubert would have been particularly drawn to the poem because, like Heine, he too was aware of having a dual nature. But whereas Heine's sprang from the dichotomy between his romantically inclined feelings and his mocking intellect, Schubert's arose from a form of manic depression which was probably exacerbated by syphilis. The depressive mood of the poet and the manic behaviour of the doppelgänger, 'aping' the poet's feelings, would therefore have been a situation he could empathize with.

As has been indicated, the ordering of the poems in *Die Heimkehr* was made after they were written. The poems covering the affair with the fisher girl and its immediate aftermath are dealt with very briefly. Interspersed between them are poems exposing and mocking the poet's doubts about himself, in particular his doubts about his ability to cope with the girl whose passion he has aroused. It is these doubts which may lead the reader to believe it was he who broke off the relationship, not the girl, and that his subsequent grief was occasioned by his sense of inadequacy as well as loss.

Significantly two of the poems between *Das Fischermädchen* and *Am Meer*, those describing the beginning and end of the affair, refer to mermaids. Heine tells us that mermaids are a threat to men in the second poem in the collection, his famous poem about the Lorelei, the mermaid who lures men to their deaths in the Rhine. In the poem after *Das Fischermädchen* he and the girl are in each other's arms on the beach. When he asks her why she is listening to the wind she replies that it is not the wind she hears but the mermaid's song, and that her drowned sisters are singing it. This is followed by a poem in which he imagines he is at sea on a small boat being tossed about by a howling gale, and that the shrieking of the seagulls on the mast seems to presage disaster. Two poems later the person on the beach with him has become a mermaid. She has emerged from the sea to tell him of her wild, passionate, all-consuming love for him.

Thereafter the image of the mermaid is dropped. After *Am Meer* the mockery of his inadequacy is made by other means. The poem which follows tells how he courted three girls living in a castle. On Saturday he kissed Jette, on Sunday Julia and on Monday Kunigunde. When he arrived on Tuesday their family was preparing for a feast but, when the female relatives discover he has brought nothing for it, they deride him.

Schubert's dual nature

Elizabeth Norman McKay believes Schubert suffered from cyclothymia, a mild form of polar disorder (manic-depression) in which 'periods of depression, hypomania (mild mania) and complete normality alternate, the latter lasting no more than two months at a time' (McKay, p. 138). She thinks he probably inherited it from his mother, and that it began to manifest itself when he was about 18 or 19. It was a condition several of his friends mentioned in their memoirs of him. 'Schubert had, so to speak, a double nature', said Eduard von Bauernfeld, 'the Viennese gaiety being interwoven with and ennobled by a trait of deep melancholy. Inwardly a poet and outwardly a kind of hedonist ...' (Mems, p. 45).

Hypomania has advantages for the creative artist, because its cognitive symptoms are enthusiasm, energy, self-confidence, speed of mental association, fluency of thoughts, euphoria, ability to concentrate, emotional intensity, a sense of well-being, rapid thinking, exapansiveness of ideas, decreased need for sleep, and increased sensory awareness. But it also involves behavioural changes: hypersexuality, talkativeness, carelessness with money, irritability and an increased need for alcohol.[5] In Schubert's case these symptoms were well documented. They were discussed by his friends as often as his moods of black melancholy.

Cyclothymia tends to get worse over the years, and as far as Schubert was concerned the condition was probably exacerbated by the onset of syphilis when he was 26. This disease also causes behavioural changes. The comments of Josef Kenner, a friend who had known him since they

---

[5] Jamison, Kay Redfield (1993), *Touched with Fire – Manic-Depressive Illness and the Artistic Temperament*, New York: Simon and Schuster, *passim.*

were schoolboys, almost certainly refer to the last few years of Schubert's life: 'Anyone who knew Schubert', he said, 'knows how he was made of two natures, foreign to each other ... one pressed heavenwards and the other wallowed in slime' (Mems, pp. 100 and 96). In saying this he was undoubtedly thinking of Schubert's heavy drinking, visits to brothels, foul temper and wretched behaviour during short periods in those years.

Schubert's dual nature had two distinct patterns. One was the alternation of depression and hypomania, the other the alternation of the cognitive and behavioural sides of hypomania. The cognitive symptoms were uppermost when his musical productivity was at its highest, the behavioural symptoms surfaced when, in Kenner's words, 'the craving for pleasure dragged his soul down to the slough of moral degradation' (Mems, p. 86).

It would have been strange had Schubert's music not reflected his mental condition; indeed the extreme contrasts he makes within the context of a single movement, especially in works composed in the last year of his life, are without parallel. Obvious examples are the middle movements of the C major String Quintet and the Andantino of the A major Piano Sonata (D959). However, in these Schubert controls the mood swings. His art compensated for what he could not control in life. This is undoubtedly why he took so much trouble with the Heine set, for the essence of *Der Doppelgänger*, the climax of the set, involves not only a harrowing vision of his other self, but an awareness that the figure represents himself as he was in the past. The recognition of this is cathartic, for at the end of the song the figure fades away and the music becomes calm. In other words, the pain that has been obsessing him has been purged.

To lead into *Der Doppelgänger* Schubert had to select poems which establish the following points: (1) the dual nature of the poet, (2) that the cause of his suffering was an unhappy love affair he himself may have terminated, (3) that he is subject to imaginary delusions, (4) that to make the denouement effective, emphasis should be given to the suffering he experiences in the present.

Texts

1. *Der Atlas*

Ich unglückseliger Atlas! eine Welt,
Die ganze Welt der Schmerzen, muss ich tragen.
Ich trage Unerträgliches, und brechen
Will mir das Herz im Leibe.

Du stolzes Herz! du hast es ja gewollt!
Du wolltest glücklich sein, unendlich glücklich
Oder unendlich elend, stolze Herz,
Und jetzo bist du elend.

(I, wretched Atlas, must bear a world, the whole world of sorrow. I bear
the unbearable, and my heart threatens to break in my body.
You, proud heart, have willed it so. You wanted to be happy, endlessly
happy, or endlessly wretched, proud heart. And now you are wretched.)

2. *Ihr Bild*

Ich stand in dunklen Träumen,
Und starrte ihr Bildnis an,
Und das geliebte Antlitz
Heimlich zu leben begann.

Um ihre Lippen zog sich
Ein Lächeln wunderbar,
Und wie von Wehmutstränen
Erglänzte ihr Augenpaar.

Auch meine Tränen flossen
Mir von den Wangen herab –
Und ach, ich kann es nicht glauben,
Dass ich dich verloren hab!

(I stood in dark dreams, gazing at her portrait, and mysteriously those
beloved features began to come alive.
Around her lips there played a wondrous smile, and her eyes glistened as
if filled with melancholy tears.
The tears flowed down my cheeks too. And ah, I cannot believe that I
have lost you.)

3. *Das Fischermädchen*

Du schönes Fischermädchen,
Treibe den Kahn ans Land;
Komm zu mir und setze dich nieder,
Wir kosen Hand in Hand.

Leg an mein Herz dein Köpfchen,
Und fürchte dich nicht zu sehr;
Vertraust du dich doch sorglos
Täglich dem wilden Meer.

Mein Herz gleich ganz dem Meere,
Hat Sturm und Ebb, und Flut,
Und manche schöne Perle
In seiner Tiefe ruht.

(Lovely fisher maiden, ply your boat to the shore; come and sit beside me,
and hand in hand we shall talk of love.
Lay your little head on my heart, and be not too afraid; every day you
trust the turbulent sea without fear.
My heart is like the sea, it storms, it ebbs and flows, and in its depths lies
many a lovely pearl.)

4. *Die Stadt*

Am fernen Horizonte
Erscheint, wie ein Nebelbild,
Die Stadt mit ihren Türmen
In Abenddämmrung gehüllt.

Ein feuchter Windzug kräuselt
Die graue Wasserbahn;
Mit traurigem Takte rudert
Der Schiffer in meinem Kahn.

Die Sonne hebt sich noch einmal
Leuchtend vom Boden empor,
Und zeigt mir jene Stelle,
Wo ich das Liebste verlor.

(On the distant horizon, like a misty vision veiled in the evening light, the
town with its turrets appears.
A damp wind ruffles the grey stretch of water; with mournful strokes the
boatman rows my boat.
The sun rises radiantly again from over the land, and shows me the place
where I lost my love.)

5. *Am Meer*

Das Meer erglänzte weit hinaus,
Im lezten Abendscheine;
Wir sassen am einsamen Fischerhaus,
Wir sassen stumm und alleine.

Der Nebel stieg, das Wasser schwoll,
Die Möwe flog hin und wieder;
Aus deinen Augen, liebevoll,
Fielen die Tränen nieder.

Ich sah sie fallen auf deine Hand,
Und bin aufs Knie gesunken;
Ich hab von deiner weissen Hand
Die Tränen fortgetrunken.

Seit jener Stunde verzehrt sich mein Leib,
Die Seele stirbt vor Sehnen; –
Mich hat das unglückselge Weib
Vergiftet mit ihren Tränen.

(The sea glittered far and wide in the dying rays of the sun; we sat by the
fisherman's lonely house silent and alone.
The mist rose, the water swelled, a seabird flew hither and thither. From
your eyes, full of love, tears fell.
I watched them fall on your hand and sank on my knee. From your white
hand I drank those tears away.
Since that hour my body has been consumed, my soul has died of
longing. That unhappy woman has poisoned me with her tears.)

6. *Der Doppelgänger*

Still ist die Nacht, es ruhen die Gassen,
In diesem Hause wohnte mein Schatz;
Sie hat schon längst die Stadt verlassen,
Doch steht noch das Haus auf demselben Platz.

Da steht auch ein Mench und starrt in die Höhe,
Und ringt die Hände, vor Schmerzensgewalt;
Mir graust es, wenn ich sein Anlitz sehe,
Der Mond zeigt mir meine eigne Gestalt.

Du Doppeltgänger [sic]! du bleicher Geselle!
Was äffst du nach mein Liebesleid,
Das mich gequält auf dieser Stelle,
So manche Nacht, in alter Zeit?

(Still is the night, the streets are at rest. In this house my dearest once
dwelt. She has long since left the town, but the house still stands in the
same place.
There too stands a man staring upwards and wringing his hands in
anguish; I shudder when I see his face, for the moonlight reveals it is
mine.
You ghostly double! You pale companion! Why do you ape the pain of
my love which tormented me in this very place on so many nights in the
old days?)

The overall musical structure

Schubert's first four songs, like those in his four-song sets, are divided into related pairs of opposites. By placing a light-hearted song third, Schubert may have had in mind his Op. 3 set (*Schäfers Klagelied, Meeres Stille, Heidenröslein, Jägers Abendlied*). When this was discussed in the Introduction and Part One it was suggested that its design was not unlike a four-movement instrumental work in that the first song is dramatic, the second reflective and the third the equivalent of a scherzo. However, to be suitable for a song set the finale had to be intimate rather than extrovert. In this Heine set, instead of having a single song for a finale Schubert has three.

Several reasons suggest that *Die Stadt, Am Meer* and *Der Doppelgänger* constitute a single musical unit. Schubert may mark the first *Mässig geschwind* 3/4, the second *Sehr langsam* 2/2 and the third *Sehr langsam* 3/4, but the pace of the crotchets in each song varies only slightly from one to the next. In effect all are slow movements, and all begin and end softly. In addition Schubert has composed them so that *Die Stadt* can run into *Am Meer*, and *Am Meer* into *Der Doppelgänger* without a break. Equally important is the way the dyad of D♯ (or E♭) and F♯ contained in the very distinctive and unusually handled chromatic discords that characterize the prelude and postlude of *Die Stadt* and *Am Meer* ultimately finds its resolution at the end of *Der Doppelgänger*. It is in this last song that the repetitiveness of the typical finale occurs. Edward T. Cone describes it as 'a passacaglia or chaconne that finally breaks out into a freely composed peroration' (Chusid, pp. 81–2).

All these facets contribute to the impression that we are listening not to the voices of different people, as the first three songs may suggest, but to the inner thoughts of a single person. This resembles the sequence of five poems beginning with *Die Stadt* and ending with *Der Doppelgänger* in *Die Heimkehr* (numbers 16 to 20). Poems 17 to 19 relate to the poet walking sombrely and introspectively through the streets of the town searching for the places associated with his beloved. However, the short, four-line poem preceding *Der Doppelgänger* has a sting in its tail as bitter and even more self-revealing as the one at the end of *Am Meer*: 'Ich trat in jene Hallen, / Wo sie mir Treue versprochen; / Wo einst ihre Tränen gefallen, / Sind Schlangen hervorgekrochen.' (I trod through those porticoes where you spoke to me of fidelity – where your tears once fell, serpents crawled out.). In other words, although Schubert substitutes *Am Meer* for poems 17 to 19, he retains the spirit of the texts he rejected.

As in all his sets other than Op. 12, each song is in a different key – G minor, B♭ minor, A♭ major, C minor, C major, B minor. These were undoubtedly selected because of the associations they had for the composer. G minor (*Der Atlas*) is the key of Mozart's restless and highly charged Symphony No. 40, which he so much admired. It is also the key he chose for *Amphiaraos*, *An Mignon* and *Erlkönig*, songs about battling against fate. B♭ minor (*Ihr Bild*), the key he used for *Gretchens Bitte*, *Im Walde* and *Luisens Antwort*, appears to be specifically associated with tears. A♭ major (*Das Fischermädchen*) he associated with situations which were likely to have a happy outcome, especially those involving love. Typical are his setting of three of Klopstock's 'Cidli' songs: *An Sie*, *Furcht der Geliebten* and *Das Rosenband*. C minor (*Die Stadt*) he associated with deep melancholy such as in *Wonne der Wehmut*; C major (*Am Meer*) with stillness, particularly, as *Meeres Stille* bears witness, the ominous stillness of the sea. With Mozart's 'Dissonance' Quartet as his example, he also employed C major when he wanted to alternate between mysterious, chromatic music and simple, 'open', diatonic music, a prime example being *Dass sie hier gewesen*. B minor (*Der Doppelgänger*) was Beethoven's 'black' key which Schubert selected for 'physical and mental suffering, loneliness, alienation, derangement' (SSC, p. 492). By moving into B major at the end of this last song, he goes into the key he almost invariably used for the transcendence of suffering.

Yet although each song inhabits its own tonal world, they are nevertheless co-ordinated, for they all give special attention to F♯ or its enharmonic equivalent G♭. Essentially this pitch functions as a pivot, a note around which its neighbour notes turn. When unstable in G minor, C minor and C major, it finds resolution by moving up to G; when unstable in B♭ minor and A♭ major, it moves down to F. It becomes stable only in *Der Doppelgänger* where F♯ is the dominant of the B minor/major tonality. Here it is present as an inner pedal in all but six of the song's 63 bars. The six bars are those when it moves either up to G or down to E♯, the enharmonic equivalent of F.

Schubert had explored this highly innovative technique in Opp. 6 and 58, but in this Heine set his pivot creates a dynamic. It may not be as strong as the 'pull' of a tonic, yet by emphasizing the instability of F♯/G♭ in the first five songs he creates a sense of expectation, the expectation that ultimately its stability will be achieved. When the final song arrives and F♯ becomes the dominant of the B minor/major tonality, it may be subservient to the tonic in terms of its melodic function, but as a member of the tonic triad it shares the tonic's stability and so the expectation is fulfilled.

In B minor both G and E♯ pivot around F♯ and produce the double neighbour-note figure.

Dominant   F♯-G-F♯-E♯-F♯
Tonic   B----------------

The pattern over the course of the six songs is as follows:

Oscillation	F♯-G	F♯-E♯	F♯-E♯	F♯-G	F♯-G	F♯-G-F♯-E♯-F♯-G-F♯
Enharmonic change		G♭-F	G♭-F			
Tonic	G----	B♭---	A♭----	C----	C----	B--------------------B
Song number	1	2	3	4	5	6

The first three songs are ternary in design. *Der Atlas* modulates to B major for its central section, *Ihr Bild* to G♭ major, *Das Fischermädchen* to C♭ major. By this means Schubert hints at the ultimate destination of his harmonic progression, for C♭ major is the enharmonic equivalent of B major, and G♭ major the enharmonic equivalent of F♯ major, B major's dominant. By stabilizing F♯ or G♭ in the central sections he reinforces the pitch's instability in the outer sections. The nature of the instability depends on F♯'s position in the scales of the different keys. The differences in its position enable Schubert to encapsulate the essential character of each song.

The relationship of the degrees of the scale to the tonic triad can be summarized as follows. The major seventh, the major and minor seconds are pulled into the tonic, the minor third and fourth into the major third, the sharp fourth, major and minor sixths, and minor seventh into the dominant. To get to the dominant the minor seventh has to go through one of the sixths. Sharps added to the notes of the diatonic scale pull the note up a step, flats down a step. The note exercising the greatest pull of all is the tonic, the most important pitch in the hierarchy and the goal to which all the others are drawn. Tensions which resolve on the dominant are therefore in a context of flux, while those resolving on the tonic are in a context of finality.

In *Der Atlas* Schubert exposes the double neighbour-note figure at the end of the song. But in this instance it oscillates round the tonic rather than the dominant: G-A♭-G-F♯-G. He therefore places it in a context of finality. By this means he can indicate that the Titan feels his pain to be irredeemable, and can emphasize that it is being experienced in the present. He holds back A♭ for the climax of the song when he has the Atlas sing 'Schmerzen' (pain) at the top of his voice. Until then he stresses F♯ which as the key's leading note expresses a high degree of upward-thrusting tension when accented. The tremolo conveys the Titan's intense agitation, and in the context of the song the augmented triad (the second inversion of B♭-D-F♯) his raw energy (see next page, *Etwas geschwind*). According to Schoenberg, the augmented triad came into use in German music with Wagner, notably with the Valkyries' Cry.[6] Schubert's use of it

---

[6] Schoenberg, Arnold (1911), *Harmonielehre*, Vienna: Universal Edition, English translation (1978) by Carter, Roy E., London: Faber and Faber, p. 390.

26 years earlier is evidence that as well as being influenced by the vocal style of *Der Atlas* Wagner also found in the song the harmony to characterize his redoubtable war-maidens.

In B♭ minor, the key of *Ihr Bild*, G♭ lies on the minor sixth degree of the scale. Tension on this is traditionally associated with anguish or grief of a less hopeless kind than that on the minor second at the climax of *Der Atlas*. The passage in which it first occurs is unharmonized, a feature, according to Martin Chusid, usually associated with loneliness or isolation (Chusid, p. 129). The A-B♭ (major seventh to tonic) for the word 'Träumen' is a reference to the previous song, but the goal of the music is G♭ resolving on to F.

In the song's central section G♭ is stabilized as a tonic and F becomes its leading note. But at the end of the song the relationship of G♭ and F takes on a different and totally unexpected meaning. Instead of drawing attention to G♭, he hammers out F as if to stress its greater importance. In the context of a song where the dynamics rarely rise above *pianissimo* and the texture has never been as full as in the closing passage, the volte-face is surprising because there is nothing in Heine's text to supply a reason for it. It would appear that Schubert wanted to bring back the vehement quality of the first song and to secure an even stronger relationship between them.

In the next song, *Das Fischermädchen*, transformations of this ending appear in bars 13–15 and 17–19. They result in a phrase used to

encapsulate the lover's winning charm. Since the minor seventh resolves
on to the dominant via the sixth degree of the scale, Gb will be less effective as an appoggiatura than F in the context of Ab major. The appoggiatura on F in bar 22 resolves by falling in the vocal line and rising in the
accompaniment. As a major sixth it has none of the sorrowful associations of the minor sixth, and by handling its resolution in this manner
Schubert has it represent caressing – 'Wir kosen Hand in Hand'. For his
part, Fischer-Dieskau thinks that the lilting way the singer leaps to Gb is
also 'a caressing gesture' (DF-D, p. 281).

The diminished seventh chord harmonizing the Gb in that passage (A-C-
Eb-Gb), will be transposed down a minor third (F♯-A-C-Eb) and when this
is rearranged it will become the chord representing the mournful strokes
of the boat man in *Die Stadt* (C-Eb-F♯-A). It will be further transformed
for the ominous chord opening and closing *Am Meer* (C-D♯-F♯-Ab). These
are the only incidences when F♯ occurs in *Die Stadt* and *Am Meer*. Schubert's
ploy is evidently to reduce its appearances so that when it becomes the inner
pedal in *Der Doppelgänger* its significance will be the greater. Nevertheless,
although limited in its presence, F♯ is still an essential note in the gesture
defining the inner core of *Die Stadt* and *Am Meer*. In *Die Stadt* the rapid
up-and-down arpeggiation of the diminished seventh conveys not only the
plying of the oars and psychological disturbance, but also, according to
Prawer, 'a mood of utter desolation' (Prawer, p. 28). The F♯ and A in it lead
into the hushed entry of the voice speaking of the town as a misty vision
on the distant horizon. Here Schubert leans heavily on Ab, the minor sixth.
He reserves the sense of hopelessness for when the material comes back in
the third section of the song and he places even greater weight on the flattened
supertonic, Db. As at the end of *Der Atlas* he has the double neighbour-
note figure turning about the tonic (C-Db-C-B-C) so that once again the
context is one of finality; once again the protagonist considers his pain to
be irredeemable.

At the end of *Die Stadt*, the diminished seventh remains unresolved. It
finds its resolution in the opening chords of *Am Meer* where A is lowered
to Ab and Eb changes to D♯ (see over).

In *Die Stadt* the F♯'s resolution up to G was not overt. Here it is, but what is less prominent is the presence of A♭ resolving down to G in the pianist's left hand. Although condensed, it brings back memories of the double neighbour-note figure in *Der Atlas* (G-A♭-G-F♯-G) except that G is now the dominant not the tonic. Another reason for the return of A♭-G becomes clear at the end of *Am Meer*.

Although A♭-G may not be in a prominent position in those closing bars, when *Der Doppelgänger* opens it will be heard that its first four bars come directly out of them. The short theme, B-A♯-D-C♯, derives from A♭-G raised an augmented second (the equivalent of a minor third) and then another minor third (see next page, *Sehr langsam*).

It may have been a coincidence or was Schubert perhaps deliberately drawing on the theme he used in his E♭ Mass for the words 'Lamb of God, who takest away the sins of the world …' when he selected this to represent the ominous presence of his doppelgänger. The Mass is dated June 1828, that is to say, two months before the date on the manuscript containing the Rellstab and Heine songs. This, of course, is no proof that he composed the Agnus Dei before the songs; the dates may simply refer to when he wrote out the fair copies. However, it is possible he felt the poem had personal connotations and that the meeting with his doppelgänger would be an encounter with himself as he was in those times when, according to Josef Kenner, his soul was dragged down 'to the slough of moral degradation'. If this were so, then he would certainly have wanted forgiveness for his sins and to end the song in a manner reflecting the words 'give us peace'.

In *Der Doppelgänger* the theme is presented in double octaves with an octave F♯ lying between them. The first time F♯ moves up to G occurs after 40 bars when the watcher sees he is looking at himself.

Nine bars later comes an even greater climax. The pitch rises stepwise from B minor to D♯ minor, and swings between this chord to its dominant, A♯ major. It then takes the oscillating F♯ and E♯ within these chords and combines them with a move from G to F♯ in the bass so that the features which have taken it in turns to be present in all the songs at last come together (see next page, bar 47ff).

The melisma on the first syllable of 'alter', and the rapid switch from triple *forte* to *pianissimo* over four bars heralds a complete change of mood. The opening of the song is recapitulated, but C natural is substituted for C♯, the harmony slips into B major and trepidation is replaced by quietude (see over).

was äffst du nach mein Lie-bes-leid, das mich ge-quält auf die-ser Stel - le

so man - che Nacht, in al - - - ter Zeit?

Edward T. Cone has drawn attention to another way of looking at the metamorphosis of the phrase at the beginning of *Der Atlas* to the one that dominates *Der Doppelgänger*.[7] The clearest way to elucidate it is to refer to the degrees of the scale. The opening phrase in *Der Atlas* uses 1-3-7-1, the opening one in *Ihr Bild* amplifies this, 1-3-(2 1)-7-1. The passage in *Das Fischermädchen* Cone refers to is also in the key of Bb minor, 1-3-(2)-7-1-(5).

Der Atlas

Ihr Bild

Das Fischermädchen

The other three songs make use of the inversion of the pattern, that is, 1-7-3-1. The first example is taken from opening phrases of *Die Stadt*, (1-2-)-1-7-(1)-3-(2)-1. The opening phrase of *Am Meer*, however, reverts to the original, 1-3-(2 1-)-7-(2)-1.

---

7   Cone, Edward T. (1974), *The Composer's Voice*, Berkeley, CA: University of California Press, p. 40.

Die Stadt

Am Meer

Later when the key modulates to D minor both the original and the inversion are present, 1-(2)-7-3-(2)-1-7-1. Confirmation (enhancement) of the inversion is achieved in *Der Doppelgänger*, 1-7-3-(2)-1.

Am Meer

Der Doppelgänger

One of the most outstanding features of the set is the role of the piano. In no other set and in neither of the cycles does Schubert use it so im-aginatively. In essence it becomes the equivalent of the narrator in a nineteenth-century novel, as the orchestra was to become in Wagner's Ring Cycle. It not only establishes the character of the song, accompanies the singer and sets the scene, it also moves in and out of the protagonist's mind, relating his inner world to the outer world, and drawing parallels between one situation and another.

The individual songs

1. *Der Atlas*

G minor. Fairly fast 3/4.

Although Schubert entitled the song The Atlas rather than Atlas to show that the poet was assuming the role of the mythological figure, he wrote it as if it were the actual voice of the gigantic Titan raging against his punishment and himself. To emphasize this he repeats the first stanza after the second, less vehement one to make an ABA structure, so that the song ends with the cry, 'Die ganze Welt der Schmerzen muss ich tragen' ('I must carry the whole world of sorrows'). In the first part Schubert repeats this line, but omits the words 'Die Schmerzen' on the repetition. Jack Stein is severely critical of both this and of Schubert's approach to the poem as a whole. 'Heine's preposterous image of himself as Atlas', he says,

> has been taken seriously by Schubert, as though the figure were another Prometheus. In fact, the Atlas image is a highly personal, self-ironizing hyperbole, not a grandiose generalization such as Schubert makes of it. Heine's Atlas is bearing his own world of pain on his shoulders, so that the pathos in the poem is narcissistic. That Schubert misses the point is clear not only in the mood of the musical setting, but also in his repetition of the second line. Because the musical idiom requires expansion, both of the first two lines are repeated. In the repetition, though, Schubert omits the words 'die Schmerzen', and the line is sung 'Die ganze Welt muss ich tragen'. In the context of the poem this is absurd .... (Stein, pp. 81–2)

In the last part of the song Schubert brings the whole line back again. Stein believes that in making 'Schmerzen' the climax of the song the pathos becomes 'almost maudlin'.

Stein treats the poem and the song as being separate from their contexts. He fails to mention that *Der Atlas* is one of several poems in that part of *Die Heimkehr* dealing with the affair with the fisher girl in which the poet blames himself for the breakdown in their relationship. He never explicity says so, never directly exposes this fact; in most of them, as we have seen, he hides behind a mask of parody. But in this case he uses Atlas as his mask. Heine's purpose in selecting Atlas could only have been because Atlas's suffering was his own responsiblity. It was he who decided to wage war against the gods.

Another reason for the seriousness of Schubert's tone is that, even if he had been able to express 'self-ironizing hyperbole', it would have been totally inappropriate for the dramatic structure of the set. *Der Atlas* can be and frequently is performed by itself, but it is also part of the larger design. It has to convey the behaviour of someone 'acting' under extreme emotional pressure. In so doing it prepares the ground for the encounter with the doppelgänger who is also 'acting' under extreme emotional pressure. It is no coincidence that the vocal styles of *Der Atlas* and *Der Doppelgänger* are so similar. Everyone who writes about Schubert's songs singles these out as looking forward to the declamatory vocal writing of the future. According to Dietrich Fischer-Dieskau they 'held enormous importance for the development of dramatic singing, particularly so far as Wagner is concerned' (DF-D, p. 281).

Wagner never confessed any debt to Schubert. He maintained his mentor was Beethoven. It so happened that as far as this song is concerned Schubert also looked to Beethoven for inspiration, for it was

Beethoven's last piano sonata that Schubert must have had in his mind when writing the vocal line of *Der Atlas*.[8]

The corrections in Schubert's manuscript indicate that the Ds in bars 4–7 were originally Gs, so that, as Martin Chusid has pointed out, the first two phrases resembled 'more closely Beethoven's head motive' (Chusid, p. 127).

Schubert's vocal line is directed towards the B♭s in bars 12 and 14, the first syllable of 'tragen', the sentence's verb. B♭ is the pitch that more than any other defines the key's minor mode. When Schubert modulates to B major for the central section of the song, his purpose is not only to stabilize F♯, but to raise B♭ to B so that when the first section returns the minor mode will be enhanced.

Throughout the song, the piano, in its role of narrator, illustrates the character of the would-be Titan by means of gestures representing his physical appearance and mannerisms. In the outer sections the thundering octaves, agitated tremolos, and dotted rhythm in conjuction with the appoggiaturas and augmented harmony vividly convey his gigantic frame and towering rage; in the central section, when he turns to the aspirations he had in the past, the strutting rhythm, softer dynamics and discords capture his pride, his willingness to challenge fate. But we look at him from the outside. It is as if the piano were simply presenting us with the necessary background for his performance.

---

[8]   The relationship was first pointed out by Hugo Riemann in (1917) *Ludwig van Beethovens sämtliche Klaviersonaten, ästhetische und formaltechnische Analyse mit historischer Notizen*, Berlin: Max Hesse (3rd edn), vol. 3, p. 453.

2. *Ihr Bild*

B♭ minor. Slow 2/2.

Although there is nothing in the poetry to suggest that the poetic voices in *Der Atlas* and *Ihr Bild* are those of the same person, Schubert's music suggests that they are. By transposing the two pounding crotchet Gs lying in the bass in the penultimate bar of *Der Atlas* up a minor tenth, slowing them down, separating them and having them played *pianissimo*, Schubert may lead the listener to believe that the vehemence of the Titan figure has been suddenly transformed. As yet there is no reason to believe the key is anything other than G minor. Perhaps the man has unexpectedly caught sight of something that grips his attention. The distinguished Austrian analyst, Heinrich Schenker, in his discussion of the song, was somewhat bemused by these opening B♭s. He maintained that from a structural point of view they could have been dispensed with. However, like so many commentators he was looking at the song as a separate entity and not as part of a set. To explain their presence he had to abandon his strictly formal approach to analysis, and find a poetic reason.

> No one could possibly think of this as a motif; so the question arises, what is the function of these two notes? Are they to establish the tonality, or to give the singer his first note, or both? Whatever the answer, there is still the question why the master sounded the same note twice, when it would have been possible to have held the note over two bars. In fact the answer to this last question provides the solution to the puzzle as a whole. To repeat the same note in a slow tempo and furthermore to repeat it after a rest is not unlike the process of staring at something, and in doing this we feel ourselves miraculously transported to the side of the unhappy lover who stands 'in dark dreams' staring at the portrait of his beloved. We stare at the portrait with him. A simple procedure, is it not, this separation of a single note held over two bars? Yet it takes a genius – it is only given to a genius – to grasp its effectiveness, for it has arisen from his ability to project himself deep into the spiritual experience. With one stroke, Schubert has proved himself to be a magician capable of binding together in a single gesture the external circumstances (in this case the staring at the portrait), the soul of the unhappy lover and ourselves, a gesture containing prospects which will go beyond its initial manifestation.[9]

As far as the unhappy lover is concerned, the whole song concerns the reverberations the portrait produces in his mind. Schubert sets each line

---

[9]   Schenker, Heinrich (1921), 'Franz Schubert "Ihr Bild" ', *Tonwille 1*, Vienna: Universal Edition, pp. 46–9.

as a two-bar phrase combining two of them to make a four-bar period. Since the poem has three quatrains, the vocal line consists of six periods of equal length. The first – the one presented in bare octaves and containing the first reference to Gb-F – establishes the model. In the fourth period, when the lover imagines that the eyes in the portrait are glistening 'as though with melancholy tears', the key has changed to Gb major and the harmony is full and warm, especially in the penultimate bar where Gb becomes a suspension noticeable because it is not sustained over the bar line.

und wie von Weh - muts - trä - nen er - glänz - te ihr Au - gen - paar.

After each four-bar period, the piano echoes (but never exactly) its last two bars. Here, however, it echoes only the vocal line's last two notes (Db-Bb). It does so three times. The purpose is clearly to reflect the protagonist's switch from thinking about the girl's tears to thinking about his own. The two Bbs are a recapitulation of those that opened the song, but now they are harmonized so that the Gb-F in the pianist's left hand are empty fifths.

These empty fifths prepare for the return of the bleak octaves when the lover says, 'My tears, too, flowed down my cheeks'. This suggest that he now sees himself in the portrait, that it has, in a sense, become a mirror. Was it for this reason that Schubert cast the form and bar structure of the song as a mirror image? The only deviation from the pattern of four-bar period plus two-bar echo comes after the third period when the echo takes place in one bar. This bar is therefore the axis of the periodic structure's reflective symmetry.

A	B	A
2-4-2-4-2	4-1-4	2-4-2-4-2
Bbm	Gb	Bbm

Another strange feature of the song is that Schubert uses virtually the same music for the sixth period ('And ah, I cannot believe that I have lost you') as he does for the second ('And that beloved face began mysteriously to come alive'). For each he goes into Bb major, but whereas he remains in this key after the second period for the piano's echo, after the sixth period he transposes what was originally in the major into the minor. This ending to the song was quoted earlier on page 256 when the changed relationship of Gb to F was discussed. One can only assume that on this occasion the piano as narrator is drawing a parallel with the mood of *Der Atlas*.

In his analysis of the basic line of this song (the Urlinie), Schenker made no mention of this strange ending, nor did he pay much attention to the significance of Gb. It is tempting to wonder how his graph would have looked if he had treated the song as an entity in a much larger work.

3. Das Fischermädchen

Ab major. Rather fast 6/8.

Ihr Bild ends with the notes Bb-Eb-F-Gb-F in the piano's upper line, the most prominent being Eb and F falling on the strong metric beats. And it is with Eb and F that Schubert begins *Das Fischermädchen*. They too are in the piano's upper line and are on strong metric beats. He turns to the other notes of this five-note figure in bars 13–14 when he introduces the key's supertonic (Bb minor) and has the first of the three appearances of Gb-F, the last being when he uses them for the caressing gesture which characterizes the song.

The song is the first in the sequence of three with the sea as their back-cloth. This one adopts the persistent trochaic rhythm of the barcarolle throughout its course. In that a barcarolle is supposed to evoke the rocking motion of a gondola on the canals of Venice, the use of the genre for a poem describing events in a fishing town on the North Sea coast is somewhat ironic. Fischer-Dieskau also sees irony in the 'nonchalant slurs' at the end of each stanza, the transposition of the second stanza into Cb major and the word repetitions. These, he thinks, lend 'a touch of impertinence to the setting' (DF-D, pp. 280–81).

The regular trochaic metre and equally regular phrase lengths of the typical barcarolle can easily become boring, but as Martin Chusid has pointed out Schubert shows considerable skill in frustrating 'the inherent regularity of the four- and eight-bar rhythmic units' (Chusid, p. 133). He does this in three ways: by eliding or overlapping phrases and periods (as when at the end of piano's introduction he has the voice enter over the piano's cadence), by having the piano echo what the voice has just sung, and by extending periods. Chusid's example for this is Schubert's repetition of the last line in each stanza in order to float the voice up to top Gb for the caressing gesture.

Schubert also varies the song's strophic form. By transposing the second strophe up a minor third into Cb major, he can both emphasize Gb and provide it with a large measure of stability. He can also make the home key sound brighter and relaxed when it returns. It is a trick he uses over and over again in his music. By raising the pitch he can make the same music sound a little more intense, and by lowering C, Ab major's major third, to become the root of Cb major, he can 'lift' it when it has to be a major third again. However, the transposition is not exact. Had it been, the voice would have had to sail up to Bbb for the slurred leap, and in a soft dynamic this would have been impractical for a high baritone. Instead Schubert leaps from Cb to Gb, a fifth rather than a seventh. This means the phrase loses much of its caressing quality. Furthermore in the next bar there is no appoggiatura in the vocal line on the first beat; 'täglich' ('daily') lacks the expressive quality that 'kösen' ('caress') received. This is another reason why Schubert transposed the central strophe up a minor third. Here the lover is not asking the girl to sit hand in hand with him as he did in the first stanza, he is asking her to trust him. He must therefore modify his advances.

Schubert has been criticized by Prawer for not taking into account Heine's cynical scepticism when he suggests at the end of the third stanza that the girl could be won over by the promise of pearls. According to Prawer, Heine believed that, like his Hamburg cousins who had rejected him for well-heeled suitors, most women were prisoners of the social conventions and materialist thinking that hedge in the lives of philistines (Prawer, p. 16). In other words, Heine's lover looks down on the girl, treats her as being culturally inferior. But although Schubert makes no attempt to convey this, the tone of the song, its easygoing lightness, is not that of someone who is emotionally or intellectually committed to the person he is addressing. Like the Atlas figure in the first song, he is acting a part.

4. *Die Stadt*

C minor. Moderately fast 3/4.

As in *Ihr Bild*, we now encounter a reflective self. Once again the protagonist becomes a person who gazes. He looks at the town shrouded in mist, at the ruffled water and the mournful strokes of the boatman, then at the town again, this time visible in the last rays of the sun. What he sees mirrors his mood, and Schubert has two types of music to convey it. One conveys the outer world, the other what goes on in the man's mind. The song opens with an introduction in which the pianist's left hand suggests the ruffled water and right hand the pulling of the oars.

The song is a vivid example of Schubert's capacity to bind together what Schenker called 'the external circumstances, the soul of the unhappy lover and ourselves'. We hear the splash of the oars just as the lover does. Schubert also intends us to imagine that the sound continues even when we have entered the lover's thoughts. For this there is another type of music. It is based on the dotted rhythm used in *Der Atlas*. The tightness of this rhythm, the rudimentary harmony, the restricted range of the vocal line and the instruction to sing the passage 'under the breath' (leise) suggest that the protagonist has his feelings strictly under control.

During the second stanza, when he turns his attention to the water and the rowing boatman, the piano's introductory music returns to accompany him, the notes of his vocal line being mainly those of the instrument's diminished seventh. The third stanza reverts to the other type of music. The mist has lifted and the poet can see the place he is looking for. His awareness that he has lost the girl floods his mind. He can no longer control his emotions so tightly. The singer has to cover a much greater range, sing strongly (stark) and to leap to top G. The double neighbour-note figure revolving around the tonic last heard at the end of *Der Atlas* comes back, but now, as the upper line of the piano part indicates, it is extended to become two phrases: C-Db-C-B and C-Eb-D-C. Schubert harmonizes the Db as a Neapolitan sixth, a chord used to reinforce the depressed quality of the minor mode as the final cadence approaches. In this context it throws the whole of the second phrase into relief, making the protagonist's feeling of irredeemable loss more intense than it had been at the end of *Ihr Bild*.

As that last bar indicates, the song ends with the return of the introductory music. The boatman continues to row unaware of what the lover feels. The diminished seventh chord, however, remains unresolved at the end of the song. It finds its resolution at the beginning of the next.

5. Am Meer

C major. Very slow 2/2.

A correction in the autograph shows that the augmented-sixth chord that begins this song was written as E♭ rather than D♯. E♭ would have been the orthodox way of spelling a German augmented sixth, and it would have indicated a direct link with the unresolved diminished seventh at the end of *Die Stadt*. But Schubert was looking ahead as well as back. In fact the chord does not behave as a German augmented sixth should. Instead of resolving on to a 6/4 – 5/3 over the dominant, its bass is rooted on the tonic. A♭, D♯ and F♯ are appoggiaturas. The elaboration is undoubtedly the most potent musical image in the whole set. It not only draws together memorable incidents in the previous four songs, it also sets the scene for future events in both *Am Meer* and *Der Doppelgänger*. F♯-G will recall the F♯-G running through *Der Atlas*; A♭-G the end of it. A♭-G was also prominent in *Das Fischermädchen* and *Ihr Bild*. It will also be used for the climax of *Am Meer*, and to lead into the opening bars of *Der Doppelgänger*. When F♯ is eventually combined with D♯ in the final song, the resolution of the harmonic tension throughout the set will be achieved.[10]

As an image the opening of *Am Meer* suggests the gentle yet ominous swell of the sea as well as the poet's brooding. Had Schenker analysed the song he might have said, as he said of the two B♭s at the beginning of *Ihr Bild*, why repeat the gesture? Perhaps his answer might have been the same. The man is gazing. On this occasion, however, his attention is devoted to himself rather than to looking at a portrait. He is searching his memory, trying to recall the circumstances which marked the end of the affair.

As the first four bars indicate, when the voice enters its melody is not only doubled by the piano at the unison, but also at the third above and the sixth below. The passage could therefore be considered a diatonic extension of the thirds in the opening two bars, the B-(D)-C in the fourth bar being a decorated transposition of the F♯-G in bars 1 and 2.

Schubert divides the song into two parts, the first functioning as an antecedent ending in the dominant, the second as a consequent altered to end in the tonic. This means that the same music leads to different conclusions. Both parts begin with a continuation of the simple diatonic melody quoted above. The use of parallel thirds suggests the man is remembering that at first he and the girl were in harmony with each other, that their relationship was uncomplicated and stable. His thoughts then turn to the time when the relationship began to fall apart. He thinks of it in terms of the rising mist, the agitation of the sea, the seagull flying hither and thither. The piano plays tremolando, the key changes to the minor and the parallel thirds are confined to one bar only. When the girl

---

10   Joseph Kerman (1962) in his essay 'A Romantic detail in Schubert's *Schwanengesang*', *Music Quarterly*, **48**, p. 36, interprets this song differently. For him the introduction 'does not signal ahead to a later event in the song, nor does it anticipate figuration or melody. It simply recurs; the song begins and ends with an oracle framing or glossing the poetic statement, rather than playing into it. From the Classical point of view, the introduction is non-functional; it illuminates nothing. But from the Romantic point of view it suggests everything – everything in the world that is inward, sentient, and arcane'.

begins to weep, the tremolos cease and Schubert conveys her sobbing with a twofold elaboration of a D minor chord in its first inversion, the elaboration consisting of much harsher appoggiaturas than hitherto.

The return of the diatonic music in parallel thirds and sixths for the consequent suggests that when he gets on his knees to drink away the tears from her hand the lover still feels at one with her. Up to this point words and music have also been in harmony with each other. But from the beginning of the next appearance of the agitated music to the end of the song they fall apart, as the relationship between the lovers had done. The words, cast in the present tense, convey estrangement rather than love, mock what has gone before; the music, on the other hand, conveys the opposite. The clash of the A♭ against the G for the word 'Weib' may be harsh as are the chords in the following bar previously used to express sobbing, but the piano has the climactic A♭-G not the voice, the dynamics hardly rise above *pianissimo*, and the expressive turn in bar 43, which most singers linger over, suggests unhappiness and longing rather than bitterness or self-mockery (see p. 258).

Both Prawer (p. 41) and Stein (p. 87) are critical of Schubert's failure to express in music the tone of the poem's last two lines, but once again they look at the song as a single entity rather than as a component in a larger work. It was essential for Schubert at this stage in the drama to convey the fact that although the two sides of the lover's personality have been kept separate in the first four songs, they must now be brought together, presented in the same context. And one of the most effective ways of doing this is to have the words say one thing and the music another.

By closing *Am Meer* with the same brooding chords that opened it, Schubert prepares the ground for the moment when the protagonist probes further into his memory and brings to the surface circumstances that are even more disturbing. Musically it is therefore essential that the B-A♯-D-C♯ motif which dominates *Der Doppelgänger* (see p. 259, *Sehr langsam*) should be heard as an extension of the partially obscured A♭-G figure lying within the these chords.

6. *Der Doppelgänger*

B minor. Very slow 3/4.

In *Die Heimkehr, Der Doppelgänger* is the last of the four poems in which the poet wanders through the streets looking for the places associated with his sweetheart. The loss of her was clearly not a recent event because, when he finds her house, he tells us she has long since left the town. Prawer places this in the context of other Heine poems:

> Again and again, the poet confronts his readers with a picture of a man standing outside a house where once he had been welcome, but which is now either empty or shut against him ... The significance of the 'Doppelgänger' image, presented here with such an effect of controlled hysteria, of powerful feeling held back by deliberately slow-moving self-contained lines, is not far to seek. Once again we are watching an 'outsider', a 'man outside', shut out from love and life: but this time the outsider is watching as well as being watched ... a past self watched by a present self. The lover not only suffers and reenacts past suffering, he is not only shut out and rejected – he is also condemned to watch himself suffer, to watch himself rejected. And, as he watches, the face of suffering itself becomes a mocking grimace.
>
> Du Doppeltgänger![11] du bleicher Geselle!
> Was äffst du nach mein Liebesleid.
> Das mich gequält auf dieser Stelle,
> So manche Nacht, in alter Zeit?
>
> The echoed ä, 'links mockery to suffering, äffen [to ape] to quälen [to torment, to torture], and its very ugliness robs suffering of dignity; a dignity which even the musical cadence of the final line finds it difficult to re-establish.
>
> *Der Doppelgänger* presents, with entire seriousness the dilemma of a post-Romantic poet who has lost even the naïveté of suffering; who is forced to watch his own gestures of sorrow with an all-too-conscious eye. So watched, these gestures become ridiculous, a mockery of grief that may once have been spontaneously real but has now become self-conscious and hollow. The ultimate subject of this magnificent poem is not so much grief over lost love as grief over the lost simplicity of grief. (Prawer, p. 36)

Schubert looks at the poem from a different perspective. There is no evidence that he shared Heine's post-Romantic disillusionment. He used Heine for his own purposes, and takes the poem at its face value. For him it represented the moment when the poet becomes aware of the other side of his nature, when he realizes that his suffering lies in the past. It gives Schubert the opportunity to offer hope to those oppressed by a side of themselves they find unacceptable in their periods of normality. He takes

---

[11]   This is Heine's spelling of the word. Schubert omits the 't'.

his clue from what Prawer calls 'the musical cadence of the final line', treating it as the moment when the doppelgänger slowly fades away, and a measure of inner peace is promised.

Although the music of the song comes from the last two bars of *Am Meer*, the transition from one to the other involves parallel fifths (C/G to B/F♯). These were avoided in tonal music because they undermine the independence of the parts. But in this instance their use was quite deliberate, for Schubert brings the same parallel fifths back near the end of the song (bars 59–60) when the doppelgänger is disappearing. They were clearly intended to mark the entrance and exit of something unusual, something normally considered beyond the pale.

The distinctive features of the song's opening are the octave doublings (reminiscent of *Der Atlas*), the slow, steady pace of the chords mirroring the 'slow-moving self-contained lines' of the poetry, the note-against-note style of the harmony, the avoidance of appoggiaturas, and the absence of thirds in the first and fourth chords of the four-bar phrase. In *Ihr Bild* Schubert had omitted the third from the chord leading to the recapitulation of the opening section in order to return to the poet's feeling of emptiness. The passage in *Der Doppelgänger* is therefore a description of both the external world, his plodding steps, the still night, the empty streets, the deserted house, and his inner world, his numb feelings, isolation, deep introspection.

Heine's first stanza is devoted to setting the scene, and throughout Schubert's music for it the atmosphere of the opening remains the same. He extends the initial four-bar figure by adding to it six bars terminating in an imperfect cadence with the dominant chord sustained for a furtive echo of the vocal line's last two bars (reminiscent of *Ihr Bild*). These suggest he has momentarily halted, and the empty streets are echoing his words, first 'Wohnte mein Schatz' (my beloved dwelt), then after going through the ten bars again 'Auf demselben Platz' (in the same place).

During the second stanza, when the poet recognizes that the figure wringing his hands outside the house is himself, Schubert repeats (with modifications) the music he used for the first stanza but drops the echoes so that the period is reduced from ten to eight bars. He also intensifies the dynamics; instead of being consistently *pianissimo*, they now crescendo to triple *forte* during both eight-bar periods. The effect is to suggest mounting trepidation.

Throughout these first two stanzas, the voice has articulated the man's conscious thoughts in 'lyrical declamation' (SSC, p. 263): the piano, on the other hand, has had the dual function of presenting the outside world, including his trudging steps, and his unspoken thoughts. This conforms to a salient characteristic of Heine's poetry in general. 'In Heine', says Prawer (p. 29), 'the landscape reflects the man.' Since the doppelgänger is an imaginative projection of what the poet has been brooding over, the piano becomes the medium through which its presence is experienced. In Schubert's hands it gradually becomes an object of terror. It is only when the poet realizes the figure belongs to his past and the past is behind him that he can rid himself of the image. During the third stanza, the piano, in its role of doppelgänger, moves slowly and ever more menacingly to the climax of the song, the moment of revelation. At this point the voice and piano fuse, and the motifs which have dominated both the song and the set are drawn together into a single phrase.

The arrival of this moment has been carefully planned, and it relies on Schubert's use of appoggiaturas. These have helped to define the difference between the voice and the piano for they occur only in the vocal line. Their purpose is not only to stress a particular word, but to create a pattern which has the climax as its goal. Schubert places them on the minor second (G), fourth (B) and minor sixth (D) of the key's dominant, F♯ major. With these he makes the pattern G-F♯, B-A♯, D-C♯. He goes through this sequence twice. The first time he stresses the words with umlauts on them in the poem's first six lines – 'längst' (G-F♯), 'Höhe' (B-A♯) and 'Hände' (D-C♯). On the second occasion he ignores the words Prawer thought so important, 'Doppelgänger', 'äffst', 'gequält'. Instead he stresses 'graust es' (G-F♯) then 'sehe' (B-A♯). Before continuing he builds up tension by slowly rising up a chromatic scale and accelerating the tempo. B-A♯ is held back for the word 'Stelle'; finally D-C♯ appears as the upper notes of a drawn-out cadential gesture on the piano. This is the moment when voice and piano come together for the first time in the song, for the vocal line's setting of the words 'so manche Nacht, in alter Zeit' is none other than a lyrical elaboration of D-C♯.

The following postlude, where the doppelgänger fades away and peace is attained, has also been carefully planned. The six-bar, later four-bar, phrase which follows the repetition of the song's head motif B-A♯-D-C♯ in the first two stanzas, culminates in an imperfect cadence rendered more imperfect by the dominant chord being changed into a discord each time it occurs. On the first and second occasions (bars 12–14 and 22–24) it is a second inversion of the dominant seventh (C♯-E-F♯-A♯). On the third (bars 32–3) the C♯ is lowered to a C to make a French sixth (C-E-F♯-A♯). On the fourth (bars 41–2) the F♯ is raised to G to make a German sixth (C-E-G-A♯). On each occasion the discord is preceded by a triad of D major and followed by a triad of B minor. To avoid parallel fifths between bars 42 and 43 (C/G – B/F♯), the German sixth is changed to a French sixth (from G to F♯) before moving on to B minor (C/F♯ – B/F♯). Parallel fifths are reserved for the piano's postlude when the doppelgänger fades away. This is when a chord of C major in root position drops down a semitone to a chord of B major in root position to create what was avoided at the end of the second stanza, C/G-B/F♯. Significantly Schubert adds a seventh to the B major chord. This means he can recall F♯-G, the motif with which the set began. But whereas initially this was an expression of violent longing, now it enables him to end with a cadence traditionally associated with the 'Amen'.

In assessing the Heine songs, Dietrich Fischer-Dieskau says, 'when listening to these miraculous compositions, one must have mixed feelings of astonishment and regret at the artistic breakthrough which they represent. No other prematurely deceased artist ever produced such startling innovations in the last months of his life' (DF-D, p. 280). Unfortunately, although he performed and recorded the songs as a set, he has made no comment about their value as a unit. Sufficient to say that they bring to an outstanding conclusion one of the most personally revealing yet undervalued series of works Schubert produced.

Select bibliography

Bingham, Ruth Otto (1993), 'The song cycle in German-speaking countries, 1790–1840: approaches to a changing genre', unpublished PhD thesis, University of Cornell.

Brauner, Charles S. (1981), 'Irony in the Heine Lieder of Schubert and Schumann', *Musical Quarterly*, 67.

Brown, Maurice J.E. (1967), *Schubert's Songs*, London: BBC Publications.

Byrne, Lorraine (2000), 'Schubert's Goethe settings: a reappraisal', *The Schubertian*, 29.

Cappell, Richard (1973), *Schubert's Songs*, 3rd edition, rev. M. Cooper, London: Pan.

Chusid, Martin (ed.) (2000), *A Companion to Schubert's 'Schwanengesang'*, New Haven, CT: Yale University Press.

Cone, Edward T. (1974), *The Composer's Voice*, Berkeley, CA: University of California Press.

———— (1998), '*Am Meer* reconsidered: strophic, binary, or ternary?' in B. Newbould (ed.), *Schubert Studies*, Aldershot: Ashgate.

Cooke, Deryck (1959), *The Language of Music*, Oxford: Oxford University Press.

Deutsch, Otto Erich (1946), *Schubert: A Documentary Biography*, trans. Eric Blom, London: Dent; published in the USA (1947) as *The Schubert Reader: A Life of Franz Schubert in Letters and Documents*, New York: Norton.

———— (ed.) (1958), *Schubert: Memoirs by his Friends*, trans. R. Ley and J. Nowell, London: Black.

Dürr, Walther (1979), 'Schubert and Michael Vogl: a reappraisal', *Nineteenth-Century Music*, 3.

———— (1982), 'Schubert's songs and their poetry: reflections on poetic aspects of song composition', in E. Badura-Skoda and P. Branscombe (eds), *Schubert Studies: Problems of Style and Chronology*, Cambridge: Cambridge University Press.

Einstein, Alfred (1951), *Schubert*, trans. D. Ascoli, London: Cassell.

Fischer-Dieskau, Dietrich (1976), *Schubert: A Biographical Study of his Songs*, trans. and ed. K.S. Whitton, London: Cassell.

Frisch, Walter (1986), 'Schubert's *Nähe des Geliebten* (D162): transformation of the *Volkston*', in W. Frisch (ed.), *Schubert: Critical and Analytical Studies*, Lincoln, NE: University of Nebraska Press.

Georgiades, Thrasybulos (1967), *Schubert: Musik und Lyrik*, Göttingen: Vandenhoeck und Ruprecht.

———— (1986), 'Lyric as musical structure: Schubert's *Wandrers Nacht-lied*' ('Über allen Gipfeln'), in W. Frisch (ed.), *Schubert: Critical and Analytical Studies*, Lincoln, NE: University of Nebraska Press.

Goethe, Johann Wolfgang von (1980), *Wilhelm Meister's Years of Apprenticeship*, trans. H.M. Waidson, London: Calder; New York: Riverrun Press.

Goldschmidt, Harry (1974), 'Welches war die ursprüngliche Reihenfolge in Schuberts Heine Liedern', *Deutsches Jahrbuch der Musikwissenschaft für 1972*.

Gramit, David E. (1987), 'The intellectual and aesthetic tenets of Franz Schubert's circle', unpublished PhD thesis, Duke University.

———— (1993), 'Schubert and the Biedermeier: the aesthetics of Johann Mayrhofer's *Heliopolis*', *Music and Letters*, 74.

———— (1997), ' "The Passion for friendship": music, cultivation, and identity in Schubert's circle', in C.H. Gibbs (ed.), *The Cambridge Companion to Schubert*, Cambridge: Cambridge University Press.

Heine, Heinrch (1990), *Buch der Lieder*, Stuttgart: Reclam.

Kerman, Joseph (1986), 'A romantic detail in Schubert's *Schwanengesang*', revised version in W. Frisch (ed.), *Schubert: Critical and Analytical Studies*, Lincoln, NE: University of Nebraska Press.

Kivy, Peter (1984), *Sound and Semblance: Reflections on Musical Representation*, Ithaca, NY: Cornell University Press.

———— (1989), *Sound Sentiment: An Essay on the Musical Emotions*, Philadelphia, PA: Temple University Press.

Kramer, Lawrence (1986), 'The Schubert Lied: Romantic form and Romantic consciousness' in W. Frisch (ed.), *Schubert: Critical and Analytical Studies*, Lincoln, NE: University of Nebraska Press.

Kramer, Richard (1994), *Distant Cycles: Schubert and the Conceiving of Song*, Chicago: University of Chicago Press.

Litterick, Louise (1996), 'Recycling Schubert: on reading Richard Kramer's *Distant Cycles: Schubert and the Conceiveing of Song*', *Nineteenth Century Music*, 20.

Lukács, Georg (1968), *Goethe and his Age*, trans. R. Anchor, London: Merlin Press.

McKay, Elizabeth Norman (1996), *Franz Schubert: A Biography*, Oxford: Oxford University Press; revised paperback edition 1997.

Muxfeldt, Kristina (1991), 'Schubert song studies', unpublished PhD thesis, New York State University.

———— (1997), 'Schubert's songs: the transformation of a genre' in C.H. Gibbs (ed.), *The Cambridge Companion to Schubert*, Cambridge: Cambridge University Press.

Nemoianu, Virgil (1984), *The Taming of Romanticism: European*

Literature and the Age of Biedermeier, Cambridge, MA: Harvard University Press.

Prawer, Siegbert, S. (1960), *Heine: 'Buch der Lieder'*, London: Arnold.

Reed, John (1985), *The Schubert Song Companion*, Manchester: Manchester University Press; New York: Universe Books; paperback edition (1993), London: Faber and Faber.

Reid, Paul (1998), 'The Therese Grob song collection of 1816', *The Schubertian*, 22.

Rosen, Charles (1997), 'Schubert's inflections of Classical form', in C.H. Gibbs (ed.), *The Cambridge Companion to Schubert*, Cambridge: Cambridge University Press.

Sammons, Jeffrey (1979), *Heinrich Heine: A Modern Biography*, Princeton: Princeton University Press.

Schachter, Carl (1999), *Unfoldings: Essays in Schenkerian Theory and Analysis*, ed. Joseph N. Straus, Oxford: Oxford University Press.

Schenk, H.G. (1979), *The Mind of the European Romantics*, Oxford: Oxford University Press.

Schiller, Friedrich (1951), *Über Naive und Sentimentalische Dichtung*, ed. W.F. Mainland, Oxford: Blackwell.

Schubert, Franz (2000), *'Schwanengesang': Facsimiles of Autograph Score and Sketches, and Reprint of the First Edition*, ed. Martin Chusid, New Haven, CT: Yale University Press.

Solvik, Morten (1999), *Franz Schubert: Kosegarten Cycle*, http://www.ping.be/gopera/lieder/kosegarten

Steblin, Rita (1983), *A History of Key Characteristics in the Eighteenth and Early Nineteenth Centuries*, Ann Arbor, MI: UMI Research.

—— (1998), 'Schubert's relationship with women: an historical account', in B. Newbould (ed.), *Schubert Studies*, Aldershot: Ashgate.

Stein, Jack, M. (1971), *Poem and Music in the German Lied from Gluck to Hugo Wolf*, Cambridge, MA: Harvard University Press.

West, Ewan (1989), 'Schubert's Lieder in context: aspects of song in Vienna 1778–1828', unpublished PhD thesis, University of Oxford.

Whitton, Kenneth, S. (1999), *Goethe and Schubert: The Unseen Bond*, Portland, OR: Amadeus Press.

Wigmore, Richard (1988), *Schubert: The Complete Song Texts with English Translations*, London: Gollancz; New York: Schirmer Books.

Wolff, Christoph (1982), 'Schubert's *Der Tod und das Mädchen*: analytical and explanatory notes on the song (D531) and the quartet (D810)', in E. Badura-Skoda and P. Branscombe (eds), *Schubert Studies: Problems of Style and Chronology*, Cambridge: Cambridge University Press.

Youens, Susan (1992), *Schubert: Die schöne Müllerin*, Cambridge: Cambridge University Press.

———— (1996), *Schubert's Poets and the Making of Lieder*, Cambridge: Cambridge University Press.

———— (1997), 'Schubert and his poets: issues and conundrums', in C.H. Gibbs (ed.), *The Cambridge Companion to Schubert*, Cambridge: Cambridge University Press.

Index of Schubert's music cited

Instrumental Music

Index of poets cited

General index

www.ingramcontent.com/pod-product-compliance
Lightning Source LLC
Chambersburg PA
CBHW050703280326
41926CB00088B/2434